Key Issues in Housing

Policies and Markets in 21st-Century Britain

Glen Bramley
Moira Munro
and
Hal Pawson

macmillan

First published 2004 by
PALGRAVE MACMILLAN
Houndmills, Basingstoke, Hampshire RG21 6XS and
175 Fifth Avenue, New York, N.Y. 10010
Companies and representatives throughout the world

PALGRAVE MACMILLAN is the global academic imprint of the Palgrave Macmillan division of St. Martin's Press, LLC and of Palgrave Macmillan Ltd. Macmillan® is a registered trademark in the United States, United Kingdom and other countries. Palgrave is a registered trademark in the European Union and other countries.

ISBN 0–333–96913–8 hardback
ISBN 0–333–96914–6 paperback

This book is printed on paper suitable for recycling and made from fully managed and sustained forest sources.

A catalogue record for this book is available from the British Library.

Library of Congress Cataloging-in-Publication Data
Bramley, Glen.
    Key issues in housing : policies and markets in 21st century Britain / Glen Bramley, Moira Munro and Hal Pawson.
        p. cm.
    Includes bibliographical references and index.
    ISBN 0–333–96913–8 (cloth)
    1. Housing policy—Great Britain. 2. Housing—Great Britain. I. Munro, Moira. II. Pawson, Hal. III. Title.

HD7333.A3B728 2004
333.33'8'0941—dc22   2004042093

10 9 8 7 6 5 4 3 2 1
13 12 11 10 09 08 07 06 05 04

Printed and bound in China

Contents

List of Figures, Tables and Boxes

Figures

Tables

Boxes

Acknowledgements

The authors and publishers would like to thank the following who have kindly given permission to reproduce copyright material:

The Controller of HMSO and Queen's Printer for Scotland (under click licence number CO1W0000276) for the right to reproduce Tables 4.1, 4.2, 4.4, 4.5 and 8.5 and Figures 4.4 and 8.1, and to publish updated versions of Figures 4.1, 4.2 and 4.3.

The Joseph Rowntree Foundation for the right to reproduce the table in Box 9.1 and Table 2.8.

Every effort has been made to contact all the copyright-holders, but if any have been inadvertently omitted the publishers will be pleased to make the necessary arrangement at the earliest opportunity.

List of Abbreviations

ABIs	area-based initiatives
ALMOs	arm's-length management organizations
ASB	anti-social behaviour
ASBOs	Anti-Social Behaviour Orders
BES	Business Expansion Scheme
BME	black and minority ethnic
BV	Best Value
BVH	Best Value in Housing
CABE	Commission on Architecture and the Built Environment
CBHA	community-based housing associations
CBL	choice-based letting
CCT	Compulsory Competitive Tendering
CDPs	Community Development Projects
CPO	Compulsory Purchase Order
CSP	community safety plan
DETR	Department of the Environment, Transport and the Regions
DTLR	Department for Transport, Local Government and the Regions
ERCF	Estate Regeneration Challenge Fund
ESD	environmentally sustainable development
GIAs	General Improvement Areas
HAs	housing associations
HB	Housing Benefit
HIP	Housing Investment Programme
HMA	housing market area
HMCCT	Housing Management Compulsory Competitive Tendering
HMR	Housing Market Renewal
ISMI	Income Support for Mortgage Interest
LAs	local authorities
LCHO	low cost home-ownership
LSVT	large-scale voluntary transfer
MPPI	mortgage payment protection insurance
NDC	New Deal for Communities
NHP	New Housing Partnership
NIMBY	not-in-my-backyard
NLPs	New Life Partnerships
NPM	New Public Management

ODPM	Office of the Deputy Prime Minister
PEP	Priority Estates Programme
PFI	Private Finance Initiative
PMM	plan-monitor-manage
PPAs	Priority Partnership Areas
PPGs	Planning Policy Guidance Notes
PPP	Public–Private Partnership
RDAs	Regional Development Agencies
RSLs	registered social landlords
RTB	Right to Buy
SEU	Social Exclusion Unit
SHIP	Safe Home Income Plans
SIPs	Social Inclusion Partnerships
SRCF	Single Regeneration Challenge Fund
SURIs	Smaller Urban Renewal Initiatives
TPC	Tenant Participation Compacts
UP	Urban Programme

1

Introduction

A context of change: changing times, changing places

This is a book about housing in Britain today and the changes and challenges that face everyone involved with it, whether as consumers, providers or policy-makers. It reflects on the far-reaching changes in housing since 1980 in patterns of tenure, provision and consumption and in the preoccupations of governments.

The starting point for this book is the notion of change, the pace of which seems to be ever-accelerating. Many people find change unsettling, whether it relates to their workplace, the economy, social norms or family structures. But government ministers, business leaders and managers urge us to change in order to increase our economic competitiveness.

Around the time that the Berlin Wall came down in 1989 there was much written about 'changing times'. This referred to a breakdown of old certainties, a set of intellectual beliefs and commitments that had lasted for half a century or more, defining the political Left and Right. This happened to coincide, in Britain, with the high point of public sector reforms instituted by Margaret Thatcher's government and the spread of these ideas to much of continental Europe. Also at this time in Britain, the Labour Party was radically redefining itself as no longer wedded to a traditional socialist programme but seeking instead a new 'third way' (Giddens 1998). Many commentators have pointed to changes in the nature of the economy, strongly linked to technology and labelled 'globalization' or 'post-Fordism' (or postmodernism), as key contextual factors: see, for example, Burrows and Loader (1994) and Hutton and Giddens (2001).

In some ways the agenda for housing policy debate in the last decade has been defined by the working through of these fundamental changes in the political, administrative and economic climate. Thus trends such as the continued shift towards individual home-ownership and away from social housing provision, the preoccupation with Best Value and with regulation, and the involvement of private sector finance and partnerships all follow from these critical changes.

The basic dimensions of change in British housing are well known but none the less quite dramatic:

1   In 1976 some 56 per cent of homes in England were owner-occupied and 29 per cent were rented from the council; by 2000 these figures were 70 per cent and 15 per cent (Bramley 1997b, pp.389–90; Wilcox 2000).
2   In 1976 local authorities built 140,000 new homes per year, 46 per cent of the total in Britain; by 1999 this had fallen to 165 (0.1 per cent).
3   In 1975 the government subsidized the two main tenures (owners and public renters) by more than £4 billion each (at 1995 prices), while providing £2 billion of means-tested rent rebates and allowances; in 1999 the equivalent figures were £1.4 billion for home-owners, *minus* £0.9 billion for public renters, and £8 billions for means-tested benefits.
4   In 1970 the proportion of council tenant households with no one in work was 20 per cent; by 1998 this proportion was 69 per cent (Giles *et al.* 1996, p.28; Wilcox 2000, p.131).

These rather stark figures serve to illustrate the extent of the transformation of at least some aspects of housing in Britain over recent years (Chapter 2 examines recent trends more fully).

The places where we live and consume our housing are also changing. Britain has long been a very urbanized country by international standards, but there is a well-established drift of households from cities to suburbs, and also to small towns and villages. At the same time there has been a revival in city-centre living, particularly for younger people and households without children. There is a continuing drift of people from north to south, leaving some northern cities with 'low demand' and housing abandonment (this will be discussed further in Chapter 4). Meanwhile, the more attractive parts of the country are facing growing congestion, pressures for development and high house prices. This gives rise to problems of affordability (Chapter 4), as well as problems in planning to accommodate the extra housing required (Chapter 5).

These problems can be compounded by instability in the housing market. Although governments strive to create the conditions for a stable, growing economy, the housing market has experienced repeated cycles of boom and bust (discussed particularly in Chapter 3). These have exacerbated the problems of affordability as well as introducing unfamiliar problems such as 'negative equity', which causes frustrated mobility. These cycles affect the wider economy and create other problems, including the shortage of key workers in London and the South East.

Changes in the housing system have been accompanied by changes in the ways that people think about housing and their aspirations, which in turn affect both individual behaviour and government policy. Ever-larger majorities of people aspire to individual home ownership, but not all can afford to realize these aspirations. Experiences of boom and bust, and reduced job security and uncertain career prospects, have led some to be more cautious about the extent of their commitment to house purchase. People expect more from government, and from their housing, but at the same time become more sceptical of either governments' or others' ability to deliver services effectively.

Government policy towards housing has changed substantially in response to these changes in the economy, in society, in demography and urban geography, and in political ideology and the realm of individual beliefs and behaviour. Although the basic goal of housing policy – a decent home for all families at a price within their means – has remained constant, the means adopted for achieving this have changed radically. All parties now subscribe to an agenda of 'enabling' rather than directly providing housing. The traditional local authority as a large-scale, monopolistic, bureaucratic landlord is giving way to a reliance upon housing associations. New investment is increasingly financed using private capital, while the land-use planning system is increasingly called upon to 'lever in' affordable housing as a substitute for traditional use of public land and public subsidy. The concept of *'social housing'* as subsidized rented housing of an adequate standard, provided by regulated non-profit or public bodies and allocated on criteria of need, is giving way to models offering more choice. Ideas about giving tenants more stake in their homes are being promoted. Approaches to housing for vulnerable groups are shifting from provision of special needs housing to supporting people in mainstream housing. In the face of so much change, some commentators have focused their attention on trying to define 'sustainable' housing policies (see especially Hills 1991; Williams 1997).

In the remainder of this chapter, we introduce the three main themes which inform and structure the rest of the book:

- the increasing role of *markets* in housing and the problems associated with this
- the implications of change for *consumers* and for *providers* of housing
- the roles of *government* and *other agencies* in housing policy and its evolution.

The dominance of markets

Reliance on markets

Linking many of the changes outlined above is the increasingly pervasive role of markets. Housing has witnessed the shrinking social rented sector and the increasing dominance of private sector provision. Additionally market processes have effects within the non-market sector: for example, social landlords increasingly rely on private finance for investment, requiring borrowers and lenders to make 'business' judgements about risks and returns (Chapter 7).

Sometimes, where landlords encounter serious problems of lack of demand, they are obliged to respond to market forces (Chapter 4). In these circumstances, many social landlords have moved towards allocation systems which rely more on choice, another key market concept. This trend towards the introduction of market-style processes – 'quasi-markets' (Le Grand and Bartlett 1993) – is seen across the public sector. Examples include 'internal markets' in the National Health Service, and devolved decision-making in schools.

The main 'public utility services' (post, telecommunications, water, electricity, gas) have been privatized and are now run as overtly commercial operations, often with competition mechanisms introduced. Most of these pro-market reforms survived the change of UK government in 1997. Compulsory competitive tendering in local government (affecting housing management and other services) was removed, but the replacement, Best Value, retains a strong emphasis on challenging traditional public sector methods and providers. And in procuring new investment in schools, hospitals and transport, the post-1997 New Labour government has made much fuller use of the 'Private Finance Initiative' (PFI), or Public–Private Partnerships (PPPs: see Institute for Public Policy Research 2001). Markets cannot be ignored in the contemporary scene.

A particularly important manifestation of this trend in the housing context concerns local authority housing stock transfer. As Pawson and Fancy (2003, p.6) contend: 'the policy is part of the "modernisation project" which seeks to bring commercial disciplines to bear on the running of public services. An important consequence of this is to reduce the role of locally elected representatives in directly controlling such service provision.' The pattern of stock transfer, the policy's underlying dynamics and its significance in restructuring Britain's housing system are discussed in detail in Chapters 2, 6 and 8.

Belief in markets

Why has there been such a pronounced shift towards reliance upon markets, or quasi-markets? Broader economic and social forces are influential, but ultimately these changes reflect deliberate policy decisions. This suggests that politicians, and the voting public, have come to believe that markets or market-style mechanisms work best at delivering what they want to achieve. For some politicians, particularly those on the Left and centre-Left, this is a profound change of position and approach.

In part the enthusiasm for markets reflects negative past experiences with traditional public sector models of provision. For example, the 'public corporation' nationalized industry model adopted by the postwar Labour government for public utilities and transport was never seen as a satisfactory solution. The relationship between the Treasury and these industries was a constant battleground over investment levels, price controls and efficiency (Levačić 1987). For high-profile public services such as health, it was a response to the intensive media attention on the ever-widening gap between perceived needs and aspirations, and what a cash-limited service could provide. Public housing provision has also had a deteriorating image, increasingly associated with decaying, defect-ridden and unpopular types of housing (e.g., high-rise flats) and with concentrations of poverty and 'social exclusion'.

Politicians and policymakers face difficult choices, because in general the range of good and desirable things that they want to do far exceeds the resources and powers which they have to provide them. A general 'squeeze' on public spending results from the economic and political imperatives to keep taxation and borrowing down. It is widely believed that 'globalization' implies that governments have less discretionary power to vary economic policies (Hutton and Giddens 2001). It is also apparent that politicians believe that taxation levels and policies are sensitive electoral issues, although opinion poll evidence on this is ambiguous (Jowell and others 2000).

The reliance on markets does not, however, just stem from negative reasons and impersonal economic forces; in reality, there is enthusiasm for the positive virtues of markets including:

- increasing *consumer choice* and control
- *responsiveness* to the needs and preferences of consumers
- *diversity* and *innovation* in provision
- greater economic efficiency and hence *value for money* (see Le Grand and Bartlett 1993)

Unlike services like health and education, in housing public provision is not dominant. The existence of a well-established market makes it relatively easy to envisage what a greater reliance on markets might involve. And some pro-market policies have simply involved giving certain households a helping hand in making the transition (the Right to Buy has been a notable example of this).

Just as a large existing market makes it easy to see the advantages of markets, however, it also offers experience and examples of the problems and snags that can arise, with markets in general and with housing markets in particular. Basically, markets only clearly have the beneficent properties attributed to them, in terms of promoting choice and efficiency, if certain assumptions are fulfilled. If in reality these assumptions do not hold, then the effectiveness of markets is more questionable (although one needs to consider what the alternatives are: see Hill and Bramley 1986, chs 1 and 6; Le Grand, Propper and Robinson 1992). The key reasons why markets may fail include the following:

- *lack of competition*, and hence lack of choice and lack of incentive for the providers to provide quality services and low costs
- *externalities*, whereby provision to/consumption by one individual/group affects the welfare or costs of other individuals/groups

- imperfect or absent *information* about the goods and services available in the market
- failure to deliver an acceptable *distribution* of services/benefits to all members of society because of the unequal distribution of income and wealth or because of inequalities in access

These problems apply to varying degrees to different sectors. For example, issues of lack of competition and specialist expertise are more acute in healthcare than housing. Nevertheless, this framework still points to a number of ways in which markets may fail in housing: for example, neighbourhood externalities associated with bad housing; lack of information about some aspects of housing (e.g., financial products); uncertainty about the future state of the market; and inequalities in access and outcomes.

Extremes of the housing market

Market failure underpins one of the main themes of this book: the tendency of the housing market to display extremes. The housing market is characterized by extreme swings, over time periods of a few years, from boom to slump. It is often also characterized by extreme differences between different regions and localities. The housing market of some London boroughs, for example, is literally a 'different world' from the market in some northern urban areas. In 1999 the average price of terraced houses sold in Hartlepool was £28,062; in the London Borough of Kensington and Chelsea it was £528,451 (Land Registry data). At about this time the MP for Hartlepool and cabinet minister, Peter Mandelson, got into considerable difficulty over his purchase (with assistance from a colleague) of a house in that London borough. Journalists commented – without exaggeration – that for the price of the London house he could have bought a whole street in Hartlepool. By 2002 that 19-fold difference had doubled again to no less than 41-fold (£1.32 million as against £32,100). In 1995 the ratio had been a mere 14:1.

We are used to economic and other differences between different parts of the country, but they are rarely as stark or extreme as this. The authors' recent research on 'low demand' found that even these local average prices fail to give a sense of the real extremes. In the poorer terraced housing areas of Liverpool, Burnley and Salford, for example, there were plenty of examples of houses changing hands for between £2,000 and £5,000, at auctions or even 'in the pub'. These areas were dropping out of the normal housing market, with neither mainstream first-time buyers nor mainstream mortgage lenders interested.

In the early 1990s, hundreds of thousands of households in southern England were stuck with 'negative equity', namely houses worth less than the size of their outstanding mortgage debts. In 1991 some 76,000 households in

Britain lost their homes through repossession, and many of them were living in the (normally prosperous) South. Such extreme variations in market conditions naturally beg the question, why? There are some structural reasons why housing markets, like other property markets, may be more unstable and more extreme than some other markets (Ball 1996a and 1996b; Gibb, Munro and Satsangi 1999). This has to do with the extremely durable nature of housing assets, their spatial fixity and the difficulty in adjusting quantities of housing quickly. The causes and dynamics of housing booms are explored further in Chapter 3 and low demand in Chapter 4.

Why it matters

Does it matter that housing markets vary so much? We would argue that it matters quite a lot, for a number of reasons, but perhaps this could be summed up by saying that housing is too important to be left wholly to such an unstable market:

1 The largest part of personal wealth is wrapped up in housing assets, but the housing system makes some millionaires whilst reducing others to penury, purely on the arbitrary basis of place of residence.
2 At a time when people are being expected to make more personal provision for the contingencies of life, such as higher education, pensions, old age care and so on, a system which generates such large inequities in wealth outcomes is unhelpful and de-motivating (see Ford, Burrows and Nettleton 2001 for a discussion of home-ownership in a 'risk society').
3 Cities depend upon a wide range of workers in different occupations to provide the services upon which 'civilized life' depends. Teachers, nurses, police officers and refuse disposal operatives are needed in central London, as well as investment bankers and media stars, but they will always find it hard to compete in the open market in areas such as central London.
4 The economy depends increasingly upon a flexible and mobile supply of skilled labour, discouraged in a housing market characterized by episodes of extreme negative equity, and co-existing areas seen as a 'no go' for investment, while others are totally unaffordable.
5 The gyrations of the housing market, led by London, can disturb the balance of the national economy (Maclennan 1997; Maclennan, Muellbauer and Stephens 1998).
6 Low demand for housing and its consequences (vacancies, abandonment, vandalism and disorder, disinvestment in stock maintenance, etc.) has a range of wider costs in terms of writing-off public sector assets, and the running down of other services such as education and retailing (Bramley, Pawson and Third 2000).

So we believe these phenomena of extremes in the housing market do pose real problems, for individuals, for local communities, for the economy and for government.

Implications for consumers and providers

Consumer as sovereign

In a perfectly competitive market, the consumer is sovereign; the producers of goods and services compete to provide what consumers want at the lowest price. Of course, this model is an 'ideal type'; nevertheless it contains an important truth, which is of tremendous significance in understanding the politics of the last 20 years or so.

Much of the change in housing policy and the housing system over the recent period can be understood as a deliberate attempt to shift control from producers to consumers. Above all, the emphasis on owner-occupation as the preferred and increasingly dominant tenure has substituted individual responsibility and self-management for reliance on landlords.

Other changes have reinforced this shift towards more consumer-oriented markets. For example, subsidies have been shifted from a 'bricks and mortar' supply orientation to being predominantly individual assistance with the cost of housing. Private rented housing, having previously been regulated and taxed almost to extinction, has been deregulated and revived (to some extent). Considerable efforts have gone into the encouragement of tenant participation in the management of social housing, a collective form of consumer involvement.

Power, information and foresight

For the notion of consumer sovereignty to have any reality, then certain conditions have to pertain. First, there should not be a great inequality in the power of different actors in the market. In reality, there are at least two kinds of inequalities of power. On the one hand, purchasing power varies with the enormous variation in income and wealth, and it is the purchasing power of the rich which dictates the price of housing, particularly in regions of scarcity. On the other hand, individual consumers are small compared with large organizations such as local authorities, housebuilding companies or banks. This suggests both a need for regulation and a need for individual consumers to act collectively.

Some individuals have less power than others, because of the urgency of their need and their lack of bargaining power; this is the characteristic position of the homeless. Some vulnerable groups also traditionally reliant on public support, such as the frail elderly, disabled people or those with learning difficulties, may be less able to exercise choice without significant support. Second, there should be adequate information about the products which are in the market: what is their quality, how do they perform and do they represent value for money? Although people have experience of living in a house and know what sort of features they do or do not want, what lies underneath the plaster may be difficult to assess without the expertise of a surveyor. The quality of the location, neighbourhood and neighbours may also be a trickier aspect of housing decisions.

It may not be the housing per se which presents the greatest problem for consumers, but some of the products which are indirectly associated with it. The range of 'financial products' which owner-occupiers (in particular) use to finance and underpin their house purchase – mortgages, savings plans, endowment schemes, life assurance, mortgage protection insurance, structure and contents insurance – are highly diverse and relatively technical, making it a hard for consumers to compare and choose (Chapter 7).

The third aspect of what consumers need to be effective in the market is foresight. The durable nature of housing assets makes knowledge of the future vital, but the future is inherently unknowable. The extreme instability and variability of the housing market may make buying a house rather like staking most of your wealth on a highly uncertain lottery.

Who are the providers?

Important though the consumption perspective is, we also need to consider the implications of the changing context of housing for the providers of housing. But who are the key providers of housing in the early 21st century? The different roles involved are:

- developers of land
- architects, designers, planners, surveyors
- housebuilding companies
- repair and maintenance organizations
- residential landlords
- managers of housing assets
- financiers
- insurers

Particular organizations may combine several of these roles. For example, a typical 'volume' housebuilder in Britain will act as land developer, designer and construction company, and will employ a range of skills including some professionals who also work in the public sector (e.g., planners). These roles are not always combined in the same way in other countries. For example, in Australia and the USA it is common for the development and housebuilding roles to be separate.

It is also important to note that these structures of provision have changed substantially and may change further. It has been noted above, for instance, how the local authority's role is being increasingly replaced by housing associations. In the owner-occupied sector, individual households themselves take on the management and maintenance responsibilities, a form of self-servicing, but at the same time their use of mortgage finance and insurance is very important. A large public landlord can pool many of the risks, whereas an individual household cannot do this without recourse to external insurance. The general changes in tenure and provision structures which have taken place are described in more detail in Chapter 2. In discussing and evaluating provision structures, a distinction is drawn between 'development' roles (Chapter 6) and 'management' roles (Chapter 8).

Changing face of social housing

The wide-ranging significance of the government's stock transfer policy has already been noted above. It is also important to highlight a number of other key changes in the nature of social housing which accompany its quantitative decline. These have implications for professionals working in the social housing field.

First, the declining size of the social rented sector means that social housing providers have to come to terms with managing a declining industry, which can create extra pressures for economy and efficiency as well as problems of morale and motivation for staff. Second, social housing has come to house a growing proportion of the poor within society, a process described as 'residualization' (Forrest and Murie 1988; Murie 1997; and see Chapter 2).

Third, social housing accommodates a disproportionate share of individuals and households who are in some degree vulnerable and need appropriate forms of support. Thus, social housing management may become more closely allied to social services and social work, symbolized in some local authorities by these departments being combined. Fourth, the concentration of deprivation in social housing estates with their attendant problems of crime, disorder, drug abuse and 'anti-social behaviour', puts housing managers in the front line when dealing with them (Chapter 8).

Taking these problems in social housing estates in conjunction with the growing backlog of disrepair and defects within social housing, it becomes clear why these areas are in the forefront of regeneration activity (as discussed in Chapter 9).

At the same time that these pressures have to be faced, social housing managers also have to come to terms with the growth of consumerism. Tenants have higher expectations of the housing on offer and the services provided, and central government has responded to this by mandating a raft of mechanisms to give effect to consumer concerns, including 'citizen's charters', performance indicators, league tables and more elaborate regulatory and inspection regimes (Chapter 8).

Government and housing policy

The state: from provider to enabler and regulator

In housing, as in other areas of public policy, government has explicitly sought to shift local authorities towards an 'enabling' approach which implies a reliance upon other agencies such as quangos (quasi-autonomous non-governmental organizations), to deliver policies and services. Elements of the enabling role include a greater emphasis on the formulation and monitoring of local housing strategies, allied to wider developments of 'planning' (e.g., 'community planning'), and the development of partnerships. Enabling is likely to work only if local authorities have a suitable range of levers to influence what the other agencies actually do (Bramley 1993a; Goodlad 1998). The important levers in relation to housing include:

- finance in the form of grants
- land for development
- the use of planning powers to influence what is provided on land owned by others (see Chapter 5)
- information (e.g., on housing needs and demands)
- orchestration of the views of tenants and communities
- other legal and regulatory powers, including building standards, tenancy regulation, physical conditions

The increased emphasis on regulation reflects central government's nervousness about the effectiveness of service delivery, a central focus of electoral competition in an era of consumerism.

From government to governance

National governments have also shifted significant parts of the policy implementation function to quangos operating at arm's length, of which the notable examples are the Housing Corporation in England and Scottish Homes/ Communities Scotland in Scotland. The term 'policy communities' is often used to describe the looser networks of stakeholders and representative organizations that are routinely consulted about policy development (Richardson and Jordan 1979).

Although the post-1997 Labour government signed up to the European Charter of Local Self-Government (Bailey 1999), the period since 1980 has been one in which local authorities have lost powers and resources to act independently. In housing, as in other sectors, local authorities have come under greater central control whilst also ceding more of their responsibilities to other agencies, such as registered social landlords (RSLs) and the Housing Corporation. They are under constant pressure to do more for less.

Devolution to Scotland and Wales has been a very significant development, politically and constitutionally, and represents a decentralizing move which to some degree contradicts the strongly centralizing tendencies of recent times. Housing policy in Scotland had in any case followed a somewhat separate course for many years, but the expectations associated with the new Scottish Parliament and Executive are that this separation will become more pronounced. Similar differences have opened up between Welsh Assembly policies and Westminster policies. The devolved Scottish (or Welsh) policy process may be qualitatively different from that at Westminster, with (for example) more consensual policymaking, partly because of the use of proportional representation and coalition-based government, and partly because of the role of committees in the new Parliament. It is also clear that rather complex interactions can arise between policies developed north of the border and matters that remain reserved to Westminster, such as social security and financial regulation. These are potentially quite significant for housing.

Although we recognize the importance of devolution, and reflect this strongly by frequent contrasts between the Scottish and English systems and policies, we do not claim to provide comprehensive coverage of policy differences in all parts of the devolved UK. Coverage of Northern Ireland and Wales is in practice much more limited.

Overall, the way Britain is governed has changed significantly. It is commonplace to characterize these changes as entailing a shift from government (a top-down administrative bureaucracy) to governance, a more complicated and diffused network of interacting centres of power which must negotiate with each other to achieve action (Stoker 1993; Leach and Percy-Smith 2002). Accountability for decisions and performance is more difficult to track in such a structure (Chapter 10).

The social economy

Given the emphasis on markets discussed above, it is not surprising to find that the private sector is taking on more, in housing as in other areas. But it is also noticeable that other agencies are increasingly important, which do not fit neatly into the category of either state or private.

This 'third sector' consists of agencies which are not formally constituted as part of the state but which are not private either, in the sense of being commercial, profit-oriented organizations. This third sector, 'the social economy', is an increasingly significant player, particularly in sectors relevant to social policy but also in others relating (for example) to the environment. The social economy includes, among other things:

- most RSLs or housing associations, which typically operate on a not-for-profit basis
- charitable organizations, which collect contributions from the public and voluntary effort from members, and which engage in a range of activities including campaigning for particular causes and groups and providing services and benefits to particular clients
- mutual organizations, ranging from small-scale local co-operative undertakings such as credit unions up to very large-scale national organizations such as building societies and mutual insurers
- local community-based trusts which take responsibility for particular social, environmental or heritage amenities
- co-operative enterprises, including local housing co-ops, retail co-ops and so on

It is clear from this list that the social economy is very significant in housing. It plays a major role in both mainstream and specialized provision, in housing finance, in services addressing the needs of groups such as the homeless and young unemployed, and in local community-based associations which are an important part of the 'social glue' which binds people to local communities and engages them with their local environment.

However, while the third sector is advancing in some areas, other trends are more negative. In particular, there has been a major movement towards de-mutualization in the financial sector, with the majority of former building societies and mutual insurers converting to public limited companies (plcs). This reflects the broader shift towards marketization discussed earlier. At the same time though, many large corporations make considerable play of their efforts to act in a socially responsible manner and devote significant resources to activities such as charitable giving, sponsorship and environmental improvements.

Private sector: master, servant or partner?

This leads on to the role of the private sector in the development and implementation of housing policy. The New Labour government under Tony Blair has placed considerable emphasis on a new and more positive attitude towards the private sector, but there remains considerable unease on the Left about this new attitude. It is felt that there may be a naive and overdeferential attitude towards corporate business, and that involving the private sector more in core public services such as health and education can be seen as threatening the public service ethos and democratic character of those services.

Where does housing sit within this debate? Housing is not a core public service in the sense of having public provision as the dominant mode. It has always been a 'mixed economy', and even in the heyday of the postwar welfare state public provision was never a majority (at least in England). The key markets for existing housing, new housebuilding and housing finance are generally very competitive, so there are fewer concerns about monopoly power than would apply in other cases. The issue is, then, more one of ensuring that consumers are well informed and that appropriate quality standards are maintained through regulation. Housing also provides opportunities for partnerships between the public and private sectors, significantly within RSL provision using private finance and (separate) procurement of buildings from private firms and partnership mixed tenure developments involving local authorities, RSLs and private housebuilders.

Housing policy 'out of the box'

It is a mistake to see housing policy as something neatly self-contained. Bramley (1997b) argued that housing policy was thriving but living at a different address, or rather at several different addresses, having diffused across the boundaries of a number of other policy sectors. Below are given a few examples:

1   As the main form of subsidy to housing is through Housing Benefit (HB), which is integrated with the main forms of social assistance devised by the Department of Work and Pensions, debates about the reform of HB have to be seen as part of wider debates about social security, means testing and (increasingly) taxation and tax credits involving the Treasury and Inland Revenue.

2   Energy efficiency in housing is important both for longer-term environmental sustainability (reducing CO_2 emissions) and for more immediate relief from poverty caused by high fuel bills and from adverse housing conditions including damp and condensation. Overall energy policy rests with the Department of Trade and Industry; environmental affairs are now with the Department of Environment, Food and Rural Affairs; poverty rests primarily with the Department of Work and Pensions; whilst housing rests with the Office of the Deputy Prime Minister (ODPM), and these are just the English departments; some but not all of these responsibilities have devolved equivalents. This is a particularly 'diffused' area of policy where 'joined up government' poses particular challenges.

3   Increasingly, people with a range of particular needs – frail elderly people, people with physical disabilities, learning difficulties or mental illness problems – are expected to live within the community with appropriate support, rather than in special purpose institutions. Social

housing organizations have a major role both in housing such groups and in organizing and connecting appropriate kinds of social support and care. This role entails close co-operation with social services and health services. Organizations such as 'Care and Repair' schemes help elderly and other householders to get essential repairs and adaptations to their homes and again connect them to other services (e.g., through welfare benefits advice), as well as the private sector.

So we would argue that housing policy is concerned not just with those core activities that normally have that label, but with a considerably wider agenda of issues and activities which interact in some way with housing but which go under a different label. We suspect that the most effective policymakers and practitioners will be those who realize this and who operate through a wide and diverse network of organizations and forums in order to make these connections.

Now read on

Guide to this book

The purpose of this first chapter has been to provide a context for the book, providing an overview of the bigger changes in housing itself, the economy, society and governance which have created the key issues facing housing policymakers and practitioners in early 21st-century Britain. In doing so we have referred to areas where later chapters will expand on particular themes. Therefore it is not perhaps necessary to give a detailed, step-by-step guide to the rest of the book. However, it may be worth just pointing up one or two features of the overall structure and approach.

The book falls broadly into two parts. The first part (Chapters 1–4) is more concerned with describing and explaining recent developments, whilst the second part (Chapters 6–9) adopts in turn the perspective of particular actors. Chapter 5 contains elements of both: what is happening in the geographical and environmental sense, and the perspective of particular actors concerned with these matters, the planners.

Within the first part, Chapter 2 enlarges on some of the trends briefly touched on in this chapter, with a particular emphasis on the changing size, profile and roles of each tenure. The next two chapters (3 and 4) take up the theme of market processes and influences, and focus on the most striking, and in many ways dysfunctional, feature of the British housing market, its tendency to extremes; it also considers the twin phenomena of booms and 'low demand'.

Chapter 5 looks at the major issue of where the growing number of households should be housed. It relates this to environmental sustainability questions, and considers debates about how to plan, as well as what to plan for.

Chapter 6 looks at the development process more from the point of view of the developer, whether public or private. The housebuilding industry is distinctive and in this chapter we discuss the factors which make it so. We also look at the development role of the new-style social housing organizations, in particular in relation to stock transfers from the public sector. Chapter 7 adopts the consumers' perspective and considers how changing household structures and lifestyles are affecting what people want from their housing and their ability to pay for it.

Chapter 8 focuses on the managers' perspective, mainly in the management of social rented housing, and analyses management responses to the variation in demand and the growing burden of regulation.

Chapter 9 looks at regeneration. Regeneration is a challenge, perhaps by definition because one is trying to turn around areas which the market is generally not favouring. We review the history and recent evolution of regeneration and the current scale of problems. Key issues here include what are the best ways of mixing people and activities in different urban settings, and how to involve local communities who may both need and fear change.

Chapter 10 returns to the process of policymaking in housing, which we have touched on in this chapter. The core question addressed is whether the housing policy system is adequate to the task of responding to the challenges outlined in this book.

Guide to further reading

This chapter has been pretty general and wide-ranging, so it is difficult to know where to start or stop with recommended reading. General texts on housing which are reasonably up to date include Cowan and Marsh (2001), Gibb, Munro and Satsangi (1999), Malpass and Murie (1999) and Balchin (1996a). Williams (1997) is a useful collection of essays examining and anticipating some of the issues addressed in this book, as is O'Sullivan and Gibb (eds) (2002) with a more economic slant, while Cole and Furbey (1994) reflect on the key structural changes in housing provision. McCrone and Stephens (1995), Balchin (1996b) and Kleinman, Matznetter and Stephens (1998) put British housing policy in a European context.

On current housing policies, the best official sources are the relevant government Green White Papers (e.g., the Department of the Environment, Transport and the Regions, or DETR 2000c), together with commentaries on these produced by bodies such as the Housing Quality Network (http://www.hqnetwork.org.uk) and in policy/practice-oriented journals such as *Roof, Inside Housing* and *Housing Today*. The ODPM (2003b) Sustainable Communities plan provides the latest official analysis and proposals for policy in England, drawing strong links between housing, planning and urban regeneration. The Scottish Executive (2001a, 2003c) provides a resumé of current housing policies in Scotland.

Wilcox edits the annual *UK Housing Review* (formerly *Housing Finance Review*), which not only provides an invaluable collection of statistical series relating to housing, but also contains useful short articles discussing current housing policy issues or reviewing trends. The Council of Mortgage Lenders' journal *Housing Finance* and the ODPM's *Housing Signposts* perform similar functions. Wilcox is especially valuable for containing data relating to all parts of the UK. Devolution as an influence on the evolution of housing policy was the theme of a special issue of the journal, *Housing Studies*, in March 2003.

2

The Changing Housing System

Background and introduction

This chapter provides a statistical background to current issues in British housing policy. Focusing mainly on trends in the housing system over the last 25 years, it sets the scene for the rest of the book.

Generally, the chapter takes the turn of the 1970s as its starting point. This is convenient partly because it coincides with the establishment of some statistical series. More importantly, it marked a substantial shift in government policy, with public housing reaching its high water mark, and the onset of a period of housing market restructuring. State intervention on a massive scale had already transformed the postwar housing legacy, clearing the slums that had blighted the inner cities and all but ending the acute shortage of housing which dominated housing policy thinking from the late 1940s through to the 1960s. By 1980, housing conditions, as measured by traditional indicators such as the absence of amenities, were also much improved; with overall numerical shortage ended, households generally could choose to live independently of others, whether as older people, or as young married couples and families. They could look to the state to help cover reasonable rents, subject to a means test. Alongside the overt commitment to good quality public housing there had also been a quiet expansion in owner-occupation.

With hindsight it is clear that, far from having achieved a stable and satisfactory housing system, the 'success story' which seemed apparent at the end of the 1970s was facing pressures which would lead to enormous instability and change over the next 20 years. This book explores and explains the way that housing problems have re-emerged in different guises over this period, particularly focusing on issues that are most pertinent at the start of the new millennium.

First, we look at the restructuring of housing tenure since 1981 and discuss the factors which have contributed to some of the major changes such as the post-1988 revival of the private rented sector. Next we examine the way that Britain's shifting demographic structure has influenced the overall demand for housing as the typical size of a household has continued to decline. We then review briefly patterns of housing disrepair. Lastly in this section we look at the changing patterns in income distribution and poverty seen over the past 20 years, a crucial part of the backdrop to so many housing and regeneration policies preoccupied with ensuring better housing prospects for the least well-off.

Partly because so much of housing policy relates to the social rented sector we then focus on the way that the sector has been evolving since 1980. In particular, we examine the impact of the Right to Buy and then the more recent transfer of ownership through Large-Scale Voluntary Transfer (LSVT) on the make-up of the public sector housing stock and the tenant population. Lastly, we look at the housing association sector's recent evolution and the way that LSVT is progressively transforming this segment of the housing system.

The big picture: the changing housing system since 1980

The restructuring of housing tenure

As the national stock of dwellings has grown since 1980, Britain's housing market has been substantially restructured (see Table 2.1). In part these changes reflect the continuation of long-term trends. In other respects, however, they represent reversals of postwar patterns.

The most significant aspect of tenure restructuring has been the expansion of home-ownership, now overwhelmingly the dominant tenure across the country, accounting for more than two-thirds of all homes. Between 1981 and 2001 the number of owner-occupied homes rose by 40 per cent, though this is only the most recent phase in a long-established growth trend.

The rise in home-ownership since 1980 results from two processes: new housebuilding (see Table 2.2) and the sale of former public housing to sitting

Table 2.1 *Change in stock by tenure, Great Britain, 1981–2001 (thousands)*

	Private sector		Social rented sector		
	Owner-occupied	Private rented	Housing association (HA)	Local authority (LA)	HA and LA
1981	12,171	2,340	470	6,115	6,585
1986	13,660	2,205	550	5,655	6,205
1991	15,162	2,150	701	4,966	5,667
1996	16,036	2,450	1,078	4,369	5,447
2001	17,190	2,434	1,624	3,558	5,182
% change 1981–2001	+41.2	+4.0	+245.5	−41.8	−21.3
% change 1991–2001	+13.4	+13.2	+131.7	−28.4	−8.6

Sources: Data from ODPM *Housing Statistics 2003*, Table 102; ODPM website, www.odpm.gov.uk/housing.

Table 2.2   *New housing construction by tenure, Great Britain, 1975–2001 (housing starts)*

	Local authorities		Housing associations		Private sector		Total
	No.	%	No.	%	No.	%	No.
1975	133,567	44.2	19,369	6.4	149,128	49.4	302,064
1980	34,493	23.3	14,799	10.0	98,837	66.7	148,129
1985	20,863	10.5	12,428	6.2	165,628	83.3	198,919
1990	7,784	4.8	18,438	11.3	137,066	83.9	163,288
1991	3,873	2.4	22,381	13.7	136,708	83.9	162,962
1992	2,160	1.4	32,942	21.2	120,190	77.4	155,292
1993	1,734	0.9	41,576	22.6	140,368	76.4	183,678
1994	1,195	0.6	41,177	20.9	154,364	78.5	196,736
1995	912	0.5	32,743	19.5	134,231	80.0	167,886
1996	652	0.4	29,399	16.8	145,008	82.8	175,059
1997	445	0.2	26,344	13.9	162,296	85.8	189,085
1998	233	0.1	22,262	12.6	154,199	87.3	176,694
1999	331	0.2	21,521	12.0	156,783	87.8	178,635
2000	328	0.2	18,468	10.4	158,147	89.4	176,943
2001	324	0.2	16,768	9.4	161,695	90.4	178,787

Source: Data from *Housing and Construction Statistics* as reproduced in Wilcox (2002), Table 19g.

tenants. The tenure transfer of formerly private rented housing, important in boosting home-ownership in earlier decades, has played only a relatively minor role.

Whilst home-ownership has continued to expand throughout Britain, there is a contrast in the scale of this expansion between England and Wales, on the one hand, and Scotland on the other. As shown in Table 2.3, owner-occupation north of the border more than doubled between 1981 and 2000. In part, this is because the historic home-ownership rate in Scotland was relatively low. The effect has been to reduce – though not quite eliminate – the difference between Scotland and the rest of Britain in terms of the rate of home-ownership (see Table 2.4).

As the rise of home-ownership has continued, renting from social landlords (i.e., local authorities and housing associations) has contracted overall. The combined size of the social rented sector fell by 21 per cent between 1981 and 2001 (see Table 2.1). Whilst social rented stock accounted for nearly one-third of all homes in 1981, this had shrunk to little more than one-fifth by the end of the century (see Table 2.4).

At the same time, however, the relative size of the two sub-sectors – local authorities and housing associations (or registered social landlords, RSLs) – has changed dramatically. Mainly as a result of sales under the Right to Buy (RTB), local authority housing dwindled by over 40 per cent between 1981 and 2001. Over this period the RTB facilitated the sale of some two million former public sector homes across Britain. Council stock losses have been

Table 2.3   *Change in size of housing tenures, 1981–2001*

	Home-ownership	Private renting	Housing association	Local authority	All tenures
	% change in no. of dwellings by tenure, 1981–2001				
England	+37.4	+6.1	+247.3	−41.4	+17.7
Wales	+35.3	+5.7	+129.2	−35.2	+15.9
Scotland	+109.7	−18.3	+311.1	−47.9	+19.0
Britain	+41.5	+4.1	+246.2	−42.2	+17.7

Sources: Calculated from ODPM *Housing Statistics 2003*, Tables 104, 106 and 107; ODPM website, www.odpm.gov.uk/housing.

Table 2.4   *Tenure distribution by country, 2001 (dwellings) (%)*

	Home-ownership	Private renting	Housing association	Local authority	Total
England	69.8	10.2	6.7	13.3	100.0
Wales	72.2	8.7	4.3	14.8	100.0
Scotland	64.2	6.7	6.3	22.8	100.0
Great Britain	69.4	9.8	6.6	14.2	100.0

Sources: Calculated from ODPM *Housing Statistics 2003*, Tables 104, 106 and 107; ODPM website, www.odpm.gov.uk/housing.

compounded by transfers into RSL ownership and – to a smaller extent – by increasing number of demolitions (see Chapters 4 and 9). A consequence, however, has been that the RSL stock has increased (see pp.33–41 and Chapter 7).

Changing tenure patterns have also been driven by new construction. Between 1980 and 2001 more than 80 per cent of new homes were built for sale (see Table 2.2). In the late 1970s private sector output accounted for only around half of the total.

The private rented sector

Having been in virtually continual decline since the early 20th century, the private rented sector staged something of a revival after 1990 (see Figure 2.1). For more than 70 years the tenure had been consistently losing stock through demolitions and sales into home-ownership, involving both sitting tenants and open market transactions. Between its nadir in 1988 and 2001, however, the sector in England grew in net terms by some 350,000 dwellings (nearly one-fifth). In Wales, as illustrated in Figure 2.1, the upward trend has been even sharper.

Figure 2.1   *Trend in number of privately rented dwellings, 1981–2002*

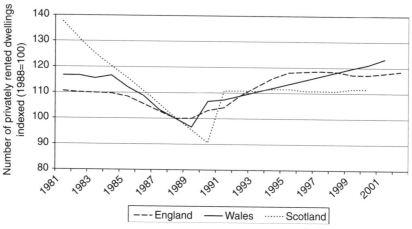

Sources: Data from ODPM *Housing Statistics 2003*, Tables 104, 106, 107; ODPM website, www.odpm.gov.uk/housing.

In part, the private rented sector's revival is probably attributable to the effect of deregulation introduced by the Housing Act 1988. This reduced security of tenure and abolished rent control for new lettings. The timing of the new regime coincided with the housing market slump of the early 1990s which resulted in many owner-occupiers who needed to move choosing to rent out rather than sell their homes. A more recent phenomenon has been the 'buy to let' trend whereby homes are bought specifically as an investment to be rented out. The co-existence of (post-1999) falling stock markets with strongly rising house values underpins the current popularity of such ventures. A third factor relevant during the early 1990s was the government's temporary extension of its Business Expansion Scheme (BES) regime to private renting. Under this regime, in force from 1988 to 1993, companies investing in 'housing to be let on assured tenancies' enjoyed substantial tax concessions. However, whilst this generated some 81,000 homes, many of these were built or acquired on behalf of housing associations and others were sold – some probably into owner-occupation – when BES restrictions were re-imposed in 1993 (Crook and Kemp 1995). Whether BES had a lasting effect on the private rented sector is, therefore, debatable.

Particularly in areas severely affected by low demand, some landlords have also taken advantage of 'rock bottom' prices to expand property portfolios (see Chapter 4). It is, however, notable that the sector's renaissance has been somewhat patchy: in Scotland, for example, the number of privately rented homes remains well below its 1981 level (see Table 2.3 and Figure 2.1). More generally, the restrictions on the availability of Housing Benefit introduced during the second half of the 1990s (e.g., the 'local reference rents' regime) may have restricted the sector's continued growth.

Current thinking emphasizes the valuable economic role played by the private rented sector in facilitating labour mobility, as well as its social role as an 'easy access' tenure: 'The PRS [private rented sector] has an importance for housing policy which far outweighs its size' (Houston, Barr and Dean 2002, p.6). In policy terms, therefore, the general post-1990 revival outlined above can be counted as something of a success. In spite of the recent expansion of the buy-to-let market (see above), the prospects of attracting a greater flow of private investment into privately rented housing in the future remain uncertain. The government's 1995 proposal for Housing Investment Trusts failed to take off and expanded interest in private renting among financial institutions remains conditional on the development of 'tax-transparent investment vehicles' as well as an industry-wide code of practice on property management (Crook and Kemp 1999). The turn of the millennium boom in property values has also dampened potential investors' interest in the sector as typical rental returns have failed to keep pace with rising sale prices: the case for 'buy to let' investment has come to depend largely on anticipated capital appreciation.

Household formation

The numerical demand for housing nationally is driven by the total number of households. We therefore discuss here the factors underlying household growth. However, the implications of this growth for the planning of new housing provision are dealt with in Chapter 5.

It is generally accepted that contemporary household growth in Britain is driven by three main factors (Department of the Environment 1995b, 1996; Bramley and Lancaster 1998):

- increased life expectancy of the population
- net international in-migration
- the trend towards living in separate, smaller households, across all age groups, including the decline in marriage rates and the prevalence of divorce/separation

Table 2.5 shows the total number of households since 1981 and the projected numbers up to 2021, while Figure 2.2 shows the main components of change in the number of households in England over the 25-year period to 1996 and projected for the next 15 years. The projections from 1996 shown in the latter are lower than the actual likely outcome, because population estimates have since been revised upwards. Figure 2.2 shows that in both periods the largest single factor has been sheer growth in the size of the population. The ageing

Table 2.5 *Household estimates and projections, 1981–2021*

	Total number of households				Average household size, England
	England	Wales	Scotland	Britain	
1981	17,306	1,017	1,854	20,177	2.67
1991	19,213	1,128	2,052	22,393	2.47
2001	20,750	1,192	2,192	24,134	2.34
2011[a]	22,519	1,277	2,408	26,204	2.24
2021	24,000	1,342	n/a	n/a	2.15
% change 1981–2021[b]	+38.7	+32.0	+29.9	+37.5	−19.5

[a] '2011' figure for Scotland refers to 2012.
[b] '% change, 1981–2021' figure for Scotland refers to 1981–2012.
n/a = not available.

Sources: Data from ODPM *Housing Statistics 2003*, Table 401; ODPM website, www.odpm.gov.uk/housing. Figures derived from Office for National Statistics (ONS) household estimates and projections. Figures for 2001 and subsequent years are 1996-based projections (except for Scotland which are 1998-based).

Figure 2.2 *Components of projected net increase in households, England, 1971–2010*

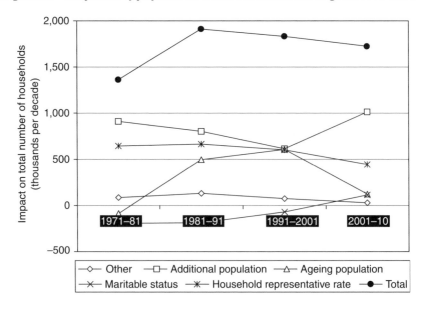

Source: Authors' calculations using data underlying 1992-based Department of the Environment household projections.

of the population also increased household numbers. However, in the previous 25 years, the trend towards separate living, represented in this diagram by 'household representative rates', made a much bigger contribution to growth than it is projected to in the next period. The process of households splitting into ever-smaller units appears to be slowing down (see also Holmans 2000). Change in marital status (including cohabitation) was a negative factor in the 1971–96 period, but becomes a neutral factor in the following period.

Until the late 1980s Britain generally lost more population through international emigration than it gained from international immigration. In the 1990s this situation turned around, and it is now expected that this pattern of positive net immigration will persist into the future. Between 1991 and 1998 international migration added 93,000 per year to the population of England and Wales (Champion 2002, Table 9). Between 1996 and 2021, it is projected to add 869,00 households (about 2.1 million people), an annual gain of 87,000 persons or 35,000 households (Champion 2002, Table 16). International migration comprises a number of distinct flows, including moves within the EU (not restricted), return migration from the 'Old Commonwealth', migration by dependents of previous migrants, migration to take up work or study opportunities in Britain, and the increasingly controversial flows of refugees and asylum seekers. These flows are subject to different influences, but a common underlying factor is the generally favourable economic and employment situation in Britain since the early 1990s. International migration is heavily concentrated on London, increasing pressure on its housing market and spilling over into the surrounding South-East region.

There is a long-established upward trend for people of any given age to live as separate households. This propensity is measured by 'headship rates' (the proportion of a given age/sex/marital status group to head a separate household) or, as they are now known in some contexts, 'household representative rates'. Figure 2.3 illustrates the trends for household headship rates for 'non-family' groups (i.e., excluding married couples and lone parents). Rates rise steeply with age to around 30, then reach a plateau until middle age, after which they rise further. Successive cohort groups born in later decades display generally higher rates at given ages. Older age groups are close to the maximum attainable levels of 1.0 (as one married couple families, not shown), but there remains considerable scope for more younger, non-family groups to live separately (Bramley and Lancaster 1998).

The trend towards separate household formation arises from a combination of socio-cultural factors (such as changing expectations) and economic factors (including higher incomes). Changing patterns of further/higher education and labour force participation link these two sides together. For example, more people leave their parental home to study at university, and are then more likely to continue living away from the parental home as they establish a career. More women are pursuing qualifications and employment careers, allowing a greater degree of independence. A key feature of household

Figure 2.3   *Non-family household headship rates by birth cohort*

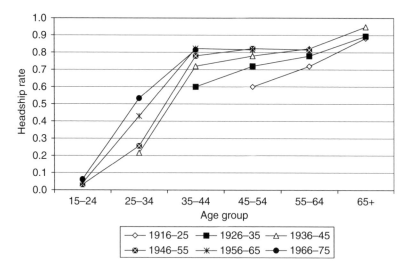

Source: Authors' calculations using data underlying 1992-based Department of the Environment household projections.

change is the general decline in marriage (fewer people marrying, and many marrying later), only partially offset by rising cohabitation.

For housing, one key consequence of these trends is that most of the increase in household numbers will take the form of single person households (Figure 2.4). There will also be some increase in lone parent households, and in childless couples, but a large fall in couples with children. This has potentially major implications for the type of housing to be provided, although it should be noted that most of the growth will be in single and childless households in the middle and older age groups (Figure 2.5). More of the increase in single person households will be 'never married' people (although some may have cohabited), rather than widowed or divorced (Holmans 2000, p.14). However, rising incomes and expectations mean that it cannot simply be assumed that the growing numbers of smaller households translate into an inevitable future demand for more small dwellings. An increasing proportion of small households want – and can afford – larger homes. While the ageing population contributes to the upward trend in single person households, much more significant for the immediate future in terms of the implications for health and social services is the projected rise in the over-75 cohort. Members of this group are now estimated to account for 41 per cent of older people, up from only 26 per cent in 1951 (Malpass and Murie 1999).

At the same time, other types of 'non-traditional' household (such as 'cohabiting couples' and 'other multi-person' households) are expanding.

Figure 2.4 *Changing household type distribution, England, 1981–2021*

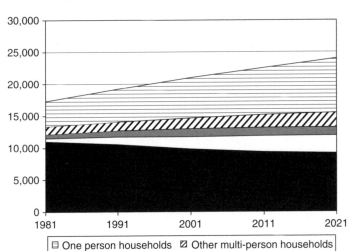

Source: Based on data in Table 1, DETR (1999d).

Figure 2.5 *Household growth by household type and age, England, 2001–21*

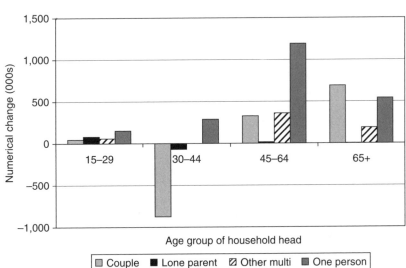

Source: Authors' calcuations based on data in Table 4, DETR (1999d).

From a housing policy point of view, lone parents are a particularly significant group since they are grossly overrepresented among those near or below the poverty line and among those requiring state housing assistance of one kind or another. However, whilst lone parent households are estimated to have doubled between 1981 and 2001, the numbers in this category are now forecast to level off (see Figure 2.4).

Economic influences   A recent review of relevant research suggested that if incomes were 10 per cent higher household formation could increase by 1.4 per cent (Bramley, Munro and Lancaster 1997; Bramley and Lancaster 1998), although another study (DETR 1997) suggested a higher figure of 3.3 per cent. Similarly, these studies suggested that if house prices were 10 per cent higher household formation could shrink by 0.8–1.8 per cent. Because higher incomes tend to push up house prices, these effects tend to counteract each other. So economic factors do influence household growth at the margins, and this is given some official recognition in government projections (DETR 1999c, pp.86–7). As the housing system becomes more market-oriented, these influences may become stronger. However, their effects are probably less powerful than the basic demographic forces of population numbers and age structure.

Policy influences   More controversial are suggestions that certain policy factors can influence household growth. There is some evidence that the supply of affordable/social housing has an effect on household growth (Bramley and Lancaster 1998), although this is disputed by Holmans (2000). The supply of social housing since 1980 has been relatively restricted, particularly in London and the south of England. In the late 1990s household formation rates grew less than expected, on the basis of past trends, in London. This could be further evidence that restricted housing supply, or rather the tightness of supply relative to demand and the high level of prices resulting, does affect household numbers.

   Other policy areas which influence household formation include:

- housing subsidies, particularly those targeted at lower income or more marginal groups
- Housing Benefit (HB) specifically, as it is the most important UK mechanism subsidizing rental costs (within some limits in the private sector) (Gibb, Munro and Satsangi 1999, ch. 8)
- other social security benefits which can influence the ability of different kinds of household units to live separately (e.g., there is some, albeit mixed, US evidence that more generous welfare schemes in some states are associated with higher rates of household formation)
- family policy, including the legal framework governing divorce, guidance/ mediation services, and the Child Support Act/Agency, which may all have some impact on the propensity for marriages to break up

- higher education, which increased massively in scale in the late 20th century, has wide-ranging implications for household formation and housing demand, some positive (e.g., more independent living away from home) and some negative (e.g., increased student debt)
- community care, which is intended to help a growing number of dependent elderly, disabled and other groups to live in mainstream housing with appropriate support.

Overall, Bramley and Lancaster (1998, p.28) concluded that, although many social and economic policies influence household formation, they exert only limited leverage on total household numbers, and that many of these policy levers are already set in a fairly 'negative' fashion (e.g., social security, affordable housing provision).

Homelessness

Homelessness is linked to household formation because a substantial proportion of households counted as having 'become homeless' each year involve young people leaving the parental home but failing to find or sustain independent accommodation. Demographic trends associated with changing volumes of new household formation therefore exert an underlying influence on homelessness numbers. The official homelessness figures are perhaps the single most widely cited indicator of housing need; however, these figures, collected by local authorities, are to some extent an artefact of the legislation (originally passed in 1977) which defines councils' rehousing responsibilities towards homeless households. Essentially, councils are required to 'secure housing' for households without access to their own accommodation and which contain dependent children, a pregnant woman or person(s) deemed 'vulnerable' in relation to their ability to access housing (say, in terms of old age, disability or mental ill health).

Councils are obliged to monitor all housing applications made on the grounds of homelessness (see Figure 2.6). However, these 'applications figures' are generally regarded as unreliable because of inconsistent local recording practices. In making comparisons between areas and tracking trends over time, more weight is generally placed on the concept of 'homeless acceptances': that is, households accepted (by local authorities) for rehousing as 'unintentionally homeless and in priority need'. Whilst changes in these figures are probably indicative of wider trends in homelessness, they inherently understate the scale of the problem because they exclude able-bodied single people and childless couples of working age who do not meet the 'priority need test' qualifying them for statutory rehousing.

Although demographic factors affect the incidence of homelessness, a more important driver of short- and medium-term fluctuations is the state of

Figure 2.6   *Households assessed as homeless and in priority need, 1991/2–2002/3: Scotland and England compared*

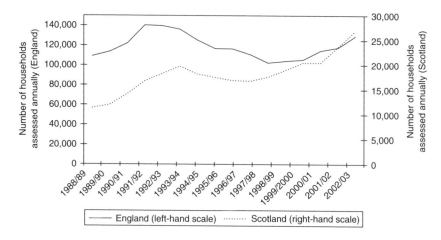

Sources: Data from ODPM *Housing Statistics 2003*, Table 621; ODPM website, www.odpm.gov.uk/ housing; Scottish Executive homelessness statistics HSG 2003/5, Table 2a and Wilcox (2003) Table 87. Figures for 1988/9–1990/1 (and 1991/2 for Scotland) are for calendar years. Scotland figure for 2001/2 interpolated.

the housing market: low income households are liable to be 'priced out' of the private housing market in 'boom' periods when house prices run ahead of incomes (see Chapter 3). The overall improvement in 'affordability' seen during the mid-1990s (see Figure 3.2) helps to explain the parallel decline in homelessness.

Housing conditions

British postwar housing policy until the 1970s was dominated by the drive to tackle the crude shortage of dwellings which was exacerbated by war damage and subsequent slum clearance. This imperative underpinned the 'numbers game' played by successive administrations during the 1950s and 1960s, each seeking to outbid one another in terms of annual new housing output.

By the 1970s, however, with the crude deficit in dwelling numbers having been eliminated and with 'slum' clearance increasingly encountering resistance from committed owners and residents, the national policy focus switched to the improvement of house conditions embodied in area improvement approaches such as the General Improvement Areas and Housing Action Areas of the Housing Act 1974. Indicators on access to basic amenities as well as on overcrowding assumed key importance in measuring the extent of housing deprivation and as yardsticks against which progress could be assessed.

Table 2.6   *English housing conditions: unfitness*

	1986			2001		
	No. (000s)	% of tenure	% of total	No. (000s)	% of tenure	% of total
Owner-occupied	769	6.6	46.3	424	2.9	47.9
Private rented	361	25.4	21.7	207	10.3	23.4
Local authority	281	6.8	16.9	110	4.1	12.4
Housing association	23	4.9	1.4	40	3	4.5
Vacant	228	28.1	13.7	106	16	12.0
Total stock	1,662	8.8	100.0	887	4.2	100

Sources: Data from Wilcox (2002) Table 23a (original data from *English House Condition Survey 1986*) and ODPM (2003a).

Measured in this way, housing renewal and new construction during the last quarter of the 20th century could be seen as having almost obliterated poor physical conditions. Even by 1991, for example, the number of dwellings in England lacking basic amenities had fallen to only 205,000, or less than one-tenth of the number 20 years earlier (Leather and Morrison 1997). Up until the early 1980s, much of this change resulted from the continuing decline in private rented housing.

Whilst homes classed as 'unfit or in serious disrepair' (Below Tolerable Standard, or BTS, in Scotland) have probably been declining since the 1970s, the number of dwellings affected remains considerable. In England, for example, properties classed as 'unfit for habitation' continued to account for 4.2 per cent of the total stock in 2001, despite the unfitness rate having been halved since 1986 (see Table 2.6). More broadly, there are questions about the adequacy of these kinds of house condition measures, perhaps reflecting the problems of the postwar era rather than the 21st century.

Whilst the incidence of poor dwelling conditions remains highest in the private rented sector, almost half of the homes classed as unfit today are owner-occupied. To some extent, this reflects the numerical dominance of home-ownership and the relatively marginal presence of private landlords (see Tables 2.1 and 2.4). It also reflects the point made in Chapter 1 that the owner-occupied sector has become increasingly diverse and now contains 'half the poor' (Burrows and Wilcox 2000; Burrows 2003a and 2003b).

There is a strong association between low incomes and poor housing conditions. In England in 1991, for example, more than one in ten households with an annual income of less than £4,000 lived in an unfit dwelling, compared with only one in 35 of those with an income of £24,000 or more. Older people are also disproportionately represented in poor quality housing: 13 per cent of households headed by a person aged 85 or more in 1991 lived in unfit housing (Leather and Morrison 1997).

In 2002 central government in England introduced its 'decent homes standard' as the primary yardstick for measuring the physical condition of social housing. Under the standard dwellings must satisfy four broad criteria (ODPM 2002b, pp.6–9):

- fitness for human habitation (as defined by the Housing Act 1985)
- disrepair (a dwelling fails this test if either (a) it has one or more key building components which are old and, because of their condition, needing replacement or major repair, or (b) two or more other building components which are old and, because of their condition, needing replacement or major repair)
- having 'reasonably modern facilities and services' (e.g., kitchen 20 years old or less; bathroom 30 years old or less)
- providing a 'reasonable degree of thermal comfort' (including both 'effective heating' and 'effective insulation')

It is estimated that in 2001 around 1.7 million social rented sector dwellings in England (41 per cent of the total) were 'non-decent' on this measure (ODPM 2002b). Central government's target of upgrading the entire stock to meet this standard by 2010 is one of the main drivers for the stock transfer programme (see Chapter 6). The Scottish Executive and Welsh Assembly Government have also established Quality Housing Standards based on principles similar to those developed by ODPM (Scottish Executive 2003a; Welsh Assembly Government 2003).

Income distribution and its changing nature

A crucial aspect of the background to changing housing and regeneration policies since 1980 is the relatively high incidence of poverty and the increasing polarization of household incomes. Almost one-fifth of UK households (19 per cent) were 'at risk of poverty' in 1999 in terms of receiving incomes below 60 per cent of the UK median value (Dennis and Guio 2003). This compares with the EU-wide average value of 15 per cent. Among EU member states only Portugal and Greece recorded higher poverty rates on this measure. Further, 11 per cent of UK households were, during the period 1996–8, at 'persistent risk of poverty' (i.e., subsisting on incomes below 60 per cent of the national median value for two years in this three-year period). Again, this figure is high in relation to the EU-wide average (9 per cent), and was surpassed only by Greece and Portugal.

As far as income polarization is concerned, the 12 years to 1991 saw incomes in the lower 20–30 per cent of the national income distribution remaining static or increasing only marginally, whilst the average figure across the distribution as a whole rose by 36 per cent. By the mid-1990s income inequality in Britain was greater than at any time since the 1940s (Hills 1998). Since 1997, however, there has been a modest reduction in income inequality resulting from rising employment levels and from changes in benefits and tax credits. These latter developments have particularly benefited households with children. Nevertheless, the reduced number of 'low income' households seen since the late 1990s only brings the total back to its 1995/6 level; the number of people below the low-income threshold remains almost double that of 20 years ago (Palmer, Rahman and Kenway 2002; Piachaud and Sutherland 2002).

There is also evidence that generally widening income differentials have been accompanied by growing spatial polarization. Dorling and Rees's analysis of 1971–2001 census data demonstrated an ongoing tendency for neighbours to become more similar in social and demographic terms, whilst neighbourhoods (local authority districts) are becoming more dissimilar (Dorling and Rees 2003).

The changing public sector

Council housing: the postwar legacy

Since the early 1980s, some of the policy focus on 'sub-standard dwellings' has switched from the private rented to the local authority sector. Whilst the incidence of unfitness in council housing remains relatively low (see Table 2.6), structural and design defects have become an increasingly familiar problem. To some extent, these problems are attributable to the 'numbers game' of the immediate postwar period: that is, the overriding housing policy concern with quantitative output and limited unit costs.

Mainly because it facilitated the rapid construction of large numbers of dwellings, but also because it embodied a vision of 'modernism', the large-scale pre-fabrication and 'system-building' of multi-storey blocks came to symbolize the housing policy of the 1950s and 1960s (Muthesius and Glendinning 1994). Between 1965 and 1972, half of all new municipal dwellings in England had involved flats, with the proportion of these made up by 'high flats' (five storeys or more) peaking at around a quarter in 1966–7 (Merrett 1979). However, spurred by the partial collapse of the Ronan Point tower block in 1968, and by growing doubts about the cost-effectiveness of high-rise housing, the proportion of new council dwellings being built in the form of high flats declined dramatically in the late 1960s. Although the era of high-rise construction was relatively short-lived, and although the overall proportion of council dwellings accounted for by tower blocks was always relatively small, the resulting legacy has had a lasting impact. The physical and social problems popularly associated with tower blocks – as well as with other 'non-traditional' architectural forms – have blighted the image of council housing, as well as providing a continuing financial and managerial headache for the local authorities concerned.

Whilst the stock of council homes peaked in 1980 (see Table 2.1), the start of the sector's decline can, perhaps, traced to the mid-1970s when investment in new construction was sharply cut back following the public spending crisis of 1975–6. Further cuts followed the election of the Thatcher administration in 1979 so that, by 1985, the number of council homes being built across Great Britain had fallen to 21,000 (from 134,000 a decade earlier). By 1990, the figure had fallen to below 8,000, and by 2001 to virtually zero (see Table 2.2).

The Right to Buy

As noted earlier in this chapter, the shrinking size of the council sector since 1980 results mainly from the sale of council houses under the Right to Buy scheme, introduced in the Housing Act of that year. In terms of its impact on reshaping social housing over this period, the RTB far outweighs any other. Although sales to sitting tenants had been taking place before the election of the Thatcher government in 1979, the 1980 Act removed local discretion (Forrest and Murie 1988). Just as important, the Act specified very attractive levels of discount which made the Right to Buy a desirable financial option for many tenants.

With a few limited exceptions the RTB applied to all council tenants with tenancies of three years or more. The level of discount relates to the length of the tenancy, with such rates under the initial regime rising from 33 per cent to 50 per cent. Throughout the 1980s, discounts were increased to provide further incentives to potential purchasers. Discounts of up to 70 per cent were introduced in 1986. These were related to property type as well as to length of tenancy: flat residents benefited from higher discounts than people living in houses.

At the same time, throughout the 1980s, central government used the local authority subsidy regime to push up council rents. Although this was justified by the need to target subsidy towards meeting need, the reduced cost advantage of renting over ownership enhanced the attraction of the Right to Buy.

The two million homes sold under the Right to Buy since 1980 represent around one-third of the stock in council ownership at the start of this period. By comparison, only 250,000 council homes (and about 500,000 RSL homes) have been built since 1980, with most of the additions to the local authority stock being before 1985. Seen in this context, the impact of the RTB, though considerable, is perhaps not quite as dramatic as is sometimes argued.

In general, RTB sales have tended to be slightly higher in rural areas and in urban areas with relatively small amounts of council housing. In a few districts of this kind more than half of the 1980 stock has now been sold (Jones and Murie 1999). In large cities where a high proportion of council housing is flats, however, sales rates have been low. In Glasgow, for example, 1980–95 sales amounted to only 17 per cent of 1980 stock, or about half the national average; and in a number of inner London boroughs, the comparable figures were even lower. The effect of this has been to accentuate the contrast between districts in terms of the size of the public sector stock, so that those areas which started out with a below-average proportion of council housing are now further below the average.

The Right to Buy and residualization

Apart from reducing the number of council homes, and contributing to the increase in home-ownership, the RTB has changed the nature of council housing and the make-up of council tenants. Purchasers have tended to be better-off families and older tenants whose long tenancies have qualified them for higher discounts. Properties purchased have tended to be houses (especially those in more popular areas) rather than flats (especially those in less popular areas), so that what remains of council housing is more dominated by flats in less popular areas and by poorer tenants.

In terms of property type, rates of sale have generally been higher among more desirable homes, particularly larger houses. Nearly half (46 per cent) of the 1980 stock of council houses had been sold by 2001, compared with less than a quarter (22 per cent) of council flats. The RTB has also had a selective impact in terms of the purchasers. For example, whereas 13 per cent of 1981–4 purchasers in England were classed as 'professional/employers and managers', this group accounted for only 6 per cent of all council tenants at the time. On the other hand, only 21 per cent of purchasers were in the 'semi-skilled/unskilled manual' category, whereas this group accounted for 38 per cent of all tenants. More dramatically, 76 per cent of purchasers were employed, compared with only 35 per cent of all council tenants being in work. Some 72 per cent of purchasers were aged between 30 and 59, whilst this was true for only 40 per cent of all tenants.

Over time, these aspects of the RTB process have tended to sift out more and more of the better properties and better-off tenants and this has contributed to a process known as 'residualization': that is, leaving the council sector as a 'residual tenure' providing welfare housing only for more vulnerable people (e.g., single parents, people with disabilities, and others with a marginal economic position).

Since its appeal has also been selective in terms of age, the RTB has also had a profound impact on the demographic structure of the council sector. Murie, Nevin and Leather (1998) have described this as 'hollowing out' the age structure, so that the tenure is increasingly dominated by the relatively old (households headed by persons aged over 65) and the relatively young (households headed by persons aged under 30: see Table 2.7 and Figure 4.4).

However, whilst it has been an important driver of change since 1980, the RTB has not been the only cause of the transformation in the composition of council housing in the late 20th and early 21st century; trends within wider society have also played a part. For example, whilst the proportion of council tenant households containing no earners rose from 37 per cent in 1980 to

Table 2.7   *Age of household heads by tenure (%)*

	Tenure	Under 25	25–29	30–44	45–64	65–74	75 or over
Age in 1980	Outright owners	0	1	8	40	32	20
	Home buyers	4	13	48	33	2	0
	Council renting	4	7	22	36	21	12
	HA renting	7	11	15	20	25	23
	Private renter, unfurnished	4	5	13	27	26	25
	Private renter, furnished	40	24	20	10	4	2
	All tenures	4	8	26	34	17	10

	Tenure	Under 25	25–29	30–44	45–59	60–69	70–79	80 or over
Age in 2000	Outright owners	0	0	6	23	30	28	12
	Home buyers	2	10	48	33	6	2	0
	Council renting	7	7	26	20	13	17	9
	HA renting	7	6	29	20	11	16	11
	Private renter, unfurnished	12	17	36	19	6	6	5
	Private renter, furnished	29	20	34	9	3	3	2
	All tenures	4	7	21	36	14	12	6

Source: Data from Table 30a in Wilcox (2003) – original source ONS General Household Survey.

66 per cent in 1993, the comparable figure for 1962 was only 11 per cent (Holmans 1995). Post-1980 changes in the household characteristics of council housing as compared with other tenures are also mapped out in Table 2.8. This shows the demographic hollowing out of social housing (see also Figure 4.4).

Other factors likely to have contributed to the residualization of council housing include demographic change due to the ageing of the national population, the tax advantages which have tended to be afforded to home-ownership, and the rise in incomes and expectations which has accompanied decades of economic growth. As a contributor to residualization, therefore, the RTB should be seen as one among a number of processes with compound effects.

Managing a residualized sector

Residualization involving the reduction in the number of houses as opposed to flats has a number of important management implications. It reduces the chances of the remaining council tenants needing larger accommodation

Table 2.8 *Employment status of household heads by tenure (%)*

Year	Tenure	Employed		Unemployed	Retired	Other economically inactive
		Full time	Part time			
1981	Outright owners	37	4	3	44	11
	Home buyers	92	1	3	2	2
	Council renting	43	4	9	28	15
	HA renting	42	4	6	34	14
	Private renter, unfurnished	51	4	4	30	10
	Private renter, furnished	65	1	9	5	20
	All tenures	58	3	5	24	10
2000/01	Outright owners	24	6	1	63	5
	Home buyers	86	4	1	5	4
	Council renting	23	8	6	37	26
	HA renting	24	9	6	34	27
	Private renter, unfurnished	57	8	4	16	16
	Private renter, furnished	56	11	7	4	23
	All tenures	54	6	2	28	10

Source: Extracted from Table 33 in *Housing Finance Review* 2002/3 by Steve Wilcox, published for the Joseph Rowntree Foundation by the Chartered Institute of Housing and Council of Mortgage Lenders. Reproduced by permission of the Joseph Rowntree Foundation. Original data from housing trailer to 1981 *Labour Force Survey* and *Survey of English Housing 2000/1*.

getting a transfer to a more suitable property. New applicants are also affected, with large families amongst the homeless facing longer periods in temporary accommodation because of the need to wait longer for a suitable property among the diminished stock of larger homes.

With a higher proportion of remaining residents being from vulnerable groups, the housing management task is made more difficult. Social residualization also adds to the stigma that council housing equals poverty housing. Especially where low demand reduces the power of landlords to filter applicants through rationing (see Chapter 4), problems such as anti-social behaviour tend to assume a higher profile (see Chapter 8). And because the tenure is – in all areas – increasingly stripped of tenants in the residentially stable middle-aged groups (households headed by persons aged 30–65), there is an underlying tendency towards rising rates of turnover which add to management costs and undercut community coherence (Pawson and Bramley 2000).

Figure 2.7   *Losses to council housing in England, 1981–2003*

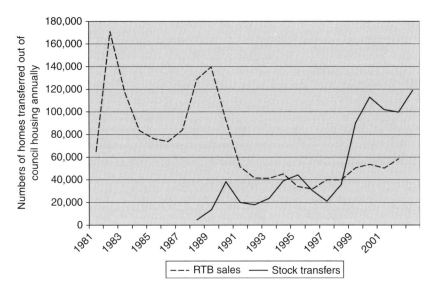

Notes: 1. Post-1990 RTB figures are for financial years. 2. Graphic excludes demolitions.

Sources: RTB sales – data from *Housing Statistics 2003*, ODPM website, Table 643 and Wilcox (1996) Table 19a; Stock transfers – data calculated from ODPM stock transfers table, ODPM website, www.odpm.gov.uk/housing (2003 figure projected).

Stock transfer

Most of the shrinkage of council housing since 1980 has resulted from the Right to Buy. Increasingly, however – in England, at least – continuing stock reductions result from ownership transfers from councils to housing associations and similar bodies (Figure 2.7).

The transfer of council stock under LSVT rules began at the end of the 1980s. Whilst they were facilitated by recent housing legislation (Housing Act 1985), and generally encouraged by central government, the early LSVTs were driven by individual local authorities for mainly financial reasons (Perry 2000). In the early days, transfer was seen as a particularly attractive prospect by authorities with a low residual housing debt: that is, where the original loans for the stock had been largely paid off. In these circumstances, the capital receipt generated allowed councils to clear their housing debt and generate significant 'windfall' gains. These sums could be ploughed into the council's investment priorities, including the funding of new social housing. For other authorities, the greater freedom available in the post-1988 financial regime for housing associations was a more important consideration.

In order to proceed with a transfer, a local authority must consult its tenants and must obtain central government consent. Although there is no specific legal requirement for a ballot, there is an understanding that ministerial consent will be given only where an authority can demonstrate, through a majority vote of tenants, that there is popular backing for the proposal (Mullen 2001).

Through the requirement for ministerial consent, central government can shape the transfer programme in favour of its own objectives. One such objective has been to discourage proposed transfers leading to the replication of large stockholdings. The objection here follows from the widely held view that large, monopolistic public sector landlords tend to be inefficient and insensitive to the interests of tenants as customers. Consequently, larger authorities considering transfer have been required to develop plans under which stock is handed over to two or more successor landlords (though the precise rules on the maximum permissible stockholding of LSVT housing associations have varied over time).

At first, LSVTs were overwhelmingly concentrated in rural districts in the South – and particularly the South East – of England. With the passage of time, however, transfers have become more widespread in England. Mainly due to changes in government rules regarding housing debt and the governance of successor landlords, post-1995 transfers have increasingly involved areas containing substantially deprived communities and, in some cases, poor quality housing stock (Murie and Nevin 2001). In 2001, Sunderland, with the transfer of its 36,000 homes – a considerable number subject to low demand – became the largest city authority in England to transfer its housing.

By 2001, nearly 100 of the 354 local authorities in England had terminated their landlord function and the annual volume of transfers was rising steeply (see Figure 2.4). In 2002, however, the programme suffered a major shock as Birmingham's transfer proposal was heavily defeated in a tenant ballot. At the time of writing it is not entirely clear whether the earlier momentum can be quickly re-established.

In addition to whole stock transfers, a cohort of estate and neighbourhood transfers have been implemented in support of the inner-city regeneration objectives. These 'partial transfers', particularly common in Inner London, have so far resulted in the handover to housing associations of some 60,000 homes in around 40 packages (see pp.195–201).

In Scotland and Wales the picture has been rather different from that in England. Few councils have so far transferred their entire housing stock. With the recent handover of Glasgow's 80,000 homes, however, this might be set to change, although a substantial majority of Scotland's councils had examined but rejected the transfer option in the 1998–2002 period (Pawson 2002b). It should, however, be noted that around 50,000 former Scottish properties have been handed over to housing associations since 1989, generally in small parcels of less than 2,000 homes. In Wales, with Bridgend tenants recently endorsing the country's first whole stock transfer proposal, there is also a possibility of a new trend being established.

The housing association sector

In describing the changing face of social housing over the past 20 years, stock transfer forms the bridge between a focus on the local authority sector and housing associations. Along with a significant volume of new completions, ownership transfers more than doubled the overall size of this sector during the 1990s (see Table 2.1). The majority of this increase – about two-thirds in England – has come about through transfers, with about one-third being attributable to new construction.

Housing associations have a variety of origins – charitable, campaigning, self-help or professionally-based – but exist in their modern form mainly as a product of the Housing Act 1974. The Act introduced a common regulatory framework and access to generous development grants. RSLs are sometimes categorized as part of the 'voluntary sector', reflecting their governance by an unpaid Board or committee of management. At the time of writing, however, there are indications that the Housing Corporation will in future allow English associations the option of paying Board members. This is justified mainly on the grounds that the responsibilities of Board membership have become increasingly onerous, and that there is a need for incentives to attract 'high quality' candidates for the task. Issues surrounding RSL Board membership – particularly in relation to stock transfer – are discussed further in Chapter 7.

In the 1970s and 1980s, RSLs tended to play a complementary role to local authorities, specializing in housing particular groups (e.g., elderly people, people with disabilities), or in rehabilitating older inner-city housing. Since around 1990, however, associations have tended to take on a more general social housing provision role. Nevertheless, the differing origins and experiences of these bodies contribute to continuing diversity within the sector. Some associations remain locally based while others play a regional or national role, and the extent to which this happens is strongly influenced by the policies of national funding bodies (e.g., the Housing Corporation). Some retain charitable status, whilst others have the status of a company limited by guarantee. Increasingly, associations are forming sometimes elaborate group structures, with different subsidiaries responsible for different functions, such as the provision of low cost home-ownership or of residential care homes for the elderly. A growing proportion are actually descendants of local authority housing departments, having emerged from LSVTs (see above and Chapter 7).

What they have in common is a commitment to social housing in the broad sense, being not-for-profit organizations, and being subject to a common regulatory framework (although this is becoming similar to that applying to local authorities). They can be regarded as an important and relatively successful example of the 'social economy' in action.

It is in some ways insular to regard the emergence and growth of this sector as noteworthy, let alone some sort of aberration. From a European comparative perspective, housing associations and similar bodies are very much more the 'norm' in the provision of subsidized rented housing. It is Britain,

with its heavy traditional reliance on local authorities, which was more anom-
alous (McCrone and Stephens 1995). Having said this, however, it should be
noted that the situation elsewhere in Europe is far from static. For example,
in Germany organizations akin to British RSLs lost much of their special status at the end of the 1980s and moved closer to the private sector, whilst in
the Netherlands the levels of subsidy support to social housing have been
drastically scaled down in the 1990s (Van Kempen, Schutjens and Van
Weesep 2000).

The rise of housing associations as central government's preferred 'main
provider of new social housing' dates from the 1987 Housing White Paper and
the subsequent Housing Act 1988. The new financial regime created by the
Act opened up both greater opportunities and greater risks for associations
(Randolph 1993; Malpass 2000). Rather than having their capital costs wholly
underpinned by the state, association investment was now to be financed by
a combination of government grant and private borrowing.

As it has developed, the post-1988 housing association sector has lost some
of its distinctiveness as compared with council housing (see above). Partly
due to stock transfers, the equation between associations and small-scale
operation has become less and less accurate. By April 2003 there were 107
English-based associations, each managing more than 5,000 homes, of which
29 owned more than 10,000 properties. (The comparable figures for local
authorities in April 2002 were 171 and 82.)

By comparison with councils, housing associations have been seen as having
a somewhat privileged status in funding terms since the 1980s. This is shown
by the relative scale of the housing association and local authority development
programmes (see Figure 2.2). It is also reflected in the quality of the housing
stock managed by associations (see Table 2.5). Their general exemption from
the Right to Buy has also helped them to preserve their most popular stock
intact (although this will change in Scotland with a limited Right to Buy for
housing association tenants which was legislated in 2001 and set to take effect
in 2011). In any case, in spite of being so far sheltered from the RTB, associations have also been affected by the residualization of social housing, and the
incidence of socio-economic disadvantage among their tenants is similar to that
for local authorities. And because – in England, at least – their rents tend to be
somewhat higher than those charged by local authorities, the poverty trap experienced by their tenants is, if anything, even deeper. (The phrase 'poverty trap'
here refers to the effect of the Housing Benefit system which blunts work incentives for unemployed tenants paying high rents: see Wilcox 1996.)

Conclusion

The last 20 years of the 20th century saw fairly dramatic changes in the
structure of British housing. Home-ownership continued to expand whilst the
decline of private renting was reversed. Council landlordism contracted

sharply, whilst housing associations burgeoned. One important consequence of this tenure restructuring is that, whilst social housing is ever more closely associated with poverty, the owner-occupied sector's expansion has increasingly drawn in poorer households.

The changing character of social housing – particularly council housing – has major consequences for the nature of the housing management task. These are further discussed in Chapter 8. Stock transfers into housing association ownership are now having a profound impact on social housing both in terms of property condition and organizational governance. The mechanics of transfer as one among a range of possible techniques for facilitating new development and property renewal are considered in more detail in Chapters 7 and 9.

Further reading

Much of the factual basis for this chapter is drawn from housing statistics accessible via the Office of the Deputy Prime Minister (ODPM) website at www.odpm.gov.uk/housing/(statistics page). This site carries a wealth of figures relating to Wales and Scotland, as well as England. Many of the data are also published in the annual *Housing Review* (formerly *House Finance Review*) edited by Steve Wilcox for the Joseph Rowntree Foundation (and others). Merrett (1979) and Malpass (2000) provide highly readable accounts of housing policy in a historical perspective. From more of an architectural viewpoint, Muthesius and Glendinning's (1994) history of tower blocks and system-built housing is a fascinating contribution both in text and illustrations.

3

The Boom Phenomenon

Introduction

The UK housing market has had a long history of price instability. There have been three major price cycles in the past 30 years: booms in 1971–3, 1977–80 and 1986–9, followed in each case by a slump, when prices (in real terms) fell back over several years. At the time of writing (spring 2003) the market appears to be in the upswing phase of another cycle. Average prices in the UK as a whole increased from £69,000 in 1996 to £144,500 in the fourth quarter of 2002 (Council of Mortgage Lenders 2003: mix adjusted house prices – i.e., an average that reflects the different types of property sold in each period), an increase of nearly 110 per cent. Prices in Greater London over the same period increased 140 per cent to an average of £219,400. Through 2002 average price growth was strong, at 19 per cent and 24 per cent in the last two quarters of the year. Commentators anticipated a slowing of the market in 2003, pointing to the slower growth of prices in London which tends to lead the market (see below). Despite the obvious implications of such high prices rises for affordability, booming housing markets are typically treated quite favourably in the press. Although high and fast-rising prices may be difficult for new entrants to the market, for the great majority of home-owners these conditions provide windfall wealth gains, which require no effort and can be very significant (as seen above, the occupiers of the average UK house has seen their house value grow by £75,500 between 1996 and 2002). Given that the great majority of UK households own their homes it is not surprising that house price inflation is popularly welcomed.

Even cyclical house price reductions have not always been painful for most owners. The trading conditions in the market change, from being a seller's to a buyer's market, thus affecting market traders depending on their role. But the wealth effects are not inevitably severe. The 1970s booms coincided with high general price inflation, so that the real fall in house prices occurred as nominal (money) prices stabilized or even rose, but more slowly than general inflation. In the early 1980s nominal prices again levelled off rather than fell. However, the slump of the early 1990s was accompanied by falls in *nominal* prices for the first time in the memory of most house buyers. This caused

Figure 3.1 *House price trends, UK, 1971–2002*

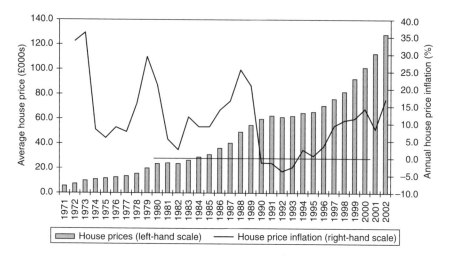

Source: Data from Building Societies Association/Survey of Mortgage Lenders, as reproduced in ODPM *Housing Statistics 2003*, Table 502, ODPM website.

severe, real consequences. As people found that the value of their house was falling, sometimes by a considerable amount, a new phenomenon – negative equity – emerged. Some owner-occupiers found that the amount they had borrowed was greater than the value of their house. The received wisdom, that buying a house was the ultimate safe investment, was shown to have been dramatically wrong. National trends in prices are illustrated in Figure 3.1.

Figure 3.1 traces the shape of the three earlier booms and the significant price rises year on year through the late 1990s. A key factor to note in interpreting these changes, however, is the underlying rate of inflation, which in the early 1970s was at a historically high level (reaching a peak of nearly 25 per cent per annum) and in the late 1990s at a much lower level (being successfully maintained near the Monetary Policy Committee's target of 2.5 per cent per annum). So, although the price rises appear to be much more marked in the earlier booms, in fact, in relation to the underlying changes in prices and earnings, the more recent boom is nearly as great in real terms. Despite this, much of the commentary on recent house price trends has discounted the possibility of another major crash (Cutler 2002; Pannell 2002; and see below).

The purpose of this chapter is to examine the causes and effects of housing market price instability. The boom and bust housing market cycle has become almost taken for granted in the UK context (although perhaps booming conditions seem more natural than the bust), but it is worth examining the fundamental question as to why this market performs so differently from those of other consumer goods. In particular, a contradiction that persists in relation to the owner-occupied housing market is examined. On the one hand, the strong attachment to owner-occupation is partly underpinned by a belief in the value of housing as an investment, as a safe way of accumulating wealth, allowing progression 'up the ladder' to attain ever bigger and better quality housing. Yet the evidence demonstrates that such gains are not always available and certainly not equally available to all. Further, in a low inflation economic climate, the real costs of investing in housing (usually requiring significant long-term borrowing and the large overall interest payments that this entails) are also becoming clearer to consumers; lenders are now obliged to show the total cost of borrowing in their information to borrowers. This chapter discusses the systematic inequalities between different types of buyer through the phases of housing market boom and bust.

Individual differences in the potential for wealth accumulation are, however, only part of the story. The scale of borrowing for housing and the amount of stored wealth it represents in the consumer sector have meant that house price instability has had serious and significant knock-on consequences for the rest of the economy. Housing market outcomes strongly influence consumers' willingness to save, to borrow and to spend. These effects are exacerbated by other mechanisms allowing the release of housing equity into the economy directly, most notably through housing inheritance and the use of new mortgage products. These phenomena are also explored in this chapter.

What causes house price instability?

Econometric work examining the causes of house price change has consistently shown that real incomes are the major, long-term explanation of the house price trend (Meen 1996; Munro and Tu 1996). This is not surprising; housing is an essential purchase and a major element of household consumption. As incomes rise people are willing and able to spend more on bigger or better housing. Unlike other goods (such as, say, computers, where rising demand has linked with increased supply and technical advances to *reduce* real prices through time) the supply of housing is relatively fixed. Each year, new building adds only about 1 per cent to the existing housing stock and, of course, houses remain spatially fixed. Thus, there is an ageing housing stock (over 20 per cent of owner-occupied property in the UK was built prior to 1919 and over 40 per cent before 1939) which was chiefly built to reflect the needs and demands of previous generations.

New building is unable to change the housing stock quickly in response to changes in contemporary demand. Some commentators (A.W. Evans 1991) point to the planning system as the key culprit in increasing house prices, by restricting the market's ability to respond more fully to the growing demands of house purchasers (and see the discussion in Chapter 5). But the tradition in Britain of preserving and renovating houses over many decades (in contrast, say, to Japan) means that this is only part of the explanation. It is clear that the long-term upward trend in incomes, and the general growth in household numbers (caused by an ageing population, divorce and separation and later marriages: see Chapter 2) creates an upward demand pressure that outstrips new supply and inflates prices. While this may seem to indicate a steady upward path for house prices, the relatively fixed supply also makes the housing market vulnerable to bigger price swings when demand exhibits shorter-term volatility overlaid on this long-term trend. And this also means that patterns at a regional or local level can vary sharply from national averages.

Examining the history of house price changes in Britain clearly shows the very broad range of factors that can create demand volatility. Muellbauer (1990) argued that booms need some sort of initial 'shock' to set them in train. For example, the 1986–9 boom was preceded by a major financial deregulation that had profound effects on the mortgage lending business. Whereas the building societies in the 1970s had exercised rationing policies to maintain a steady flow of credit on to the housing market, the 1980s saw a loosening of the restrictions that they had faced and, more significantly, a major influx of competitors, especially banks, looking to capture what appeared to be a lucrative and relatively risk-free business. Consumers suddenly found it significantly easier to access mortgage credit than previously. The changed regulatory framework allowed a more liberal attitude to the extent to which equity could be released at the time of the transaction (i.e., by not insisting that all of the sales proceeds of the previous home was invested in the next). As the boom gathered pace, borrowers took ever higher multiples of income to afford the higher prices (see Figure 3.2). This can be seen as indicative of

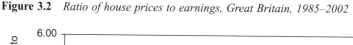

Figure 3.2   *Ratio of house prices to earnings, Great Britain, 1985–2002*

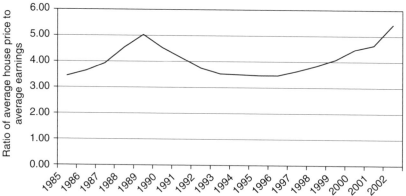

Source: Data from *Housing Finance* (various editions) as collected in *Survey of Mortgage Lenders*.

what Muellbauer has dubbed a 'frenzy' effect: as house prices become higher people become increasingly desperate to buy, because they fear that if they wait then prices will have accelerated beyond their ability to pay. Ironically the fact that house prices are rising *increases* demand for housing as an asset since the prospect of ever-greater and faster capital gains encourages people to stretch their borrowing to the limit to capture a greater share of this (apparently free) wealth.

These major changes in the mortgage market, allied to the growing prosperity caricatured as the yuppy, 'loads of money' culture (especially in London and the South East) would no doubt have been sufficient on its own to fuel a housing market boom. In addition, a direct policy measure stoked the pressure even further. Mortgage interest tax relief, which allowed borrowers to offset the cost of their interest payments against tax, was limited to the first £30,000 of any loan. A concession, however, allowed joint, unmarried purchasers each to claim up to the £30,000 limit on the same property (while married couples could receive relief on only £30,000). In the March 1988 budget the Chancellor announced that this difference in treatment would be abolished in August of that year, so that subsequently tax relief on loans up to £30,000 would be available on any single *property* (while those who had bought under the earlier arrangement could keep their tax concession until they moved/re-mortgaged). This provided a real incentive to cohabiting couples and groups of friends to rush to buy a property before the deadline.

By August 1988, the booming housing market and economy appeared to be running out of control and sharp increases in interest rates were implemented to constrain spiralling credit and consumer spending. Mortgage interest rates increased from around 9.7 per cent in May 1988 to a high of 15.5 per cent in February 1990. This magnitude of change has an enormous effect on mortgage repayments, particularly relatively new repayment mortgages (where the majority of payments in the early years is interest) and all interest-only (endowment) mortgages (which had become the most popular type of mortgage through the late 1980s, representing 83 per cent of all advances in the third quarter of 1988, for example). Effectively, this interest rate increase of nearly 60 per cent would lead to a direct and proportionate increase in payments on such mortgages by nearly 60 per cent. Such an increase would have a major impact on most family budgets, even when a prudent safety margin in borrowing had been preserved. But, for those in the very early years of a mortgage, where borrowing capacity had been stretched as far as possible to achieve a toe-hold in the booming market, such an increase was potentially catastrophic. The year 1988 marked the height of the boom, though prices were still to increase by an average of 11.9 per cent and 7.1 per cent in 1989 and 1990 respectively. Higher interest rates reduced the affordability of new loans, so that new borrowers were seeking to borrow less and some marginal borrowers were forced leave the market altogether. Prices were still rising, but the pre-conditions had been set to replace the boom with a slump.

Figure 3.2 shows clear peaks in house prices relative to earnings associated with each of the booms in marked contrast to a relatively stable long-term ratio somewhere around 3.25. At the height of previous booms, the ratio approached 5, a level regarded as being unsustainable in terms of the burden of mortgage repayments on household income. This high level is again evident from 2000. It is less easy to see the precursors for the late 1990s boom; some upward price movement was clearly just a cyclical correction to the prolonged slump of the early 1990s. Even though confidence in the housing market had been severely dented, in the medium term the basic reasons for buying houses re-emerged: to allow people to set up new households, to move as their household changes size, or for work. Economic conditions through the period have been broadly favourable for house price growth, with high employment and steadily growing incomes. Consumer confidence has also been relatively high. For most of this period, there has only been really rapid (double figure) price inflation in London and the South East, although by 2002 average rises did reach double figures in all regions and a high of 30 per cent in East Anglia (Council of Mortgage Lenders 2003). Special pressures on house prices in the South East reflect the co-existence of strong economic growth, in-migration and an inadequate supply response from the housebuilding industry.

A new phenomenon, of widespread buy-to-let, has also emerged in the 1990s as a possible factor exacerbating the asset demand for housing (which could be expected to heighten booms and deepen slumps if it continues). Several factors might account for the strong growth in the sector. There was a group of 'reluctant landlords' created during the slump of the early 1990s when home-owners, faced with losses if they were to sell, chose instead to rent out their own property and move into another. Additionally, there seems to have been a growth in individuals choosing to invest in this way, presumably attracted by the potential capital growth and facilitated by the availability of customized mortgage products. Other factors may include investor disillusionment with other investments, due to the relatively poor performance of the stock market, low interest rates on savings accounts and mis-selling of pensions and endowments. As likely pay-outs from even well-regarded pension schemes look increasingly uncertain, the attraction of 'bricks and mortar' for 'secure' long-term investment is likely to increase.

However, there is more caution as to whether, in 2003, high borrowing ratios replicate the 'unsustainable' level of 1989. Cutler (2002), Pannell (2002) and Wilcox (2002) all argue that the prevailing low inflation climate means that there is scope to adjust to a higher equilibrium price to earnings ratio. When interest rates are at a much lower level (base rate has been sustained in recent years at a historically low 3–5 per cent), higher multiples of income can be borrowed for a similar repayment burden on household incomes. Further, these commentators note that an increasing proportion of buyers are dual-earning households. So, in 2002, first-time buyers' initial payments consumed only 13 per cent of their income compared with over 25 per cent for the first-time buyers of 1989. Against this must be set another significant impact of the low inflation environment, that of maintaining the real burden of debt for longer. Inflation can quickly erode the proportion of income that is required to service any debt burden, but when inflation is low, the initial repayment ratio will remain for much longer. It is very different to have to commit over 20 per cent of income to mortgage repayments for a short period (say, for the first five years) than to imagine this continuing for 10 years or more.

Housing market slump

In the same way that demand volatility causes price rises, the demand side largely explains house price falls. Two key factors have created demand volatility, precipitating downward pressure on house prices: housing affordability and macroeconomic conditions. Definitions of 'affordability' have been hotly contested in academic and policy circles in relation to policy goals of providing housing that is accessible to those without work, or in poorly paid work (Wilcox and Sutherland 1997; Freeman, Holmans and Whitehead 1999). One possible indicator is to examine the choices made by owner-occupiers in relation to their borrowing and repayments, given that most buyers, most of the time, can choose the amount they spend on housing and the consequent repayment burden they face.

As shown above, the long-run house price to earnings ratio tends to hover between 3 and 3.5 with average mortgage advance to income ratios around 2–2.5 (these figures reflect both owners' choices and lenders' policies; lenders typically use standard income multipliers to preserve affordability and reduce their institution's risk of mortgage default). These averages, of course, conceal a substantial variation (notably between first-time buyers and subsequent purchasers, and between different parts of the country, for example: see the discussion in the following section). Booms are characterized by large increases in these borrowing ratios and create growing difficulties of affordability. Ultimately very high ratios become unsustainable, new buyers become unable to borrow any more, and so demand pressure slackens. In the late 1980s these factors coincided with a labour market down-turn where unemployment was rising and wages moderating. A significant new factor was the so-called development of 'flexible' labour markets, creating reduced job security for many workers moving from permanent positions to contracting or self-employment. This undermined willingness to borrow and created a growing group of workers particularly vulnerable to changing macroeconomic fortunes.

In the early 1990s, then, the very high interest rates and the changing economic climate put increasing numbers of borrowers to the margins of affordability, and beyond. Growing unemployment inevitably led to increasing numbers of purchasers being forced to sell, either to save money by buying a smaller property or by moving out of owner-occupation altogether.

In circumstances where the mortgage becomes unaffordable, for instance where making repayments relied on two wages where now there is only one (say, because one partner has lost a job, or they have separated), it becomes important to sell quickly. While less than full mortgage payments are being made the outstanding debt will grow, so that the borrower's financial position steadily worsens. A supply of forced sellers depresses prices. These negative signals are arguably particularly important given the psychology of the market. The house price speculative bubble is buoyed up on beliefs that prices will rise higher and, as argued above, borrowers are tempted into the market because of the fear that the opportunity to buy will accelerate away from them. The boom is supported by media stories (as reports highlight the extremes of high prices in London and the South East particularly: see Hamnett 1999) and by more local reports of high sale prices (see the Edinburgh case study below). The excitement evaporates once the stories (and the experience behind them) become more measured.

In the early 1990s this change was more severe than it had been in previous booms, because prices did not merely stabilize but actually fell. In these circumstances, people could no longer simply sell up. Recent buyers would not get back the price they paid, and where there was negative equity selling would result in a real debt that required to be repaid. Regrettably, this became a common scenario (Ford, Burrows and Nettleton 2001). One particular aspect of this problem emerged through a so-called 'flight to quality'. As housing became ever less affordable through the 1980s, one (quite rational) response was the development of more 'starter' homes; small, cheap flats (usually) aimed at providing the single purchaser, or the new couple, with access to the first step on the home-ownership ladder. When boom turned to slump, those buyers still looking to buy in the depressed conditions started to leapfrog over these properties, looking instead to buy something that would suit them for longer. This left many starter home buyers stranded in houses for which there was very little demand and which, by design, were likely to be unsuitable for very common lifecycle changes (such as moving in with a partner or having children).

Using a national sample of buyers who bought between 1988 and 1991 Dorling and Cornford (1995) exposed the widespread and significant incidence of negative equity at this time (1993). Across the whole country, 26 per cent of buyers who had purchased between 1988 and 1991 had some negative equity. The areas where prices had risen the most also saw the greatest falls, so that negative equity was commonest in London and the south of England (where over 40 per cent of buyers between 1988 and 1991 had negative equity in 1993). On average, buyers had nearly £4,800 negative equity (but around £5,500 in London and the South East). The problem was also very unevenly distributed within regions. It bore most heavily on the relatively disadvantaged, more marginal home-owners, being disproportionately found amongst young (under 25-year-old) buyers and those in junior clerical and semi-skilled

Figure 3.3   *Mortgage arrears and repossessions, UK, 1971–2002*

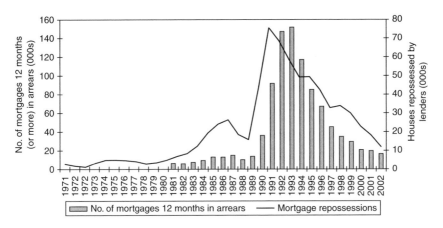

Note: Pre-1982 data for mortgages more than 12 months in arrears unavailable.
Source: Data from *Survey of Mortgage Lenders*, as reproduced in ODPM *Housing Statistics 2003*, Table 545, ODPM website, www.odpm.gov.uk/housing.

jobs. Also, inevitably, greater negative equity was found where the initial proportion of the price borrowed was greater. Thus negative equity was concentrated in households with the fewest resources (such as savings), in relatively vulnerable labour market positions and also at the greatest risk of household change (separation and divorce and the arrival of children). For such households, negative equity was not, then, just a paper loss but created real difficulties (and see Christie 2000 on the challenges of developing coping strategies in these circumstances).

Increasing numbers of households were trapped in houses that they could not sell, or (perhaps more accurately) could not afford to sell at the market price, even though they were unable to cover the mortgage repayments. Those who hoped to move into local authority housing often faced restrictions on the accessibility of this sector to owner-occupiers; for some the only way of gaining access was to become involuntarily homeless, waiting until their house was possessed by their mortgage lender. Inevitably, the scale of mortgage arrears and repossessions grew (Figure 3.3) though it fell back gradually through the 1990s.

Post-2000 trends would also lend support to the argument that an imminent house price crash need not be expected: not only are house possessions continuing to fall, but the early warning signs of rising arrears are not present. The relatively benign economic climate is also important in maintaining households' ability to pay.

Notwithstanding the misery of those who are forced out of the market during a slump, or the anxiety of the many more who accumulate arrears, it might be argued that even severe house price falls make little difference to the great majority of owner-occupiers, who do not need to move within the affected time period and who thus experience paper gains, followed by paper losses as the market price fluctuates. Lenders can also demonstrate how small a proportion of outstanding loans is ever affected by such problems (even in 1991, house possessions affected less than 0.1 per cent of outstanding mortgages). Despite this there are two main implications of price instability that deserve further examination. First, it creates a web of winners and losers for whom personal outcomes are a lottery, determined by factors largely outside their control such as an accident of timing or the spatial progression of the boom or slump, or personal misfortune such as job loss, illness or marital breakdown. Second, there are important linkages between instability of the housing market and instability in the economy as a whole. These are explored in the next sections.

Winners and losers: the consequences of house price instability

As is consistently demonstrated through this book, there is no unitary housing market across the UK. House prices at the regional and local levels show great differences and typically rates of house price inflation are also strongly differentiated (Figure 3.4). There is a well-established regional pattern to the geographical spread of upward pressure on house prices during a boom. There is a so-called ripple effect, where, like a pebble dropped on London, price ripples quickly spread to the rest of the South East, then more slowly through the rest of the country so that finally the most distant markets, in the north of England, Scotland and Wales, experience a much weakened pressure considerably later. Hamnett (1999) argues while there is often great attention paid to the phase where southern prices accelerate away from the rest of country, there is much less discussion of the subsequent catch-up phase where prices in the South moderate, restoring narrower differentials. Over time, he asserts that there is no strong evidence that price differences have tended to become permanently more divergent across the regions of Britain, though (as shown by Bramley and others) there has been a continued divergence evident since the recovery from the 1990s slump, with the South East tending to become significantly more expensive than the rest of the country while some places appear to have become cut adrift from general market recovery, exhibiting 'low demand' (see Chapter 4 and Bramley, Pawson and Third 2000).

The ripple effect is clearly shown in Figure 3.4, in that the instability is shown to be greatest in London and the rest of the South East, where price rise peaks are sharpest and falls greatest. Housing markets more distant from London, such as Scotland, have seen more steady year-on-year house prices.

There has been a long debate in the academic literature on whether the housing market creates systematic patterns of advantage and disadvantage.

Figure 3.4 *UK house price changes by (selected) region*

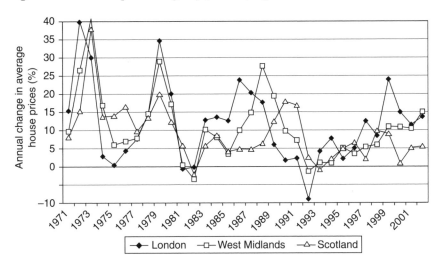

Source: Data from *Survey of Mortgage Lenders*, as reproduced in ODPM *Housing Statistics 2003*, Table 505, ODPM website.

The debate was stimulated by Saunders' (1978, 1984) contention that access to wealth accumulation through house ownership was creating a significant divide – a consumption cleavage – which created a community of economic interest distinct from that created by occupational class. If true, this has powerful theoretical implications for sociological analysis and prompted much debate between those who accepted this more Weberian view of class and those who held a more traditional view of the primacy of labour market position. Empirically, as shown above, it is clear that owners do not accumulate equity all the time and that some individuals can lose out when markets are unstable. However, it is also established that most owners remaining in the tenure over a long period ultimately have accumulated equity and wealth in real terms. (Although this does not, of course, prove that this will always be the case. The conditions that sustained a rising housing market in Britain through the second half of the 20th century may not be replicated indefinitely and not everywhere; Thorns (1992), for instance, pointed to a very different long-term experience of housing markets in New Zealand and USA.) Some debate focused on whether these were *real* gains as people have to live somewhere, arguably much of their accumulated wealth is merely a paper gain. But this is strongly countered by the increasing extent to which people can release their housing wealth through borrowing, trading down, taking equity release financial products in old age or, ultimately, passing on that wealth to their descendants through inheritance. And at younger ages housing wealth can act as security for other types of borrowing, such as a business start-up.

In Britain, though, the key point in evaluating Saunders' claim rested on whether the access to wealth accumulation creates a *different* pattern of inequality and privilege from that created by labour markets, or whether they simply reinforce each other. Does the housing market simply allow the rich to get even richer, enhancing the wealth gap between them and lower income owner-occupiers? Hamnett (1999) argues that this is broadly true. People in professional and managerial occupations tend to move more often so that, examined in cross-sectional evidence, they may not have significantly more equity than less skilled workers. Further, of course, older, retired owners have greater equity on average than those in the early years of mortgage repayment. But, he argues that over the longer term, those in higher social classes have made the greatest gains, in absolute terms, largely because they have been able to buy the most desirable and expensive properties.

This is perhaps not very surprising, but this broad conclusion should not overshadow the main argument highlighted throughout this book: namely, that there are very strong disparities in experience across the country. Owners in areas of low demand have no immediate prospect of making any gains at all. Equally, those fortunate enough to trade at the right time in local 'hot spots' can make gains that much greater than those available to others in more stable local markets.

Recent research in Edinburgh, which experienced a local house price boom in the late 1990s (see Box 3.1), shows that even for those fortunate enough to buy in a housing boom, and capture high capital gains, the experience can be stressful. Further, this research showed how the boom could be self-sustaining over a period or years. Despite people having had to pay prices well over valuations and often much higher than they had expected, most typically felt that they had made a good buy. There was also little evidence of people feeling financially stretched. A significant group largely relied on equity gained from their last property (and in buyers of the most expensive houses this contributed over one-third of the house price overall), and as this had also been inflated in the boom, the price was not hard to afford. For others with a less generous equity cushion, experiences sometimes involved having had to make some small economies and cutting back on luxuries, but this was seen as a short-term problem, with the expectation that the purchase would become affordable after the first year or so. Certainly, most buyers in the sample said that they had not borrowed the maximum that they could, confirming the qualitative accounts of feeling financially comfortable with the decisions made. Although some of this may be specific to the Edinburgh boom, it shows

Box 3.1 *A local housing boom: Edinburgh, 1996–9*

In these four years there was a strong local perception of a boom, and analysis of prices paid showed that prices in one-third of the 65 postcode sectors in Edinburgh increased by 40 per cent or more. There was a clear local geography to the price boom: the leading edge of house price rises was clustered round the centre of the city, characterized by attractive Georgian (in the New Town) and Victorian (in the South Side) residential areas. Lower house price inflation was found further towards the outskirts of the city. An Economic and Social Research Council (ESRC) funded research project sought to establish why, how and with what consequences different types of household were affected by the house price boom. This was investigated using a mix of qualitative interviews with households who had bought in sample areas across the city and with professionals involved in the exchange process, and a quantitative analysis of house price data and interviewees' financial strategies.

Economic conditions, including the expansion of local financial services and the activities associated with the development and location of the new Scottish Parliament in central Edinburgh, provided the pre-conditions for a boom. The main factors that seemed to start and then sustain the boom were:

- media attention given to exceptional cases where property sold for much more than the 'offers-over' price (Scotland has a system in which an 'offers-over' price is published and then buyers compete by putting in sealed bids)
- the difficulty professionals in the market – the surveyors and solicitors – had in predicting values and selling prices
- the sealed bidding procedure, which sometimes resulted in winning bids being far in excess of the next closest bid

Despite evidence from national slumps, there was a strong belief that Edinburgh was a special case, because the attractive city centre meant that prices could never fall and generally people did not feel they had bid 'over the odds' to get their house. But it was also clear that people involved in the process got caught up in the 'frenzy' effects of bidding and that the whole process was very difficult for all (both professionals and buyers) involved. Those interviewed for the research expressed these factors clearly

Solicitor 3: You've got Mr and Mrs Smith who have been looking for a property in Edinburgh for 3 or 4 months. They've bid for 3 or 4 properties . . . every time they've done that they've paid £4–500 on a survey . . . they're coming to their 6th [this time] whatever happens, they're going to get it, and so they bid a huge amount of money for it, just to get something.
Buyer G4: I hate the system in Scotland, really hate it . . . I think it's basically dishonest . . . the secretive bid [system] which is causing people to overbid.
Buyer G11: It's probably the most stressful thing you can do . . . It's horrible, I hate it, I won't do it again for ages.
Solicitor C: People say 'What should I be offering?' I say, I haven't a clue. And basically all you can say is, look, if you really like the property . . . then you've got to work out what's your top offer, the maximum you can afford.

And there was a strong feeling that outcomes were random and unfair:

Buyer L4: It's a total gamble.
Buyer M14: It's like a poker game.
Buyer N2: [Bidding] is like picking a lucky number.

how a 'bull market' can be sustained without households immediately facing the financial ill-consequences that might be assumed to accompany house prices accelerating ahead of wages or other prices.

Housing equity: wealth effects, equity withdrawal and intergenerational transmission

One of the consequences of this high and variable house price inflation is that owners have access to differential and variable capital gains in their property. This, allied to the general growth in owner-occupation and a population of *ageing* owner-occupiers, who own outright or have very little mortgage debt, has led to a recognition of the growing importance of housing wealth. This section discusses the distribution of that wealth and the impact that housing wealth has on the patterns and scale of inheritance. As Saunders (1990) argued, in due course a 'nation of home owners' will become a 'nation of inheritors'.

There is no direct evidence of the scale and distribution of housing equity in the UK population. In general, household wealth is less well documented than household income. Housing wealth, however, poses particular problems. The two main data sources are survey evidence and figures imputed from Inland Revenue data concerning the wealth that passes on death. Both are problematic. The difficulty with survey evidence is that unlike, say, asking households to describe how much they have in savings accounts, housing wealth typically requires a more complex calculation involving an estimate of the current value of the house and the amount that is currently owed, which is further complicated by the widespread holding of interest-only mortgages covered by endowment policies and the increasingly widespread use of second and subsequent mortgages. Inland Revenue data on inheritance is, of course, limited to those who have died and required probate on their estate, and so certain assumptions have to be made to transform this evidence into an estimate of the wealth of the living.

Hamnett and Seavers (1996) used the British Household Panel Survey data to estimate the distribution of housing wealth. They found that nearly 12 per cent of owners had £13,000 or less in housing equity and a further 54 per cent had between £13,000 and £61,000. Only a minority, therefore, had larger amounts, with just 6 per cent having more than £146,000 in total. If these sums seem relatively small in relation to average house prices at that time, the explanation lies in the great amount of mortgage debt that requires to be off-set against the total free equity as well as the fact that this cross-sectional study was within a housing market slump.

Predictably, the distribution of mean housing equity mirrored the inequality in house prices, so that buyers in London and the South East had average housing equity of over £60,000, while those in Scotland had £20,700 and the north of England £26,400 (compared to a national average of £44,900). Equally, comparing housing equity by socio-economic group (SEG) it was found that professional and managerial workers had substantially greater equity on average (£72,000) than semi-skilled workers (£42,000). The significance of these findings is a counterbalance to the perception of owner-occupation as an equalizing and in some sense democratic form of wealth; although it is true that more people own significant housing wealth than traditionally more elite wealth holdings such as land or shares, there remain deep, structural inequalities in the access to wealth afforded by housing.

This also has knock-on consequences for the distribution of inheritance. In the 1980s, the growing significance of owner-occupation prompted much discussion of the impact that this would have on inheritance. The expectation was that radical change was imminent, so that substantial inheritance would no longer be the preserve of the very rich. Instead the prediction was that increasingly a majority of people could expect to inherit, from their parents or other relatives, as the first generations of mass home-owners started to die in significant numbers (Saunders 1986). Early research argued that even if such inheritance was becoming more widespread, the likelihood of benefiting and the extent of benefit was still going to be unequally distributed, with the more affluent and those already home-owners themselves benefiting most (Hamnett, Harmer and Williams 1991). However, more recent evidence has suggested that the anticipated boom in housing inheritance did not emerge in the 1990s. Instead, Inland Revenue data show that after a steep rise at the end of the 1960s, to just under 150,000 estates passing which included housing wealth (just over half of all estates), there has been no continuing rise, but rather a 'trendless fluctuation' around this figure (Hamnett 1999). The reason seems to be that earlier predictions were based on an oversimplified expectation of the way in which housing equity would evolve. Reflecting the common practice of the time, it was implicitly assumed that the wealth tied up in housing would largely stay there, diminished only by a small amount of trading down, until the owning household dissolved (typically on the death of the surviving spouse). In the event, however, it seems that more of this equity was accessed and spent before death than expected.

There are various mechanisms by which this equity might have been extracted. Perhaps most significant, given that most deaths occur in old age, have been the changes to support available for older people in residential settings. There has been a great expansion in private residential and nursing care for older people, with state support to help with such costs being reduced. Increasingly, older people are having to fund the care themselves. With high weekly costs, few can afford them out of income and, as state help is limited to those with less than £16,000 in assets and savings, houses must be sold to pay for this. There is little doubt that many people consider this unfair: both the older generation who are very keen to see their accumulated wealth passed to their descendants, and potential beneficiaries who can argue that such rules treat unfairly the people who were thrifty and worked hard to buy a home, compared to others who spent more freely through their lives. This has led to anecdotal evidence that increasingly older people are looking for mechanisms to protect their housing wealth, particularly by giving the house to their intended beneficiaries before death. There is no direct evidence of the scale of such action, but if widespread it would affect the statistical evidence (without actually reducing the amount of transmitted wealth, of course).

A less significant route enabling older people to release housing equity has been in the development of products that specifically allow equity to be converted into income (equity release or 'home income plans'). This is a potentially useful mechanism for those seeking an improved standard of living and who are less concerned to pass on all of their wealth as bequests. Essentially such products work by giving a lender the rights over some part of the equity held in the property in exchange for an income stream. The lender receives the equity when the house is sold, anticipated to be on death or entry into residential care. These products developed a rather poor reputation. The lenders tend to take a cautious view, which ensures that the design of the product would not create losses for them, even in 'adverse' circumstances, such as the borrower living for a very long time or low housing market inflation. Thus many of the products offered rather poor value for money. In some instances, the product created risks for the borrower, where the way that interest was rolled up into the lender's equity share could lead to the outstanding debt being greater than the value of the property. Some families felt that they had been short-changed when the borrower's early death meant that only a very little income had been received in exchange for a major chunk of valuable equity. Critical publicity showing how distressing such circumstances are for borrowers can only have added to the reluctance of people to take these plans out.

Although there have been attempts to establish a quality assurance mark (SHIP, safe Home Income Plans) to ensure that fair standards were met, the products remain relatively marginal. SHIP products do, for instance, guarantee that the borrower will never owe more than the house is worth. So although there is continued policy concern to help older owners who are in an 'asset rich/cash poor' trap, and some (probably largely latent) demand amongst older owners to use housing wealth to improve their standard of living, this has never developed into a major route of equity extraction.

In contrast, more general equity withdrawal has grown enormously since the 1980s. The 1970s restrictions, which controlled very tightly the amount of mortgage funding and ensured that such funds were genuinely applied to house purchase alone, were lifted in the early 1980s. House-owners began to extract increasingly large amounts of equity from their properties. The big changes permitted by mortgage deregulation were 'overmortgaging' at the point of purchase and remortgaging *in situ*, without any control being required that the money was to be spent on improvements to the home. Some economists (e.g., Miles 1994) argue that the consequent upsurge in equity withdrawal reflected a response to a previous disequilibrium position, in which households had been forced to hold too much of their personal portfolio as (illiquid) housing wealth. Others pointed to 'wealth effects' whereby rising property values value meant that consumers felt richer and wanted to spend more (Meen 1995). Arguably, when households feel that they are 'earning' thousands of pounds in their house month by month, there is little incentive to save slowly from employment income for desired goods. A related effect is that high levels of house transactions in themselves fuel consumer demand, as buyers spend money on refurbishment, consumer durables and fixtures and fittings to customize the new house to their taste and requirements.

Consumer spending can therefore be boosted by housing equity in various ways. As well as extracting equity when trading in the market, others simply take additional loans against the inflating value of their property in order to acquire cash to fund consumer spending. Also, as lenders competed more strongly for existing mortgage business, more owners took the opportunity to move their mortgage to another provider, without moving house. At this point many also chose to increase their outstanding loan, once again freeing money for consumer spending.

The total impact of these changes was very significant. The growing numbers of owner-occupiers, the rising proportion who had been in the tenure for some time, and the marked price inflation of the previous decade meant that there was a substantial pot of housing equity (estimated at £228 billion in the UK in 1980: Wilcox 2000) available to consumers for the first time. Many remained content simply to continue to pay off their mortgages in the traditional way. But, given that annual residential transactions rose from 1.25 million in 1980 to over 2 million in 1988 (in England and Wales alone) it is apparent that even relatively modest extractions of a few thousand pounds by trading owners quickly run to billions of additional consumer spending. Holmans (1991) estimated that equity withdrawal rose from £1.5 billion in 1981 to over £16 billion in 1988. At the same time 'traditional' methods of equity withdrawal (from trading down and last-time sellers) became proportionately less important and overmortgaging and remortgaging much more so. The absolute scale of equity withdrawal appears strongly correlated to the cyclical housing market, steadily falling back from the peak in 1988 as the recession of the early 1990s began to bite.

It seems clear, however, that the propensity to extract equity is not simply a 'boom' phenomenon, as although levels fell back in the early 1990s there was still over £11 billion taken in 1990. The increasingly aggressive interlender competition has made remortgaging a very significant part of the loans business. For the lenders, this has created a phenomenon of 'mortgage churn' (Slade and Roberts 2003) in which 37 per cent of the total mortgage book turns over annually compared to 25 per cent three years earlier. The scope presented for equity release is shown in the estimate that 50 per cent of those who remortgage increase the amount they borrow, while 25 per cent of movers also withdraw equity. The average amount withdrawn by both groups was around £10,000 in 2002 and this has tended to increase over time (J. Smith 2003).

A new style of mortgage product, so-called 'flexible' mortgages, provide a new route for equity withdrawal. Indeed, they are specifically designed so that housing equity can be accessed much more easily by buyers. Increasingly as the products become *more* flexible, they also allow buyers to use their mortgage account as a savings account, which can be accessed at any point. The availability and variety of these products has grown very rapidly since their introduction into the UK in the mid-1990s (see Chapter 7).

Government (in)action?

Despite the relatively relaxed view that frequently characterizes commentary on booming house price rises, the experience of late 1980s and early 1990s, when the economic well-being of the nation seemed so strongly bound up with the fortunes of the unstable housing market, has made housing market stability a key part of the Labour government's overall strategy to maintain a stable macroeconomic environment. There is no attempt to 'micro-manage' housing market outcomes. Instead, it is anticipated that a more stable housing market will be the consequence of a low inflation environment, and an economy avoiding the extremes of 'boom and bust'. Detailed discussion of macroeconomic policy is clearly beyond the scope of this book, but it is pertinent to note that an early initiative in this strategy was the creation of the Monetary Policy Committee, an independent group of experts whose main responsibility in setting interest rates is to keep inflation at or below the Chancellor's target. No longer can the Chancellor impose the swingeing hikes in interest rates that were seen in the late 1980s. Instead, the Monetary Policy Committee has to balance the various impacts of interest rate changes, in the manufacturing sector as well as the consumption sector, to attain the (currently low) inflation target. The housing market is thus only one of many concerns, although admittedly a major one. In the 2003 assessment of the 'five economic tests' as to whether entry into the Euro was appropriate for Britain, the unstable housing market was asserted to be a key source of difficulty in the achievement of economic convergence with the rest of Europe. In the Chancellor's view the economy and consumers would be better served by the development of long-term fixed-rate mortgages, common in much of continental Europe, to reduce the sensitivity of the housing market and the economy to interest rate fluctuations.

The government also creates the climate for the operation of the housing market in other significant ways. For instance, the favourable tax treatment of home-owners has now largely been abolished with the ending of tax relief on mortgage repayments. Stamp duty imposes some progressive tax burden on the purchase of more expensive houses. The government is also responsible for shaping the planning framework and has tried to use this mechanism to ensure balance in local markets through facilitating the provision of 'affordable housing' for key workers and more generally (see Chapter 5). The government has also responded to concerns about the regulation of transactions in the housing market and has explored changing the way that contracts are created to avoid gazumping (through a move to earlier binding offers, particularly in England) or provide incentives for better maintenance of properties (e.g., through sellers' packs at time of survey). To a significant degree, then, this dominant sector of housing provision is left to the operation of the market, with policy attempting to facilitate better market operation within an overall climate of stability.

Conclusion: is instability inevitable and does it matter?

This chapter has argued that the instability in the housing market *is* important to individuals and the economy. For individuals, it creates a lottery, in which whether your house provides a painless way to accumulate wealth or a source of debt and anxiety depends on location, the timing of house moves and luck. Times of high prices and high price inflation create problems of access and affordability, reducing the quality of life for those who feel they have no option but to embark on a house move. As house price rises are funded by buyers, there is also a systematic transfer of wealth from younger to older households through this process. Lower prices, and especially falling prices, undermine confidence in the market to the extent that general mobility is deterred. For the economy, the effects of housing-fuelled expenditure can exacerbate economic cycles, either where the upswing continues to pump extra consumer demand into the economy, or where, in the downswing, there is the associated demand reduction across the consumer sector. The very significant inequality in prices can make it difficult for people to move to where jobs are most plentiful, exacerbating regional economic disparities.

It is, however, hard to imagine that house price fluctuations could ever be completely smoothed out. The mismatch in the possible pace of change in demand and supply-side response leaves open the possibility of local hot (or cool) spots in response to short and medium term shifts in local economies.

This is not to dispute that the growth of owner-occupation can be interpreted as having brought widespread wealth and benefit to those who have been able to access it. It should also be remembered that, while it is technically difficult to adjust accurately for changing quality, the rise in house prices has been associated with a continuing improvement in the quality of housing, most of which has been funded by private owners. Although it was noted that the British housing stock is old, the purchaser of a pre-1919 house today would expect to enjoy many amenities not available to Victorian occupants of that house: bathroom(s), central heating, double glazing and so on. To this extent, then, the rise in house prices has not been a completely unearned windfall for occupants, but reflects some continuing investment in maintaining and improving the housing stock to meet modern aspirations.

Further reading

Hamnett (1999) provides a research-based overview of the patterns of house price instability and the inequity that are caused. Saunders' (1990) book, although it contains much argument and analysis that has been subsequently (and sometimes fiercely) contested, gives a flavour of the optimism associated with a view of a rising housing market giving widespread benefits to all. A counterbalance is provided by Ford, Burrows and Nettleton (2001) which brings together much of their research on mortgage arrears and house possession, showing clearly the difficult and distressing consequences for households that get caught in unsustainable owner-occupation.

4

The Low Demand Phenomenon

Emergence of the issue

'End to numbers game as estate is abandoned'; 'Demand lessens as more homes are bulldozed'; 'Estates to be levelled as demand keeps shrinking'; 'Ghost town'; these are some of the housing press headlines from 1999 and 2000 which convey the stark message that by the end of the 1990s, housing demand in some areas of Britain had shrunk to such an extent that drastic action was being forced on social landlords. And although the phenomenon was most widespread in the public sector, it was also threatening the viability of some inner-city neighbourhoods where private ownership predominated.

Cases where local authorities find themselves forced to demolish blocks less than 25 years old have become relatively familiar (DTZ Pieda 2000). A lack of demand is the ostensible problem, itself arising from fundamental structural defects and/or unpopular design. By the end of the 1990s, however, RSLs operating in certain vulnerable areas were reluctantly demolishing traditionally-designed homes in sound physical condition and less than a decade old. A particularly prominent example involved Dr Henry Russell Court, a 50-unit development in the West End of Newcastle-upon-Tyne, demolished by the North British Housing Association in 1999. The scheme had been completed only three years earlier at a cost of £2 million, including £1.2 million in public funding. Some of the flats had never been let.

Rising rates of demolition at the national scale towards the end of the 1990s (see Chapter 9) reflect the growing problem of low demand in some parts of the country (Keenan, Lowe and Spencer 1999). Some large local authorities have been pursuing plans to reduce substantially their stock of council housing. In Liverpool, for example, plans were announced in 1999 to demolish up to 6,000 of the council's properties. Glasgow Housing Association plans the same fate for 14,000 homes transferred from Glasgow City Council in 2003, whilst Birmingham's ill-fated 2002 stock transfer plans envisaged clearance of up to one-third of the city's 90,000 homes to ensure the scheme's viability.

Growing concerns over low demand housing during the late 1990s is reflected in a growing body of research and policy prescription. That this debate picked up following the change of government in 1997 was only partly due to the emergence of problem itself at this time (see below). Arguably, previous reluctance to discuss the issue resulted from social landlords' anxieties that the issue would be used by central government to justify further cuts in housing investment.

Renewed interest in low demand for housing in Britain since the mid-1990s probably also reflects housing associations' increased exposure and sensitivity to the problem compared to local authorities. Associations, as independent organizations in the private sector, are more vulnerable to falling demand for housing; this represents a potential 'business risk' which could ultimately threaten their very existence (Bacon and Davis 1996). Indeed, past encouragement to associations to become involved in marginal areas makes them particularly vulnerable. Also, the small size and geographically specific focus of some associations increase the risk of serious exposure to low demand compared to the large and diverse portfolios of local authorities. This is not to say that the problem is larger for housing associations than for local authorities (see Tables 4.1 and 4.2), but only that associations may be relatively sensitive to the issue and that some individual organizations may be particularly seriously affected. All this may also help to explain how it is that regional economic decline has, in England at least, come to be construed as a housing issue, demanding housing policy responses, rather than a wider urban policy issue.

Particularly in England, the problem of low demand in both social housing and the private sector was clearly on central government's agenda by the end of the 1990s, being investigated by the Social Exclusion Unit's Policy Action Team 7 and frequently cited in the DETR's April Green Paper (DETR 2000c). Low demand is also becoming increasingly acknowledged in Wales (Inkson 1999) and has attracted the attention of the National Assembly. In Scotland, however, low demand has as yet attracted relatively little official attention.

That low demand for housing is, in general, a 'problem' is implicit in much of the media coverage of the issue. Chapter 1 (see pp.3–8) has already hinted at some of the difficulties it presents in public money terms. The latter part of this chapter (see pp.79–87) elaborates on these from the perspective of social landlords, the local residents of the areas affected, and other stakeholders. At this stage it should be emphasized that the problems have both economic and social dimensions. For landlords – and resident property owners – the absence of scarcity undermines the value of their asset and discourages investment in upkeep and improvement. At the same time, the higher managerial costs borne by landlords of low demand housing are likely to feed through into higher rents and/or poorer services, to the ultimate disadvantage of local tenants. The strong association between low demand and crime, as well as the stigmatization of affected areas, damages the quality of life for all who live in them.

The remainder of this chapter reviews the evidence of the extent and spread of low demand in England and Scotland, discusses the causes of the problem and looks at its consequences. In examining the impact of low demand, a distinction is made between 'first order' (or direct) and 'second order' (indirect) effects.

Defining, measuring and tracking low demand

Although there has been a recent upsurge in interest, low demand for housing is not an entirely new issue. There is a long-established literature on its effects in US cities such as Baltimore and Detroit, sometimes focusing on cases where whole precincts of formerly densely built housing were abandoned and then often destroyed by fire and vandalism (Steinlieb and Burchell 1974; Wilson, Margulis and Ketchum 1994; Cohen 2001). The US experience, in contrast to the UK, is coloured by the relatively small presence of public rented housing, and by the absence of an interventionist tradition in this field. The low demand phenomenon in Baltimore described by Cohen, for example, affects predominantly privately-owned housing, and the city authority's problems are compounded by its limited ability even to identify individual property owners, much less to enforce action on them.

Low demand for housing also presents problems in certain parts of continental Europe. In Germany, for example, migration to the West since national reunification in 1989 has depressed demand in the east of the country. Similarly, recent trends in Finland and Sweden have seen a growing concentration of economic activity in southern areas and an associated tendency for population drift to these regions from less favoured localities, particularly the north of each country (Magnusson and Turner 2002). This has undermined local housing markets. The late 1990s saw very substantial divergence in property values between Stockholm and northern parts of Sweden, with the latter experiencing only a very limited recovery following a national house price crash at the start of the decade (Turner and Whitehead 2001). Problems of surplus social rented stock have been sufficiently serious in some parts of Sweden to prompt central government intervention in the form of debt relief for municipal housing companies facing an unavoidable need to demolish property (partly to stem financial losses due to security and maintenance costs of vacant and unlettable blocks).

In British housing policy low demand has, until recently, been mainly perceived as a problem for council housing, where significant estates, areas or blocks of housing have come to be defined as 'difficult-to-let' (Power 1987). This perception first arose in the late 1970s (Department of the Environment 1981) and much of the housing policy effort of the 1980s was directed towards these more problematic estates, predominantly through physical improvement and management measures (e.g., those promoted through the Priority Estates Programme, or PEP). The subsequent low profile of the issue may reflect the coincidence of expanding housing need alongside limited new investment in social housing during the late 1980s and early 1990s (Bramley 1994).

'Difficult to let' housing has been officially defined in the English context as: *'dwellings frequently rejected or accepted only very reluctantly even by applicants in very urgent housing need'* (Department of the Environment, Transport and the Regions, or DETR 2001). Some social landlords work with more specific definitions, such as any vacancy refused more than three times during its current void period. However, whilst the term 'difficult to let' has been a familiar synonym for low demand in the social rented sector for some time, it has recently tended to be displaced by the phrase 'low demand housing'. The latter has the advantage of tenure-neutrality and helps to counteract the common though misguided inclination to focus on low demand as an issue confined to social housing. Whilst there is no single definition of 'low demand', it can be applied to areas where any of the following symptoms are present.

Private sector
- private property values particularly low and/or falling in relative or absolute terms
- high private sector void rate
- high turnover of population
- significant incidence of long-term private sector voids or abandoned properties
- visibly high incidence of properties for sale or let

Social rented sector
- a small or non-existent waiting list
- tenancy offers frequently refused
- high rates of voids available for letting
- high rates of tenancy turnover

Some authors (e.g., Murie, Nevin and Leather 1998) have preferred the dynamic term 'changing demand' to 'low demand', arguing that the latter 'refers to a variety of distinct processes and clouds understanding'. On the other hand, 'changing demand' could be seen as somewhat ambiguous and perhaps understating the seriousness of the problem for social landlords and others needing to confront it. Significantly, though, Murie, Nevin and Leather seek to counter the previously common tendency for the issue to be seen as specific to the social rented sector and argue that it should not be seen simply as a 'housing management problem'.

In the literature, the terms 'low demand housing' and 'unpopular housing' are sometimes used interchangeably. Our preference – consistent with the Policy Action Team reports (DETR 1999b and 1999c) – is to distinguish between these terms in relation to the scale at which the problem occurs. 'Unpopular housing' describes the stock in blocks, estates or neighbourhoods where demand is weak. This might reflect particular features of the housing involved in terms of size, design, condition or accessibility and can affect isolated pockets of (usually social rented) housing set within relatively vibrant housing markets. Within this framework, 'low demand' is reserved to describe situations where there is gross oversupply at the larger Housing Market Area (HMA) scale. This distinction differentiates between problems affecting specific buildings, streets or neighbourhoods set within generally buoyant housing markets, and those where there is overall surplus at the HMA level so that market weakness at neighbourhood level is mainly a manifestation of a broader problem.

Rae and Calsyn (1996) have coined the term 'undercrowding' to describe the phenomenon affecting areas where a pattern of persistent population loss leaves behind a large surplus of buildings and land, as in cities such as Baltimore, Detroit and St Louis (Cohen 2001). This is more akin to HMA-scale problems which would qualify as 'low demand' in our terminology.

Appropriate responses would differ between the two scenarios described above. In the former, estate-based physical improvement could stand some chance of success, whilst in the latter, there would be a stronger case for 'downsizing' the housing stock through change of use or demolition.

The incidence of low demand housing

The most authoritative national and regional figures on the incidence of low demand housing come from government-sponsored postal surveys of local authorities and RSLs carried out in 1999 and based on the definitions set out above (see Tables 4.1 and 4.2). Clearly, the national figures for England conceal very substantial variations at regional level which generally suggest the presence of a clear North–South divide within all three tenures.

In Scotland, the geographical distribution of social sector low demand housing is less straightforward. Amongst local authorities, for example, the eight councils whose 1999 'low demand score' exceeded the national average (7.2 per cent of local authority, or LA, stock) included the two main cities and two large and mainly urban authorities in the Clyde Valley, as well as a

Table 4.1 *Incidence of low demand public sector housing in England and Scotland, 1999*

	% of social landlords affected		% of stock affected	
	England	Scotland	England	Scotland
Local authorities	70	100	12	7
RSLs	66	57	8	16

Source: Reproduced from Table 6.9 in Scott *et al.* (2001b).

Table 4.2   *Incidence of low demand housing stock in England by tenure and region, 1999*

	Estimated number of dwellings affected			Estimated % of dwellings affected		
	Local authority	RSL	Private sector	Local authority	RSL	Private sector
North East	64,000	7,900	20,200	22	16	2.8
Yorks & Humberside	58,500	10,500	55,300	13	14	3.8
North West	113,000	32,600	173,700	23	19	8.6
East Midlands	31,500	6,700	33,500	11	13	2.5
West Midlands	43,000	9,100	59,800	11	8	3.9
South West	9,000	2,600	11,400	4	3	0.7
East	12,000	5,900	8,300	4	9	0.9
South East	10,500	9,200	6,000	4	4	0.2
London	35,500	7,000	7,300	6	3	0.4
England	377,000	91,500	375,500	12	8	2.6

Source: Reproduced from Bramley, Pawson and Third (2000).

former coalfield area and three remote rural councils. These findings seem to point to the impact of depopulation in its various forms as an important factor underlying the problem where it is most serious. Amongst RSLs, most of those with an above-average incidence of low demand housing at this time were Glasgow-based associations managing substantial amounts of former local authority stock.

There is no national figure on private sector low demand housing for Scotland comparable to that for England shown in Table 4.2. However, analysis of secondary indicators such as the proportion of 'low value sales' indicates the scale and geographical incidence of this problem north of the border (Bramley and Morgan 2002). Unlike England and Wales, though (where it predominantly affects private or mixed tenure terraced housing areas), in Scotland it tends to involve former public sector homes purchased by sitting tenants under the Right to Buy and located on unpopular public sector estates or in inner-city tenement-style blocks.

Recent changes in the incidence of low demand

The consensus among social landlords in most parts of England and Scotland is that low demand housing was a growing problem during the late 1990s (Bramley, Pawson and Third 2000; Scott *et al.* 2001b). In each of the three northern regions of England, for example, at least half of those authorities managing low demand housing believed that its incidence had 'increased substantially' during the period 1996–9. In London and the south east of

Figure 4.1   *LA void rates by broad region, 1990–2002*

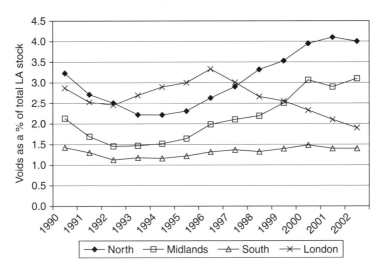

Sources: Calculated from ODPM LA Housing Investment Programme/Housing Strategy Statistical Annex returns data. Graph updated from versions in Bramley, Pawson and Third (2000) and Bramley and Pawson (2002).

England, however, most local authorities and RSLs experienced generally rising rather than generally falling demand during this period.

As far as England is concerned, the social landlord perception of increasing problems from the mid-1990s confirms other evidence and impressions. A number of studies suggest that the phenomenon developed significantly from about 1994, particularly in the North and Midlands (see Chartered Institute of Housing 1998; Murie, Nevin and Leather 1998; Holmans and Simpson 1999). On a number of key statistical indicators, the turning point was 1993 or 1994.

Perhaps the most obvious statistical indicator of demand – at least in the social housing sector – is vacancy (or void) rates. Whilst some minimal level of empty properties is needed to facilitate tenant mobility, a vacancy rate of 2 per cent is widely regarded as adequate for this purpose. Rates above this threshold are generally seen as indicating wasted resources, though these may reflect either managerial inefficiency or an absence of demand. Figure 4.1 shows trends in LA vacancy rates from 1990 to 2000 and confirms the widespread impression that problems started to increase after 1994, having previously been on a slightly reducing trend. Vacancies increased significantly in the North and the Midlands. By 2000, rates in the worst region, the North West, had almost doubled since 1994, though the cycle appeared to have peaked by 2002.

Tenant turnover provides the second key statistical indicator of low demand in the social sector. The rising turnover rates seen in the Midlands and the

Figure 4.2   *LA net re-let rates by broad region, 1990–2002*

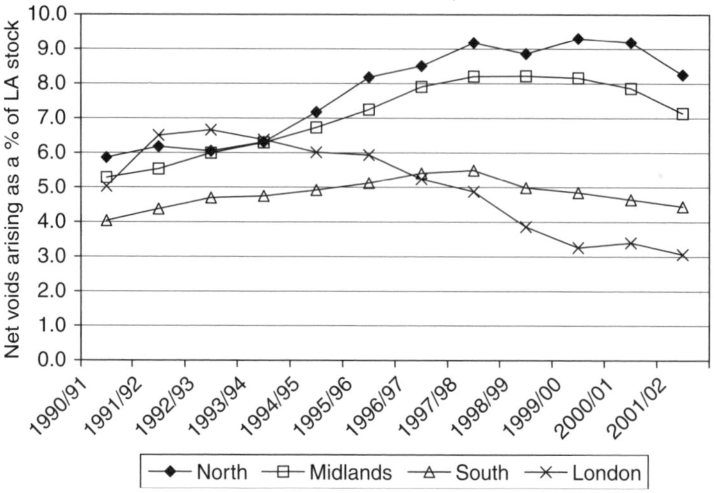

Note: Net voids arising assumed to equal ((lettings to new tenants) – (RSL lettings to LA tenants) + (change in stock of LA vacancies)). RSL lettings to LA tenants 2001/02 estimated.

Sources: Calculated from ODPM LA Housing Investment Programme/Housing Strategy Statistical Annex returns data. Graph updated from versions in Bramley, Pawson and Third (2000) and Bramley and Pawson (2002).

North of England during the past few years result largely from growing numbers of tenants 'voting with their feet' and moving to other tenures. Relets also arise because of death/old age (moves into residential homes, etc.), but it is unlikely that this factor will have increased significantly in importance over the 1990s (Pawson 1998; Pawson and Bramley 2000).

Again, the relet rate patterns shown in Figure 4.2 confirm falling demand throughout the second half of the 1990s in the Midlands and the North, with these regions increasingly diverging from London and the South in this respect. Once more, however, the figures for 2001 and 2002 suggest that interregional polarization on this measure has passed its peak. It is perhaps worth noting, however, that rising turnover in social housing is to some extent a general phenomenon, rather than being confined to 'problem' areas. Nationally, turnover rates in social housing have doubled over the past 20 years (Pawson and Bramley 2000). To a large extent, this probably reflects demographic trends closely associated with the residualization of social housing, as the more stable 'middle aged' households have become increasingly concentrated in the owner-occupied sector.

A third source of statistical evidence on changing demand for social housing during the 1990s relates to council housing waiting lists. Nationally, the

Figure 4.3 *LA Housing Register registration rates by broad region, 1990–2002*

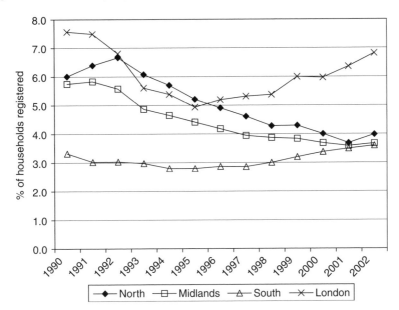

Notes
1. Registration numbers relate to 'households in need'.
2. Registered 'households in need' numbers estimated for 2001 and 2002.
Sources: Calculated from ODPM LA Housing Investment Programme/Housing Strategy Statistical Annex returns data. Graph updated from versions in Bramley, Pawson and Third (2000) and Bramley and Pawson (2002).

recorded stock of households seeking housing through local authorities has fallen somewhat over the past decade. However, as demonstrated in Figure 4.3, patterns of change at the regional level are again broadly consistent with those seen on other indicators. Downward trends in the Midlands and the North are striking, whilst the post-1995 upturns in London and South reflect the housing market recovery of the late 1990s.

The evidence reviewed here points towards the period around 1993–5 being the starting point for the emergence of low demand problems in social housing and the divergence of north and south within England. Within a longer-term perspective, however, these developments could be seen as a stronger re-assertion of a pattern seen during the early-to-mid-1980s when the problem of 'difficult to let' council housing first attracted attention (Bramley 1998a). The difference this time is that the scale of the phenomenon is greater, and its effects less confined to social housing. And within social housing, the exhaustion of 'adjustment mechanisms' involving modification of allocations

Table 4.3 *Trend in privately owned 'long-term vacant' dwellings, 1997–2002*

	Number of privately owned dwellings vacant for >12 months			Number of privately owned dwellings vacant for >6 months			2002 rate as a % of all private stock
	1997	1998	1999	2000	2001	2002	
London	39,361	33,703	34,935	40,301	45,718	40,975	1.8
South	78,447	71,081	67,472	73,701	91,173	87,418	1.3
Midlands	51,997	46,781	40,756	52,549	58,789	62,749	1.9
North	63,456	68,501	69,767	112,290	114,541	116,731	2.4
England	233,261	220,066	212,930	278,841	310,221	307,873	1.8

Source: Data from ODPM, LA Housing Investment Programme/Housing Strategy Statistical Annex returns.

and management policies means that demolition of 'surplus' stock may be a less avoidable option than in the 1980s.

Statistical evidence on recent changes in the incidence of low demand in the private sector is less plentiful, particularly in relation to Scotland. Nevertheless, figures from English local authorities' annual statistical returns show that private sector vacancies across the North of England rose by 16 per cent between 1997 and 2000, whilst the comparable figure for London fell by a similar proportion. Perhaps more significantly, long-term private sector vacancies in the North of England rose steadily after 1997 (see Table 4.3).

Causes of low demand

There is no single explanation for the low demand phenomenon. Different combinations of factors are involved in different areas. Generally, these may be grouped into three categories:

- broader regional and sub-regional effects of demographic trends, particularly migration, which are often seen as linked to economic restructuring and employment changes
- changes in preferences and behaviour, generally associated with a declining popularity of certain types of housing and with rising turnover and instability in the resident population
- micro-social processes at the neighbourhood level which lead to particular areas being stigmatized by reputations for poverty, crime and other problems, leading into processes of cumulative deterioration of conditions which may ultimately culminate in abandonment

Economic restructuring and migration

Economic restructuring and the decline of traditional male blue-collar employment in northern cities and former industrial and mining areas are widely considered to be a major causal factor leading to low demand (Webster 1998; Power and Mumford 1999). Murie, Nevin and Leather (1998) suggest that the effects of this decline, which was well advanced during the 1980s, may have been lagged: that is, its effects on housing markets may have been delayed. Holmans and Simpson (1999) suggest that the effects were damped in the early 1990s by the unusual depth of the recession in the southern economy at that time.

A variant on this theme, specific to social housing in some areas of the Midlands and the North of England, is the argument that the economic revival of the late 1990s, far from propping up demand may have further undermined it. In a study of north-west England, a strong correlation between falling unemployment and contracting housing waiting lists was found by Nevin *et al.* (2001). This seems consistent with the view that the expanding post-1995 labour market has been sucking tenants out of social housing as their incomes exceed the threshold for entry into home-ownership (as further explained below). Recent migration modelling for DTLR/ODPM shows apparently perverse effects, including the phenomenon of rising prosperity triggering larger migrant flows out of, rather than into, affected areas (University of Newcastle-upon-Tyne, University of Leeds and Greater London Authority 2002). Such effects were alluded to as long ago as the 1960s (Lowry 1966).

Longer-distance migration is another factor often cited in explanations for the spread of low demand for housing. Economic decline and the loss of employment in former industrial or coalfield areas is seen as precipitating population movement away from such areas, hence undermining local housing markets. At the interregional level, net outmigration from North to South was re-established during the second half of the 1990s as the economy of London and surrounding areas recovered from the sharp recession experienced early in the decade (Holmans and Simpson 1999). However, whilst such moves may contribute to changing demand for housing at regional level, their volume is relatively small compared with the accelerating urban–rural shift (Champion *et al.* 1998). In explaining the observed contraction in the population of cities such as Glasgow and Liverpool, short-distance suburbanization is certainly much more important than longer-distance moves to more prosperous regions. Migration trends and their relevance to housing policy are discussed in more detail in Chapter 2.

Given the link with economic decline and restructuring, some commentators (e.g., Webster 1998) have argued that low demand for housing is a symptom of a larger problem calling for re-introduction of regional economic policy of the kind familiar in the 1960s and 1970s. Central government, however, sees such an approach as being outmoded, partly thanks to globalization, the argument being that companies discouraged from locating in, say, London are more likely to re-site in Frankfurt or Milan than in Bradford or Hartlepool. In any case, EU competition rules severely restrict the extent to which public funds can be used as to 'subsidize' firms moving to or operating in peripheral or otherwise declining regions.

Changing housing preferences

The potential for 'economic revival' to undercut demand for social housing identified by Nevin *et al.* (2001: see above) is part and parcel of the general shift in preference towards owner-occupation (Department of the Environment 1994) and the increasingly accessible and affordable supply, of new as well as second-hand housing, in the lower-priced northern and midland regions (Bramley 1998a; Murie, Nevin and Leather 1998; Power and Mumford 1999). Accessibility of home-ownership is enhanced not just by low prices but also by low interest rates and attractive mortgage deals. Movement is also encouraged by changes in people's house type preferences in favour of more suburban types of houses with gardens, and against smaller housing, flats and possibly terraced housing. And a generous supply of new housing (often in suburban locations) has encouraged movement out of established areas (e.g., in inner cities). Certain types of housing, such as bedsits in social housing, are increasingly seen as obsolete by both practitioners and consumers as the impact of rising expectations feeds through into expressed demand (Barelli and Pawson 2001).

Evidence on increasing outflows from social renting and into home-ownership is readily available (Pawson 1998; Burrows 1999). Perhaps more surprising is the increased flow from social housing into *private* renting. Such movement is facilitated by the availability of Housing Benefit (HB), and may be a way of getting more locational choice, perhaps motivated by the wish to avoid the stigmatization associated with large council estates.

Some (e.g., Murie, Nevin and Leather 1998; Nevin *et al.* 2001) argue that housing providers (both social and private) have to adapt their products to a changing demographic and economic profile of demand. However, such a perspective may be misleading where there is genuine oversupply. Where scarcity no longer prevails, social housing may be used to house non-traditional client groups, people who are not in need in a strict sense, and who would not therefore be prioritized under 'traditional' needs-based allocations policies. This might include students or young childless adults, perhaps in low paid or insecure employment.

Changing tenure preferences in favour of home-ownership – in combination with official housing policies such as the Right to Buy – have also contributed to demographic change in social housing. This had led to concentrations of younger (e.g., persons aged 20–30) and older (e.g., persons over 65) groups, with a 'hollowing out' (Murie, Nevin and Leather 1998) of the overall age

Figure 4.4 *Age structure of council tenant population in England*

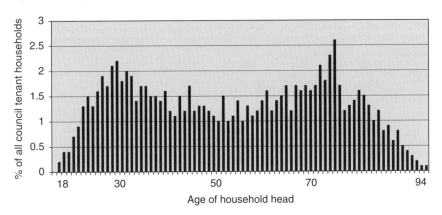

Source: Reproduced from Bramley, Pawson and Third (2000) (original data from *Survey of English Housing 1995/96*).

structure (as well as the social structure: see Figure 4.4). One effect of this is to increase social sector residential instability and turnover, since those with the highest propensities for tenancy sustainment have become substantially underrepresented among the tenant population.

Social processes and other factors at the neighbourhood level

Practitioner analyses of low demand for social housing and its causes tend to emphasize the factors which lead to poor perception or stigmatization of estates and neighbourhoods. As far as social housing is concerned, run-down or poorly designed buildings are seen as of moderate importance, whilst overall housing surplus is thought to be a significant contributory factor in only a relatively small proportion of instances (see Table 4.4). As the table shows, the perceived relative importance of the various issues is fairly similar in England and Scotland (and between local authorities and RSLs in Scotland). It may, however, be significant that stigmatization is more universally considered to be part of the problem in Scotland, but that unpopular dwelling types are a commoner ingredient in England. Another interesting contrast is the higher profile of competition between social landlords as part of the problem south of the border.

Another research finding revealed by Table 4.4 is that factors such as inaccessible location, and the quality/availability of local services are only fairly rarely considered to be important causal factors of low demand. This seems to conflict with the stance taken by the Social Exclusion Unit (SEU) which has placed considerable emphasis on the fact that many of the poorest

Table 4.4   *Perceived 'major factors' contributing to low demand for social housing, 1999 (%)*

Factor potentially contributing to low demand	Scotland		England
	LAs	RSLs	LAs
Stigma/poor perception of area	78	73	63
Anti-social behaviour/difficult neighbours	47	40	44
Drug taking/trafficking	44	49	n/a
Poor/unpopular design of dwellings and/or blocks/estates	42	30	45
Unpopularity of certain dwelling types (e.g. bedsits)	42	46	73
High levels of crime	42	44	51
Poor quality of the surrounding physical environment	39	31	26
Poor condition of dwellings and/or blocks/estates	19	16	26
Inaccessible location (e.g. with respect to public transport)	19	24	19
Overall surplus of housing (across all tenures) in area	16	16	17
Poor quality or availability of local services (e.g. schools)	13	11	10
Increased competition between different sectors of the housing market	10	12	20
Tenant concerns about quality of housing management	6	2	3
Accommodation standards unattractive compared with other landlords	3	11	11
Lack of awareness of eligibility for housing among client groups	3	4	5
Rent levels uncompetitive with other landlords	0	7	1

n/a = not available.
Note: Responses from landlords managing low demand housing.
Source: Reproduced from Table 6.11 in Scott *et al.* (2001b).

neighbourhoods suffer from 'run-down' services, both private and public (SEU 1998). So, whilst the 'poor quality' of local schools is frequently cited as a factor motivating out-migration from inner cities (e.g., SEU 1998; Boyle 1999) – and was found to be a significant factor from the perspective of low demand neighbourhood residents by Bramley, Pawson and Third (2000) – it is not regarded as particularly important as a cause of area unpopularity from the practitioner viewpoint.

First order consequences of low demand

References to 'the problem of low demand' imply that weak or declining housing markets result in various negative consequences which call for public policy responses. Discussion of these consequences is somewhat problematic because of the difficulties in disentangling symptom, cause and effect. For example, factors such as crime and anti-social behaviour are sometimes used as an indicator of low demand and are widely cited as contributing to area unpopularity. At the same time, their incidence is also liable to rise *as a result* of an area's decline, and so the cycle becomes powerfully self-reinforcing.

As well as being indicators of low demand for housing, the most significant 'direct effects' of the phenemenon are:

- high vacancy (or void) rates
- high turnover
- high incidence of very low value sales

Void rates

Drawing on case study evidence from the Bramley, Pawson and Third (2000) study of England, Table 4.5 illustrates the extent to which void rates in identified low demand estates exceed authority-wide values. For this purpose, all low demand areas in each authority are combined to produce a single average value. It is apparent that both the values and the margins (differences from the norm) are greater in the Midlands and the North.

Looking at the 1996–8 period, the DETR study found that differentials in void rates between low demand estates and LA norms had tended to widen more rapidly in areas of the Midlands and the North where the overall scale of the problem was growing compared with London where it was relatively static (Bramley, Pawson and Third 2000). This suggests that, in this phase of the property market cycle, increasing polarization at the regional level was being reflected in the local scale.

These findings are generally consistent with neighbourhood level data cited by Power and Mumford (1999) in relation to four areas in Manchester and Newcastle. They do not, however, substantiate Power and Mumford's concept

Table 4.5 *Comparison between council housing void rates at LA level and in low demand estates, April 1998 (seven case study authorities)*

LA	Region	Voids as a % of stock		Difference
		Authority-wide	Low demand estates	
Easington	North East	5.4	13.3	+7.9
Burnley	North West	6.6	14.5	+7.9
Leeds	Yorks & Humberside	3.8	6.7	+2.9
Walsall	West Midlands	6.8	12.2	+5.4
Southend	South East	3.9	5.0	+1.1
Greenwich	London	2.2	3.0	+0.8
Southwark	London	2.4	2.9	+0.5

Source: Reproduced from Bramley, Pawson and Third (2000).

of a 'tipping point': that is, accelerating decline of an area once it passes some threshold level of voids. It may be that the tipping point concept is more applicable to areas where private sector housing is predominant and where, below a threshold average property value, disinvestment sets in. There is also a question of scale here. For an individual block, group of properties or street, the arrival of a single seriously anti-social resident or the coincidence of a group of vacancies could represent a tipping point for the immediately adjacent properties, even if this is a less applicable concept at the estate or neighbourhood level.

Long-term voids in the private sector may, in fact, have been abandoned by their owners. It has been claimed that the incidence of abandonment is significant in a growing number of UK cities (Lowe, Spencer and Keenan 1998). However, whilst the rising number of 'long-term' privately owned vacancies in the North of England shown in Table 4.3 is broadly consistent with this view, it is uncertain whether a void duration threshold of this order is necessarily a sound proxy for abandonment. Abandonment should probably be defined with reference to the intentions of the owner regarding future use of the property, a matter which is very difficult to research.

Turnover rates

Turnover rate differentials between low demand social sector estates and LA-wide norms tend to be larger than void rate differentials (Bramley, Pawson and Third 2000). This adds weight to the view that turnover rates are a more consistently reliable indicator of social sector low demand than void rates, particularly in London and the South. This probably reflects the fact that in these areas the shortage of affordable housing is such that there is a healthy market for social housing vacancies, even where these are in stigmatized or otherwise less popular areas. For landlords, the problem is not attraction but retention.

At the estate level, annual turnover rates in excess of 25 per cent are not uncommon for low demand areas. In these areas the arithmetic average tenancy duration is four years. In reality, however, such estates are often characterized by a relatively stable core population alongside a highly transient cohort, typically resident for much shorter periods. In some areas a significant number of recorded lettings result in a 'real' tenancy duration of zero, as newly-signed-up tenants fail to move into their allocated home at all.

Data on residential turnover in predominantly private sector areas is much more difficult to capture, though such data ought – in principle – to be available from the Council Tax register. Complexities also arise from the fact that owner-occupiers 'trapped' by low values (and possibly negative equity) are likely to have very low rates of mobility, whilst private rented sector turnover is liable to be negatively correlated with demand (see later).

In any case, whilst there is substantial scope for further research in this area, work of this kind needs to consider carefully the appropriate area scale of aggregation to be used. Extreme conditions in particular streets in some cities would probably give rise to spectacularly high scores on indicators such as void or turnover rates. Such figures would not be properly comparable with data relating to areas such as wards or even estates.

'Very low value' sales

In analysing *the incidence of 'very low value' sales* a threshold of £20,000 is often adopted (e.g., Murie, Nevin and Leather 1998; Bramley and Morgan 2003. This partly reflects the research finding that mainstream working households may be reluctant to buy, and some lenders are reluctant to lend below a price threshold of £20–30,000. The fact that loans of under £25,000 are covered by the Consumer Credit Act is seen by some lenders as a disincentive for agreeing smaller amounts. Given the normal rules applied by mortgage lenders, such properties would be affordable to any household containing an employed person earning an annual income of £7,000–10,000.

Generally, the proportions of 'very low value' sales in neighbourhoods seen as 'low demand areas' by local authorities are well above authority-wide values. In Burnley, Leeds and Liverpool there were a number of identified postcode sectors (which typically encompass around 2–3,000 households) where the majority of transactions in 1997 involved prices below £20,000 (Bramley, Pawson and Third 2000).

Second order (or indirect) consequences of low demand

Financial consequences for local authorities, RSLs and other public bodies

Low or falling demand for housing has financial implications for local authorities and other public bodies in a number of respects. High void rates, which often result, lead to losses in rental income for landlords. Except through improving efficiency, these can be made up only by increasing rents or reducing services to tenants across a landlord's stock. High void rates also imply unusually substantial costs in security for vacant properties to prevent theft, vandalism or squatting.

As seen above, void rates due to low demand have, in the recent past, tended to be much higher in the Midlands and the North than in London and the South. In these latter areas, the financial consequences of low demand were generally more closely related to above-average rates of tenancy turnover. So whilst in the Midlands and the North losses in rental income were an important effect of weak demand, budgetary implications for southern landlords related more to higher repairs and security expenditure.

Low demand affecting the private sector also gives rise to costs which must be borne by local authorities, as well as by individual owners. Falling occupancy in private housing reduces Council Tax receipts and undermines the population base which underpins the local government grant system. In the US context, it has been observed that declining city revenues resulting from population loss can 'lead to a dynamic in which many landlords refrain from making nonessential repairs, fall behind or default on their mortgage payments, and stop paying property taxes' (Cohen 2001, p.417).

The measures needed to correct oversupply (e.g., compulsory purchase, demolition and the re-use of cleared sites) are expensive and are not all amenable to 'private finance'-based solutions such as stock transfer. Such problems become serious when falling population and housing demand is as widespread as it is in areas such as Glasgow, Liverpool and Salford, or – in the case of the USA – Baltimore, Detroit and St Louis.

Even where it is relatively localized, low or falling demand can have major financial implications for landlords if their stock portfolio is concentrated in vulnerable areas. Partly because of their smaller scale, this is a significant issue for some RSLs. Some associations, having expanded into 'marginal inner-city areas' in the North of England during the early 1990s, later found themselves struggling for financial viability as local housing markets weakened or collapsed. Stock profiles are also an issue here, with some RSLs having a high exposure to low demand because their holdings of acquired rehabilitated street properties (e.g., Liverpool) are perceived by some potential consumers as 'obsolete' (see above). Partly because of their relatively high rents, in a context of growing interlandlord competition (see below), certain RSLs have been hit particularly hard.

Collapse of private housing markets

In general, weak or falling demand for housing in the private market is reflected in low or declining property values. Falling values may follow from the peak of a housing boom where sentiment has driven prices well beyond the level justified by local incomes (see Chapter 3). Where property values fall appreciably, this often has a number of consequences for the functioning of housing markets. Owner-occupiers find their equity increasingly eroded as property prices continue to drop. Some of those with smaller mortgages sell up while they can. Recent buyers with larger mortgages are more likely to find themselves quickly trapped by negative equity and unable to move except by renting out their existing home and moving into rented housing themselves, or by selling at a loss and incurring a debt that has to be repaid. The physical and psychological stress on owners resulting from such circumstances should not be underestimated and this has some parallels with the experience of some home owners in 'boom' conditions where the extending of price differentials can make the prospect of a much-needed move increasingly remote. In neighbourhoods where many owners find themselves the victims of negative equity, the aggregate health impact on the community may well be significant.

In some areas of Salford, for example, the DETR research reported that a generation of buyers who became owners in the late 1980s found themselves living in properties whose values had fallen far below the size of their mortgages and had, by the end of the 1990s, shown no sign of recovery. By this time, repossession sales of homes built by private developers ten years earlier (in some cases subsidized by the local authority) were yielding £14–15,000 for homes originally sold for £45,000. Some neighbourhoods had seen the values of pre-1919 terraced 'two up, two down' properties fall from around £30,000 in 1990 to as little as £4,000 a few years later. Several years into the general upturn in the housing market seen across much of the country, these areas had remained untouched (Bramley, Pawson and Third 2000).

Where property values fall substantially, the housing market may cease to function in a normal way. In Liverpool, for example, research evidence suggests that across large parts of the inner city, the normal owner-occupation market had become effectively moribund by the end of the 1990s. With few conventional first time buyers choosing to buy the mainly terraced houses involved, these were being traded at auction, or through a limited number of specialist agents dealing with repossessions at £5–10,000.

Bramley, Pawson and Third (2000) found no direct evidence of explicit mortgage lender 'red lining', in the sense that mortgage applications in specified areas would not be considered. It was, however, clear that lenders were generally unwilling to lend or were wary about properties valued much below £30,000 (perhaps in part motivated by concerns about the Consumer Credit Act: see above). One factor here is that very small loans may be seen as 'uneconomic'. The main reason for lenders' attitudes, however, is that low values – particularly where they are a result of recent falls – are likely to be taken as indicative of a worsening market, where future resale values will be even lower and ability to sell even more difficult. Therefore loan finance may be difficult to obtain for anyone attempting to buy in areas where most dwellings fall below this threshold.

Partly because of problems of negative equity, many property owners in areas seriously affected by low demand are deterred from selling their homes, even when they need to move house for personal or work-related reasons. This helps to explain the observed negative correlation between the incidence of property trading and the extent of low demand (the opposite of the relationship between low demand and tenancy turnover in rented housing).

The transformation of resale markets resulting from a decline in property values beyond a certain threshold level tends to lead to the expansion of the private rented sector, as former owner-occupiers needing to move attempt to generate some income from their unsaleable asset. At the same time, the sector grows as a result of speculative landlords buying up formerly owner-occupied homes and renting them out.

In certain circumstances, there is a clear economic basis for growing private landlordism in areas hit by collapsing demand. In Salford, for example, Bramley, Pawson and Third, unearthed claims that repossessed properties were being sold at auction in the early 1990s for as little as £3,000. These homes could then be rented to people reliant on Housing Benefit for £50–75 per week. This is a gross rate of return of 75–110 per cent per annum, compared with national rates for private renting of 8–9 per cent. In some areas experiencing changes of this kind, the remaining owner-occupiers have found themselves vulnerable to intimidation and other forms of anti-social behaviour which further depress property values. Given the potential profits for speculative landlords which could result from this process, it might well be expected that such activities could, in some cases, attract the interest of organized crime. It is, however, difficult to substantiate assertions, with respect to one of Bramley, Pawson and Third's case study areas, that links developed between property speculators, local criminals and firms offering security services to residents.

As well as the potential returns to be made through private renting, there are claims that property speculation in some areas is partly motivated by the 'hope value' of eventual compulsory purchase in preparation for clearance. In some areas of Salford, for example, Bramley, Pawson and Third found expectations that repossessed houses bought for as little as £2,000–3,000 could be worth as much as £12,000 in eventual Compulsory Purchase Order (CPO) compensation value. This would seem to suggest that something is wrong with the compensation mechanism or the valuations used. Alternatively, public expectations could be completely misinformed.

As well as affecting inner-city areas of predominantly private housing (such as in Liverpool and Salford), collapsing housing markets also affect local authority estates with respect to former Right to Buy properties. Although RTB sales rates generally correspond fairly closely to neighbourhood popularity, significant numbers of homes have been sold on some estates now seriously affected by low demand. For example, the DETR study found RTB rates of around 10 per cent in low demand estates in both Gateshead and Leeds (Bramley, Pawson and Third 2000). In the latter, well over one-third of the homes involved had been resold or (probably more commonly) privately let. This ties in with evidence from Scotland suggesting a strong association between private sector low demand and ex-RTB homes on unpopular estates (Bramley and Morgan 2003).

In low demand areas where housing markets have collapsed there is typically relatively little difference in values between improved and unimproved properties. This is, to some extent, a reflection of the broader UK housing market problem that property condition is inadequately reflected in property values (Leather and Mackintosh 1997). However, whilst this may be common to high value as well as low value markets, evidence suggests that in the latter condition-related differentials are particularly small in both cash and proportionate terms.

Disinvestment (or failure to invest in major repairs or upgrading) is a logical response to the inadequate valuation differential between improved and unimproved properties. Property condition declines and it becomes increasingly difficult to relet privately rented dwellings. If rent officers then discount their estimates of market rents to take account of falling capital values or other evidence of low demand (thereby reducing the ceiling on HB payments to tenants), landlords will be further encouraged to disinvest and withdraw from the market. For this reason, expanding private renting could be just a phase in a progression towards terminal decline of a neighbourhood. In this final phase, private landlords would be effectively abandoning property which they could neither let nor sell, and which they had no further reason to maintain.

In some local authority estates, rising rates of private renting (as well as abandonment) in the ex-RTB sector blight surrounding properties remaining in council ownership, since there is little economic incentive for owners to invest in upkeep. The existence of 'easy access' private renting within social housing estates (in ex-RTB homes) can also frustrate the efforts of housing managers to displace 'disruptive tenants' through eviction, possibly backed up by exclusion from the housing waiting list.

Impact on the viability of local services

Falling demand for housing, where it leads to a decline in population and purchasing power, has obvious implications for the viability of local services, both private and public. A shrinking customer base can, for example, lead to the closure of shops and 'personal service' businesses dependent on local custom such as hairdressers and launderettes. In terms of the public sector, weakening demand for housing can have a serious impact on the viability of *schools* (see also Power and Mumford 1999). This reflects the significant diseconomies of declining scale in education as small schools become uneconomic for cash-strapped local authorities. Problems of poor morale and lack of investment are likely to result in the short term, followed by closures and 'rationalization'.

This problem is particularly relevant to primary schools which tend to be much smaller than secondaries, and which usually draw on a relatively small catchment, making them more vulnerable to collapsing housing demand even where this is relatively localized. In England 80 per cent of school funding is based on pupil numbers, though funding regulations allow local education authorities to allocate up to 20 per cent according to a number of other factors. The regulations also allow these authorities to provide some protection from the impact of falling rolls in the short term.

In a number of neighbourhoods experiencing low demand examined in the Bramley, Pawson and Third DETR study, depopulation was seriously threatening the continued existence of local schools. In Liverpool, for example, it was found that one of the six primaries serving the case study neighbourhood was facing closure, having seen its roll drop by 25 per cent in the two years to 1998. Four of the others had also seen falling rolls, in one case by 50 per cent over the same period.

Primary schools are often the most important single institution in fostering a sense of local community, particularly among the families that use them, but also because they become a natural meeting place on other local issues. They often serve as a venue for non-school community activities such as Guides and Brownies, Mother and toddler groups, and so on. The closure of primary schools serving unpopular neighbourhoods, together with the tendency of some parents to shop around further afield to find adequate education, therefore, does not augur well for the communities affected.

In Bramley Pawson and Third's (2000) Salford case study area, depopulation associated with falling housing demand was serious enough to threaten the existence of a sizeable high school. The school, which had a roll of 900 in 1987, had seen this fall to 700 by 1994 and to 375 by 1998.

Whilst primary schools, especially, are clearly vulnerable to the impact of low demand on their basis for existence, the extent of this danger is dependent on a range of circumstances, the most important factors being the severity of the low demand problem and the shape and size of catchments. Where low demand results in residential instability, there may be other second-order impacts on the quality of education, as discussed further below.

Interlandlord competition for tenants

Where local housing markets are weak this can impact significantly on the relationship between social landlords. One effect is that local authorities may cease to nominate applicants to RSL vacancies. Second, competition may develop between landlords to secure tenants. Most commonly, this rivalry is perceived as being largely within the social sector, though some local authorities and RSLs are aware that market rivals include private landlords. The wish to compete more actively with private landlords is sometimes an explicit justification for social landlords' moves to remove 'housing need' eligibility restrictions for social housing, common in much of the Midlands and the North.

From the tenant viewpoint, the development of more open competition between landlords could, of course, be seen as a good thing. With housing providers having to focus on attracting customers rather than simply rationing their product, tenants find themselves in an unusual position of power: if they are dissatisfied with the 'service' provided by their current landlord, or believe it to be 'too expensive', opportunities exist to switch their custom to an alternative provider. In the process of letting homes, landlords find themselves under pressure to negotiate rather than simply to dictate the terms of the tenancy. To secure the acceptance of tenancy offers they may, for example, need to offer inducements such as decoration allowances or rent holidays. And market competition – rather than regulatory oversight – could help to maintain competitive rent levels.

Although there is a growing realization among landlords that competition can have damaging effects in terms of maintaining social order, the emphasis on meeting short-term performance targets militates against co-operation within the social sector. In some areas the dominance of the competitive ethic has undermined trust between landlords, with little faith being placed in references provided on behalf of housing applicants seeking to move from one to another (because the current landlord of a 'troublesome tenant' may be inclined to downplay any concerns about the tenant's behaviour in the hope that any associated problems will be inherited by another provider).

In the main, competition between social and private landlords involves the former attempting to attract tenants of the latter to switch tenure. For example, using its Housing Benefit database, Leeds City Council recently carried out a mailshot to all private tenant claimants publicizing 'easy access' to council housing. Leeds also reported that enterprising private landlords were leafleting local authority blocks to solicit for tenants (Bramley, Pawson and Third 2000).

Impact on viability of sanctions against anti-social behaviour

Where significant local oversupply of rented housing leads to competition for tenants, there is an impact on the ability of landlords to apply sanctions to encourage the payment of rent or curb anti-social behaviour. Some local authorities believe that estate management difficulties affecting low demand estates are compounded by the awareness among 'problem tenants' that, in the event of eviction, obtaining a house from another landlord would be relatively easy. There is anecdotal evidence of instances involving housing applications being received from previously evicted tenants who had subsequently obtained tenancies of newly-built RSL properties in spite of their formal exclusion from council housing.

This raises a wider issue about the proper allocation of responsibility for maintaining social order in the face of growing concerns about anti-social behaviour in residential areas (see below). One argument is that, even where such problems affect mainly social rented estates, they should be handled by the police rather than by housing management staff. A second contention is that, in the effort to control and deter potentially disruptive tenants, there should be less emphasis on the social landlord's power of eviction and more stress on a local authority's corporate capability to issue Anti-Social Behaviour Orders (ASBOs) under the Criminal Justice Act 1998.

Impact on crime and anti-social behaviour

Crime is undoubtedly implicated as a cause of low demand for housing (see pp.72–6). Concern over crime tends to be the single most commonly cited factor motivating neighbourhood dissatisfaction. For example, a survey of low demand neighbourhood residents found that 52 per cent of those wanting to move to a new area mentioned crime or insecurity as a 'main reason' underlying this objective (Bramley, Pawson and Third 2000). There is also evidence that crime rates in low demand areas in England either rose or declined more slowly than the national average between 1996 and 1998. Fear of crime and neighbourhood disorders are also much more common in low demand areas.

The effects of low demand for housing can also produce an environment where crime and various forms of anti-social behaviour flourish. This is partly associated with the reduced leverage available to landlords in maintaining social order, as alternative housing opportunities multiply (see above). Similarly, faced with the need to let their properties in conditions of housing surplus, the scope for tenant selection is greatly reduced. Landlords have no choice but to relax the filtering procedures used to deny access to those with a record of anti-social behaviour. This is an issue for both social and private landlords.

High rates of empty property also act as a magnet for certain sorts of crime such as vandalism, theft or drug dealing. Not only do the vacant homes themselves attract intruders, but where groups of void properties develop, the scope for conducting illicit activities undetected increases. Theft of central heating systems from empty homes is another problem faced by some landlords managing housing in low demand neighbourhoods. In one of Bramley, Pawson and Third's case study estates the problem had spread to tenanted homes, with the thieves resorting to intimidation and bribery to secure tenant acquiescence.

Transience

As reported above, high tenancy turnover often accompanies low demand for social rented housing. In the private sector, falling property values often translate into transfers of formerly owner-occupied property into private renting. A knock-on effect is rising residential instability, given the traditional role of the private rented sector in rehousing mobile households.

As far as public sector housing is concerned, there is an argument that relatively inflexible or 'coercive' allocations systems contribute to high turnover. Some social landlords report that among tenants rehoused on unpopular estates a high proportion apply for transfers almost immediately. Irrespective of tenure, high rates of residential instability are likely to be inimical to the development of community participation and damaging to community spirit. There is a specific concern that rising private renting may result in growing numbers of residents with little commitment to the neighbourhood. This finds its expression in a number of ways, including reluctance to become involved in community activities or to contribute to the upkeep of the area (e.g., garden maintenance).

Linked with the problems of falling school rolls (see above), residential instability also has implications for children's education. In one DETR case study, for example, it was estimated by the local primary school that only one-third of the Year Six class graduating to secondary level would have attended the school since the age of five. Termly pupil turnover was sometimes as high as one in six, with many repeat movers. Often, no notice or reasons were given by parents, though crime, intimidation or debt were thought to be common factors.

Even in the context of a national curriculum, repeated school moves have a damaging impact on children's educational progress. Each move is often accompanied by a prolonged absence from school, followed by a settling-in period. Attempting to educate such a high proportion of unsettled and deprived children presents enormous challenge for a school whose entire intake is drawn from an area seriously affected by low demand.

Conclusion

The past few years have seen growing polarization of housing markets at both regional and local levels across Britain. In England the tendency towards north–south divergence has been apparent since around 1994, and at the turn of the century there was little sign of any let-up in this trend. To a large extent, the patterns seen during this recent period in England represent a re-assertion of the North–South divide which attracted so much attention during the 1980s. In the social housing sector, the co-existence of gross surpluses in the North with acute shortages in London and the South also parallels the situation of the early 1980s. Arguably, however, this most recent experience of low demand has had more damaging consequences for the landlords and the areas affected. Bramley (1998a) argues that one possible explanation for this difference is the exhaustion of 'adjustment mechanisms' (e.g., relaxation of 'tight fit' allocation rules) used to cushion the impact of the problem in its earlier manifestation.

In part, these developments reflect economic restructuring and regional variations in economic performance. Changing residential preferences in favour of suburban or rural environments and home-ownership are also relevant. At the local level, micro-social processes, particularly involving stigmatization and the incidence of crime and anti-social behaviour, also contribute, as does the antipathy for certain types of built forms.

The emergence of low demand has had a fundamental impact in undermining conventional assumptions underpinning postwar housing policy and practice. Its appearance in the social rented sector has turned on its head the taken-for-granted power relationship between landlords and home-seekers, as well as between landlords. In some areas of the country local authorities and RSLs have had to come to terms with operating in a buyer's, rather than a seller's, market. The need to embrace an approach centred on marketing rather than rationing has involved a major cultural shift for housing professionals. This has contributed significantly to the impetus for a more consumerist approach to housing management (see Chapter 8), of which choice-based lettings is just the most prominent example.

This chapter has attempted to set the scene by describing the nature and origins of the low demand phenomenon and explaining some of the problems which result from it. The policy responses which might help to address these problems are discussed later in the book, primarily in Chapters 5, 8 and 9.

Guide to further reading

Within the UK context, probably the most significant publications in addition to Bramley, Pawson and Third's study for the DETR (2000) are those by Murie, Nevin and Leather (1998), Keenan, Lowe and Spencer (1999), and Cole, Kane and Robinson (1999). The Lowe, Spencer and Keenan (1998) collection also includes a number of contributions looking at low demand from different perspectives. In the US context, the recent article by Cohen (2001), whilst focusing on Baltimore, usefully reviews earlier American work on abandoned housing and discusses a range of problems and policy responses common to a number of 'postindustrial' contracting cities in the mid-west and north east of the country.

5

Planning for Housing

Planning, household growth and urban form

In this chapter we shift the focus from housing as a national system to the geographical location and physical form of housing as it is provided, in settlements ranging from cities to isolated rural cottages. This entails looking at one particular aspect of public policy impinging on housing, namely the land-use planning system.

Land-use (or town and country) planning is very important for housing. Indeed, there is little question that it is the most important way now in which public policy affects new housing provision. This is because, as noted in Chapter 2, most new housing (about four-fifths) is built for private sector use. But the reverse is also true: housing is the most important urban land use, typically accounting for half of all urban land and half of all new urban development. Some of the biggest public debates, nationally and locally, are about where new housing should, or should not, be built (Breheny and Hall 1996; Department of the Environment 1996; Bate 1999). Planning controls affect the price and 'affordability' of housing, as discussed below in the fourth section of this chapter. Furthermore, an increasing proportion of subsidized 'affordable' housing, together with a widening range of urban infrastructure (including new roads and schools), are paid for by new housing developments.

Discussing planning takes us into distinctive areas of policy and intellectual discourse. Planning is very much about the location of housing and other activities in geographical space. Indeed the concept of 'spatial planning' is enjoying a current vogue, partly under the influence of the European Union. There is a revival of interest in the central issues of urban physical form: for example, questions about the right size and shape for urban settlements, the density of housing and other developments, how they should be juxtaposed, and the kinds of building forms which should be employed.

In the 1990s, much of this revival of interest has been motivated by a concern with an agenda of 'environmentally sustainable development' (ESD), and this can be seen as providing a new unifying intellectual theme cutting across the existing disciplines. ESD in its current form is generally seen as having been launched by the 1987 Brundtland Commission and the subsequent

UK government White Papers (HM Government 1990, 1994). It is a central theme of current government planning policy guidance in the UK. As such it has been associated with quite radical policy shifts in transport and certain other areas of planning (Royal Commission on Environmental Pollution 1995). The implications for housing are discussed further below.

To pick up on the themes of Chapter 1, planning today exemplifies regulatory and indirect means of intervening in the market, rather than traditional 'command and control' methods. This is ironic in a way, since the British town planning system was born in the late 1940s, which might be regarded as the high point of bureaucratic, top-down management of the economy in the early postwar period. Perhaps some of planning's current inadequacies reflect its failure to adapt fully to this fundamental transformation of context (DTLR 2001). Planning has, however, come to be a front-line weapon in the 'enabling' approach to housing discussed in Chapter 1. In addition to locating and regulating the 80–85 per cent of new housing which is privately promoted, planning is now being expected to facilitate (or 'lever in') the provision of a significant share of new social housing, under the banner of planning policies for affordable housing. This new approach is discussed in detail in the penultimate section of this chapter. The use of planning mechanisms to secure the provision of subsidized housing is part of a wider picture of the use of these mechanisms to secure a wide range of public infrastructure and community benefits, commonly referred to as 'planning gain'.

The planning system

Having set the scene, we now turn to the key policy system which regulates the supply of land on which new housing may be built. Britain has a long-established and comprehensive system of town and country planning, and it is appropriate to describe briefly what this system entails.

Land-use regulation is a legal or administrative system which prescribes what type of use is permitted on any given parcel of land. 'Use' encompasses both the type of activity accommodated (e.g., housing, industry, retailing) and, to some degree, the type, scale and form of buildings which may accommodate that use. Such regulation comes into play most often when landowners seek to change the use of a piece of land; a change of use constitutes 'development'.

Although planning may be undertaken by private organizations, advanced societies have generally found it necessary or desirable to interpose a public legal and administrative basis for land-use regulation and planning. Bramley, Bartlett and Lambert (1995, ch. 3) argue that the principal goals of such planning include:

- spatial containment of urban growth (prevention of 'sprawl' and protection of countryside)

- separation of conflicting land uses (e.g., housing and industry)
- maintenance of certain environmental standards (e.g., density)
- co-ordination of different kinds of urban development (e.g., housing, jobs, shopping)
- co-ordination with and efficient use of public infrastructure
- promotion of good quality urban design
- protection of natural environment
- conservation of urban heritage

In the USA and many other countries, planning primarily takes the form of 'zoning'. Under this approach the territory is divided up into zones, within each of which certain types of land use are permitted subject to certain parameters, including minimum lot sizes and building lines for housing. The essence of this approach is that the landowner has the right to develop within these parameters (and the corresponding right to expect that neighbouring plots will not be developed in a 'non-conforming' fashion: Cullingworth 1997).

This approach contrasts strongly with the British system, under which since 1947 land-use rights have been 'nationalized' and there is no automatic presumption in favour of development. Any significant development requires permission from the local planning authority, who have considerable discretion in decision-making (Grant 1992). Local authorities must have regard to a range of material considerations, including any operative local plans and national policy guidance, and are subject to an appeal process. The 1990s saw an attempt to make the British system more 'plan-led', with operative, site-specific local plans in place everywhere. But it remains true that the British system is strongly characterized by discretion, and the consequent scope for detailed negotiation between developers and planners (Tewdwr-Jones 1996). Dissatisfaction with the actual performance of this system has, very recently, led to proposals for significant reform of the planning system, the outcomes of which are unclear (DTLR 2001).

Formally the British system entails a hierarchical system of plans, ranging from national policy guidance, regional planning guidance (in England), structure plans (for county or sub-regional areas), and local plans. Only the last of these is supposed to be site-specific. The apparently comprehensive character of this policy framework and forward planning system distinguishes the British system from that found in many other countries. In principle, local development control decisions should be determined on the basis of a rational comprehensive system which works out the local spatial implications of general policies in a way which is locally sensitive and democratically accountable. In practice, the system as it operates in practice falls somewhat short of this ideal, which may in any case be unattainable in a political environment characterized by conflicting policy priorities and inadequate information. Typical shortcomings include the tendency for plans to be slow to be completed or updated, so that the currently available plans may not reflect current information or policies (School of Planning and Housing 2001), and hence there remains considerable scope for discretion. Delays in plan preparation often reflect staff resource shortages in local authorities as well as the complex requirements for public participation and the rights of objectors to public hearings. Most of the delays which characterize development control decisions, particularly on larger developments, result from the negotiations which discretion and lack of clear policy allows. These negotiations are often concerned with infrastructure provision, which increasingly developers are expected to pay for. The planning system is widely perceived as negative and controlling, rather than positive or visionary, and it has been criticized as giving too strong a platform to local interests who wish to block development (so-called NIMBYism, the 'Not-in-My-Backyard' syndrome: Industrial Systems Research 1999).

Dissatisfaction with the performance of the planning system, both in responding to the demands of the modern economy and in promoting high quality, sustainable development, have led to proposals for wide-ranging reform. Added importance is given to planning reform by the concerns of the Treasury about both its effects on economic competitiveness and specific concerns about its impact on housing supply 'inelasticity' (as discussed further below). In England the DTLR (2001) proposed streamlining forward planning, with a single policy-based 'local development framework' instead of structure and local plans, with additional 'action area plans' for areas likely to be subject to major change. In Scotland, a new system of strategic plans for city-regions has been proposed (Scottish Executive 2001b) and planning policy guidance for housing has been revised.

Whatever the outcome of these reviews, they do illustrate the point that planning is now probably the most important regulatory intervention by the state in the economy, and particularly in relation to new investment which involves the development of land. Housing is the most important urban land use and is the sector which has arguably been most affected by planning restriction. Thus it is important to understand how planning works for new housing, and to explore ways in which it could be made to work better.

Significance of household growth for planning and housing

Projections of household numbers have been routinely used in the land-use planning system as the main basis for determining how much land should be provided for new housing development. They have in practice been much less used in the process of deciding how much social housing to provide, at either national or local level. Household projections are prepared by central government (Department of the Environment 1995b; DETR 1999d) and are fed into the system through Regional Planning Guidance, which allocates numbers of housing units to be provided to different planning authorities.

Structure Plans (Unitary Development Plans in some metropolitan areas) currently refine these estimates at local level, possibly deviating from official projections where local conditions, including environmental constraints, indicate. Local Plans are expected to identify the particular sites where development is to take place (so-called 'allocations') while specifying types of housing and particular design and other requirements. Some allowance is also made for unanticipated 'windfall' sites coming forward for housing development, often on brownfield land. Structure Plans typically look forward 15 years, and Local Plans more commonly focus on a 10-year horizon.

In the mid-1990s there was increasing debate about whether the traditional reliance on household projections in land-use planning was necessarily appropriate, given policy concerns about issues of environmental sustainability and urban regeneration (Department of the Environment 1996; Bramley 1998b). It was also suggested that the process might be technically faulty, because of its inherent 'circularity' (Bramley and Watkins 1995), and/or because it did not take account of economic factors. As a response to this, the government proposed shifting from this traditional 'predict and provide' approach to a more sophisticated 'plan–monitor–manage' (PMM) approach (DETR 1998e, 2000c; Wenban-Smith 1999). What exactly this new approach entails is not entirely clear, although is closely linked to policies of trying to maximize the re-use of previously used urban land (so-called 'brownfield' land), which entails careful investigation of the potential capacity of urban areas to accommodate more housing.

While it is early days to judge the effectiveness of this modified approach, there are considerable grounds for concern that it may not in practice be delivering sufficient land for new housing, particularly in the overheated south east of England where economic buoyancy and household growth are most pressing (Monk and Whitehead 2000). One aspect of this concern is that the new approach has been interpreted as taking a shorter-term view of requirements, rather than doing what some of the critics of the traditional approach were really arguing for, which was more proactive and longer-term planning for urban development (Breheny and Hall 1996; School of Planning and Housing 2001). Another aspect is that the system of maintaining registers of available sites and ensuring that there is at least a 5-year supply of usable land available for housing has fallen into some disuse in England, as a result of the PMM approach and the emphasis on brownfield urban capacity.

It is reasonable to ask what will happen if housing provision falls short of projections of requirements based on household growth? Holmans (2000) argues that the people and households will not melt away but will still have to be accommodated somehow. A number of adjustment mechanisms will come into play, including higher prices, more affordability problems, longer commuting (from cheaper areas), more sharing and overcrowding of accommodation and, for some of the most vulnerable groups, more homelessness. Conversely, in areas of lower demand, a mirror-image question arises: what are the consequences of providing more new housing than is shown to be required by household projections? The possibility that overprovision might be a problem is a relatively recent concern, but one which has forced itself to the attention of planners as a result of the emergence of the low demand phenomenon. There have been proposals that planned provision of greenfield land in such areas should be restricted, to help bring the market back into balance (Urban Task Force 1999; Bramley, Pawson and Third 2000).

It can be fairly said, also, that the traditional emphasis on projecting household numbers neglects issues of quality, including the type and size of housing provided, as well as its cost, tenure and location. The household projections do provide some valuable information about changes in housing demand, particularly in terms of the changing mix of household types, with a strong emphasis on single person households whose requirements may be markedly different from traditional families. However, qualitative shifts in demand go beyond this, and there is no simple equation of small households with small housing units (Hooper, Dunmore and Hughes 1998). Rising incomes have some effect on numbers of households but they have a larger effect on the space and quality of housing which people look for. There is a growing demand for larger houses with more spare rooms, bathrooms, gardens, car-parking space, and so forth. Planning also has to respond to these demands, whether in terms of accommodating them or trying to moderate them. Rising incomes also increase demand for owner-occupation rather than renting. However, particularly if supply is limited, prices may rise and prevent many people from realizing these aspirations. This will bring issues of housing affordability to the fore, as a central issue which planning has to address and a somewhat different focus for planning than the traditional, demographically-dominated concept of housing need (Monk and Whitehead 2000).

Policy preoccupations

At different stages in recent history, the preoccupations of national policy-makers and local planners in approaching the planning of new housing have varied considerably. In the 1950s and 1960s there was an emphasis on catering for both backlogs of unmet need and population growth through a process of planned dispersal, alongside the establishment of 'urban containment' to prevent the kind of 'sprawl' which characterized the 1930s (Hall *et al.* 1973; Champion 2002). The two key instruments were new towns (a public-sector led initiative) and the establishment of green belts around major cities. The 1970s were a period of transition, with new concerns about the decline of the inner cities, the end of slum clearance and comprehensive redevelopment, as well as concern about booms and slumps in the private housing market. While the new towns programme was run down, new mechanisms were put in place to ensure an adequate supply of land for private development. In the 1980s, there were some moves towards deregulation, and a move away from more strategic regional planning, but local opposition prevented a mooted relaxation of green belt policy.

At the end of the 1980s, a new environmental sustainability agenda began to make its presence felt (World Commission on Environmental Development 1987; HM Government 1990, 1994), and taken in conjunction with some dissatisfaction with the haphazard operation of the planning system which was increasingly reliant on appeals, this led to the institution of the so-called 'plan-led system' (Tewdwr-Jones 1996). In the 1990s, the ESD agenda was increasingly articulated, and seen to justify a renewed emphasis on urban containment and consolidation to reduce car-based travel and emissions, together with a stronger emphasis on urban renaissance entailing a greater re-use of urban brownfield sites for housing rather than greenfield development (Jencks, Burton and Williams 1996). Another strand of thinking has focused on trying to improve the design and quality of the built environment (Urban Task Force 1999; Scottish Executive 2003a). As already noted, recent dissatisfaction with the performance of the planning system has prompted further potential reforms, motivated partly by these concerns but also by an agenda of promoting economic competitiveness (DTLR 2001; Begg 2002). While the latter focuses particularly on facilitating development by business, there is a link to housing given the inadequate supply and escalating prices evident in the areas of greatest economic growth (Bramley and Lambert 2002). Housing has become linked again to employment, and the issues of affordability of housing for key workers are a significant element in current policies for both housing and planning. Finally, the *Sustainable Communities* plan (ODPM 2003b) represents a wedding of the continued urban renaissance thrust with an attempt to correct the regional imbalances in the housing market, including planning for major new growth areas in south-east England.

The impact of planning on the market

Planning is, as we have seen, a very important and pervasive governmental intervention in the operation of the market in relation to new housing development. As such we would expect planning to have a significant impact on how the market operates and on the outcomes it produces, in terms of the number, location and type of houses built and the prices facing consumers. These effects should be considered when evaluating planning policies, and weighed alongside the benefits of planning in terms of environmental protection and enhancement and the better spatial ordering of urban settlements. But in order to assess these market impacts we have to determine what they are likely to be from a theoretical point of view, and then ideally try to measure the scale of these effects using empirical evidence. Neither of these tasks is straightforward: there are ambiguities in the theory, and considerable practical difficulties of measurement of key factors (e.g., quantifying planning restrictions) and of how to model the behaviour of the market. We consider the theoretical perspective first, and then move on to look at key empirical studies of the market impact of planning.

Impact in theory

A number of authors look at how we would expect planning to impact on the market (Fischel 1990; A.W. Evans 1991; Monk, Pearce and Whitehead 1991; Bramley, Bartlett and Lambert 1995; Cheshire and Sheppard 1997; Monk and Whitehead 1999). Planning (particularly in Britain) is seen as imposing an overall constraint on the amount of land available for housebuilding. This supply restriction reduces the number of houses which can be built, which for any given level of demand increases the price of houses. Although this impact applies most directly to new houses, because the whole housing market is connected (many consumers may be willing to buy either a new or second-hand dwelling), this upward pressure on house prices affects the whole market. Because it is land which is restricted, it is the part of house prices which reflects the value of the land which rises most, rather than the part which reflects construction costs. Housebuilders compete for the scarce available land and bid its price up. The disproportionate rise in land values has a further effect on housing supply, which is to encourage developers to try to cram more houses on to a given area of land (in other words, raising housing densities). Gardens are smaller, single-storey dwellings become rarer, and flats more common.

The long-established character of planning restriction in Britain has been to impose 'containment' on existing towns and cities, primarily through green belts around the existing built-up areas within which new building is particularly strongly opposed. Yet these are the areas which would, in the natural course of urban development, be most in demand for new building, because of their ready access to the jobs and services of the towns. This has the effect of exaggerating the effects described above, and also has implications for the spatial patterns of development which do occur. First, there is pressure to intensify housing within the existing built-up areas. Second, there is a tendency for development to leapfrog over the green belt and take place at a greater distance from the city. This is alleged to increase commuting journeys and to encourage settlements which may be more expensive to service and less sustainable than simpler expansion at the urban periphery.

This relatively simple story about the impact of planning accords with economic theory, both the basic concepts of supply and demand determining prices, and more elaborate urban economic theory about the structure of cities and the spatial pattern of densities and land values (Muth 1969; A.W. Evans 1973; Bramley, Bartlett and Lambert 1995). However, there are some complications which need to be considered.

The first complication is that planning does not just affect the quantity of housing supplied: it also should have some positive effect on the quality of the environment around that housing and the efficiency of the urban infrastructure and services to which it is connected. A well-planned city or suburb, with attractive open and green spaces, good schools and efficient transport, will be a better place to live and people will pay more to live in it. Thus, the demand side of the equation is not held constant. If we observe higher prices in a planned settlement, this may be because of these positive amenities and services rather than because of the restriction in supply.

The second complication is that the nature of the planning regulation may vary. It may, for example, be less to do with the total quantity of housing land and more to do with restrictions on the type and density of housing which may be developed on it. This is characteristic of the typical US 'zoning' control, for example, and of some local authority planning policies in UK, which seek to limit densities so as to preserve the character and amenity of suburban areas. Such regulation restricts the ability of the market to respond flexibly to demand in terms of house type and density, and so can be argued to be inefficient, although this has to be weighed against the value of the residential amenity which it protects. These policies are also criticized for having adverse distributional effects, 'excluding' poorer households from suburban housing opportunities whilst reinforcing the wealth and amenity of better-off groups. These effects may be more extreme when such policies are combined with overall containment. The effects of this kind of restriction are discussed in Monk, Pearce and Whitehead (1991), Bramley, Bartlett and Lambert (1995) and Fischel (1990).

The third complication is that allocating or zoning land for housing does not ensure that housing will necessarily be built on it, either now or in the future. Developers may choose not to build if they perceive that the price they can sell the houses for will not represent an adequate return on their outlay. The land may be nowhere near existing centres of population, employment, shopping and other services, and may lack basic infrastructure connections or good transport. The owners of the land (usually a different party from the professional developer, e.g., farmers) may be in no particular hurry to sell the land for development; they can choose to sit back and take the value at some future date, when it may (in the usual course of things) be much higher than it is today.

The idea of a world without planning is probably a little far-fetched in a country such as Britain, but certainly planning regimes and their strictness can vary a great deal. A situation where planning is not much of a binding constraint on development is not uncommon in Britain. It occurs in some areas in the north of England, for example, where low demand for housing coincides with an abundance of land allocated for new housebuilding (see Chapter 4 above; Urban Task Force 1999). It is, however, less common in the housing sector than it is in relation to industrial and business development land. For example, Bramley *et al.* (2001) found that throughout most of Central Scotland there was 20–25 years' supply of such land. In such circumstances it is the decisions of developers which determine where and when development happens, not the decisions of planners.

Measuring the impact

There have been two main attempts to measure the impact of British planning controls on the housing market. The first is that of Cheshire and Sheppard (1989, 1997), who use a methodology combining statistical house price modelling with microeconomic demand theory, and apply this to particular towns (Reading, Darlington, Nottingham) with different degrees of planning restraint. They then use these models to simulate (a) the effects of changes in the planning restrictions or other provisions for these towns, and (b) the likely impact of changes across a wider system of localities. In the first study they found that the impact of planning controls on the representative 'restrictive' locality (Reading) were to raise the average price of houses on the market by 6–8 per cent. Perhaps more significant was the finding that removing restriction on the outward development of the town (i.e., containment) would in the long run lead to a dramatic reduction in housing densities. Thus, the more important effect of planning, they argue, is to limit the extent to which people can enjoy space in and around their home. In their more recent study, they estimated that the loss of welfare from this restriction was quite substantial, of the order of 10–13 per cent of total income. They also found that restriction on the use of space within the existing built-up area of the city was a net cost to residents, even allowing for their imputed benefit from the collective open space created, equivalent to about half of the then rate of local domestic property taxation. This study also examined the distributional impacts of these effects, finding the costs borne most by the highest income group, while some middle income groups benefited. This research employs sophisticated theoretical and methodological tools but arguably suffers from some limitations in the conceptualization and measurement of planning intervention and its aims (Bramley 1998b). More broadly, its implicit policy recommendation of an American style of low density suburban development seems out of tune with the ESD agenda.

The second series of studies, led by one of the present authors, has involved a more aggregated modelling approach with more emphasis on the supply side, including testing the effects of different forms and degrees of planning restriction (Bramley 1993b and 1993c; Bramley, Bartlett and Lambert 1995; Bramley and Watkins 1996a and 1996b; Bramley 1999). These studies used district councils as the unit of analysis and experimented with various ways of simulating the feedback effects from planning policy changes to house prices. The last of these papers estimated that the elasticity (proportional sensitivity) of house prices to structure plan land release lay in the range -0.15 to -0.29. Thus, releasing 10 per cent more land could lower house prices by 1.5–3 per cent; releasing 50 per cent more could reduce prices by 7.5–14.5 per cent.

More recently, a modified version of this approach has been developed utilizing a 'panel' dataset (i.e., including variations over time as well as space). Bramley (2002) reports results from this approach which, while not directly comparable, are broadly consistent. A 10 per cent increase in land available (with planning permission) would reduce house prices in the affected zone(s) by 0.8–1.0 per cent. This suggests that the impact of planning on prices is rather lower than previously estimated, but it should be borne in mind that a general policy of extra land release, applied to whole regions or nationally, could have a bigger effect than what can be measured for a single zone.

This recent research suggests that the responsiveness of housing supply in Britain to house prices is relatively low, compared with both earlier estimates and with results from US research. Other recent British research tends to confirm this finding (Meen 1998), and indeed one study (Pryce 1999) suggests that in some circumstances housebuilding might actually respond negatively to higher prices (perhaps due to speculative behaviour). This tendency of British housing supply to be sticky and unresponsive is a cause for concern for economic and housing policy generally; it means that increases in housing demand tend to result in higher prices rather than higher output. At the time of writing the low level of national housing output, despite booming housing markets, is a growing source of policy concern (HM Treasury 2003; ODPM 2003b). This is one reason why an increasingly critical scrutiny is being applied to the planning system at the present time.

As already explained, British planning policy has become preoccupied with achieving more emphasis on brownfield development to support urban renaissance and ESD generally. As a by-product of this emphasis, and also because of political sensitivity to greenfield housebuilding in much of England, the actual amount of land made available for housing in the highest demand region of England, the South East, has been falling. Bramley (2001, Tables 5 and 6) shows that the available land supply as a percentage of plan targets in the South East fell from 159 per cent in 1992 to 114 per cent in 1996 and only 84 per cent in 1998. In the same region the flow of new planning permissions in 2001 was about half the rate in the peak of the 1988 boom (ODPM planning statistics).

Many commentators believe that brownfield sites are inherently more difficult and costly to develop and involve greater risk for developers (Breheny and Hall 1996; Monk and Whitehead 2000; Adams and Watkins 2002). Recent experience has shown that it is possible to develop a high proportion of new housing, now the majority, on brownfield land; currently 60 per cent of new housing in England is built on brownfield land, a modest increase on the levels prevalent through the 1990s. So it is clear that whatever problems there are with such sites, they can often be overcome. Nevertheless, it is reasonable to argue that this policy emphasis does have some negative impact on housing supply, and consequently some positive impact on house prices. The recent study by Bramley (2002) attempted to quantify this effect and concluded that a 10 per cent increase in the urban land share would reduce output by 1.5 per cent and raise prices by 0.5 per cent; however, further analysis of the underlying data suggests that we cannot be confident about the measurement of these effects.

The restrictiveness of planning policy towards housing varies considerably between different areas. If we can measure this effectively we have a tool which can be used both to monitor how the system is performing and to feed into economic models of the kind referred to above. Bramley (1998b) discusses this measurement issue in detail. The main conclusion is that considerable care is required in the use of some indicators. In addition, it is clear that there is a systematic tendency for local planning decisions to be more restrictive towards new housing than they are towards new business development. This is a key factor underlying the increasing tendency for job growth and economic prosperity in the more favoured areas, such as the south east of England, to run ahead of housing supply, so reinforcing the North–South divide discussed in Chapters 2–4.

Planning and affordable housing

Background

There are a number of reasons why planning policies and mechanisms to secure affordable housing have come to occupy centre stage in Britain by the early 2000s. First, as explained in Chapters 1–2, public sector investment in social housing has been cut back radically from the levels of the decades up to the 1970s (Bramley 1997b). There is little sign of these earlier levels of public investment or subsidy being restored, and recent revivals under the post-1997 New Labour government are mainly focused on improving the state of the existing social housing stock (Wilcox 2002). Planning offers a possible way of levering significant subsidy from private sources into the provision of social or affordable housing. Second, the process of planning at local level is one where local councils are particularly concerned to ensure provision to meet 'local needs'. In the 1980s many planning authorities tried to include policies to relate new housing provision to local needs, but in practice found this difficult or impossible to enforce (Loughlin 1984). This issue has proved to be particularly sensitive, and well-articulated, in the rural context (Clark and Dunmore 1990).

A third factor has been the government's attempt, throughout the 1990s, to get local authorities to shift from a direct provision to an 'enabling' role, as mentioned in Chapter 1 (Bramley 1993a; Goodlad 1998). A local authority's land use planning powers are among the few powerful tools it has to achieve desired forms of housing development through other agencies. A fourth factor, increasingly apparent as the 1990s wore on, was the drying up of traditional sources of land supply for social housing developers (RSLs), in terms of land from local authorities and other public owners, and its increasing cost. Fifth, the 1990s also saw an upsurge of concern about the social sustainability of the estates and neighbourhoods associated with new social housing (Page 1993). There has been an increasing argument that large 'mono-tenure' social housing estates are inappropriate, and that all new development should be mixed in terms of tenure, incomes and household types (DETR 1998b and 2000b). Lastly, a factor which has come on to the agenda very strongly at the end of the 1990s and in the first years of the new century has been the problem of key worker housing, particularly affordable housing for public service workers in the south of England.

To some extent most of these concerns are affected by the housing market and economic cycles. Housing booms in the late 1980s and again at the end of the 1990s have pushed the issues of affordability, rural housing, land values, and key workers to the fore, particularly in London and the south of England. The regional divide which manifests itself in many aspects of housing is certainly significant here; it is these southern areas where planning for affordable housing policies have been promoted most actively (Barlow, Cocks and Rich 1994; Monk and Whitehead 2000).

Rural local authorities especially in attractive areas with tight planning constraints (e.g., South Lakeland, New Forest), were among those most eager to develop 'housing for local needs' policies and to attempt to implement these through planning. The first official recognition of this was given by the then Secretary of State for Environment in February 1989, with the introduction of the 'rural exceptions policy'. This allowed local authorities to grant exceptional permissions for affordable housing on sites within or adjacent to small rural settlements which would not expect to get permission for general market housing, subject to evidence of need and arrangements to ensure the housing remained available for local, low income residents 'in perpetuity' (both points are discussed further below).

Two years later the Department of the Environment's Circular 7/91 introduced a more general form of planning for affordable housing policy which would be of much wider and larger scale significance. This essentially enables a local authority to seek a proportion of affordable housing provision on all new developments over a certain minimum size threshold. Subsequent circulars and Planning Policy Guidance Notes (PPGs) have both clarified and refined the policy (DETR 2000b). At certain stages there were some signs of government wavering about how strongly it wished to pursue this policy, but recently the policy has been given much stronger support from the top. These provisions related to England; Scotland had to wait until 1996 for reference to such policies in its national guidance, and this was weaker than English guidance, reflecting a general lack of interest in such policies in Scotland until around 2000.

How the policy works

How do planning and affordable housing policies work? This is best explained by identifying, in a logical sequence, the essential elements which are required to give effect to such policies:

1   *Evidence of local needs* is essential to provide a basis for affordable housing requirements, which may entail periodic special surveys; such evidence will be treated by the planning system as a 'material consideration'.
2   The policy should be enshrined in a *local development plan* (to be known in future, in England, as a 'local development framework'), which in turn requires it to be rationally based on evidence and subject to testing through local consultation and a public inquiry.
3   The policy may indicate a *target level* of affordable provision ('affordable' should be defined), and the range of site sizes and categories to which this applies.
4   The requirement for a particular site is subject to *negotiation*, based on the policy target but having regard to the particular local and site circumstances.
5   The affordable housing requirement is enforced through a *planning agreement* which attaches to the planning permission and is binding on present and future landowners (known as 'Section 106 agreements' in England, 'Section 75' in Scotland).
6   Delivery of affordable housing and its availability in perpetuity is normally ensured through the involvement of a *Registered Social Landlord*.
7   Provision on site in a *mixed development* is generally preferred, but in some circumstances financial '*payments in lieu*' (PIL, also known as 'commuted payments') may be accepted and used to subsidize provision on other sites.

These mechanisms are helpful for securing land for the development of social or other low cost housing, and for promoting mixed tenure developments. Recent research confirms that they are important for promoting intermediate tenure options, particularly low cost home-ownership (LCHO), which may in turn be particularly relevant to key workers (Bramley *et al.* 2002). However, the dominant logic driving these policies is an economic and financial one, of trying to secure not just affordable housing but also a *subsidy* towards the cost of providing it. Where does this subsidy come from? It would be careless and misleading to refer to this as subsidy from the developer; the idea is that the subsidy should come from the *land value*.

Although government policy has blown hot and cold over the years about the taxation of land values and development gains, there is general agreement among economists that land rent and land value is a special category of income/wealth. The value of a piece of land is determined mainly by its location relative to the location of other economic activities, infrastructure and environmental amenities. As such, this value is the product of the wider economy and community, including any amenities and services provided by the local public authorities, together with the effects of local planning itself. When a piece of farmland (in most of southern England, at any rate) gets planning permission for housing, its value jumps from a few thousand pounds per hectare to matter of millions, without any significant effort or cost being incurred by the existing landowner (e.g., the farmer). Because of this special character of land value, and particularly the gains in value associated with planning permission, there has long been interest in special measures of taxation to apply to these gains, particularly where these can be used to finance infrastructure, environmental compensation, or other local social requirements including affordable housing.

In negotiating planning agreements, the key factor is the so-called 'residual value' of the development: the difference between sales revenues and all the costs of building and development, other than the land itself but including the developer's normal profit margin and financing costs. This residual value is what the developer (and his or her competitors) would be willing and able to bid to secure the site, and hence the principal basis of market values of housing land in this location. And it is this residual value which planning policies for affordable housing seek to tap into.

Calculations of residual value can be used to indicate what proportion of homes on a site might be affordable and how much of the subsidy for this housing might be met from land value. In many cases, where prices are high a significant share of affordable housing can be provided at greatly reduced public sector cost. Where land values are particularly high, where the share of affordable housing is lower, or where the form of affordable housing is less subsidy-intensive (e.g., LCHO), schemes can be viable with no public subsidy at all. There are examples of local authorities negotiating schemes of this kind.

The argument for general policies and targets set out in local plans is that all developers should be making the same calculations and reducing their bids for land accordingly (the so-called 'level playing field'). This argument received further support in the DTLR's 2001 consultation paper, which proposed a more generalized 'tariff system' for planning obligations, including affordable housing. However, there are also arguments for flexibility and negotiation from site to site, because circumstances vary considerably. There is also an argument that often urban sites are more likely to have significant remediation or redevelopment costs; and also that they are more likely to have alternative potential uses which would command a substantially higher value than agriculture, even if probably a lower value than in housing use (Monk and Whitehead 2000).

Controversy over the policy

Although the policy has been up and running for over a decade in England, it has been subject to ongoing controversy, with commentators questioning its legality, its appropriateness in principle, the range of its applicability, its effects on the market and its impact on provision patterns. The issues were rehearsed extensively (e.g., in Joseph Rowntree Foundation 1994), and there have been a number of landmark court challenges to particular planning decisions. On the whole, the courts have been minded to treat this as a matter of policy, and to accept that affordable housing is a material consideration in planning and that the government's policy guidance is legitimate. This is notwithstanding the arguments of Healey, Purdue and Ennis (1993) and others that affordable housing is fairly well down the list of potential claims on 'planning gain'. It is not strictly necessary to enable a particular site to be developed, and neither is it compensating for a specific environmental impact of a particular development. The justification is more indirect, and applicable to the whole area of a local plan: the policies of restraint/containment in that plan have contributed to the overall shortage and higher price of housing, and therefore the policy may be seen as compensating lower income local residents for this impact. There are also implicit 'social engineering' assumptions, namely that enabling people to remain in the communities where they grew up, and ensuring some mixing of tenures and income groups at local level, is desirable and brings about longer-term social benefits. One of the more interesting recent debates has been about the desirability of extending affordable housing policies and agreements to commercial developments, both on 'level playing field' grounds and to strengthen the link between housing and employment, as a response to the key worker crisis (Monk and Whitehead 2000).

It is fair to argue that planning agreements for affordable housing, like other aspects of 'planning gain', are, up to a point, a form of taxation. However, as argued above, they may be an appropriate tax, given the special character of development gains, and it is not true to assert – as some do – that this 'tax' is arbitrary and unaccountable (i.e., it is based on a public policy framework agreed through a process involving local public inquiries, etc.). We would argue that planning agreements are significantly different from typical taxes in a number of respects, as set out in Box 5.1.

While from a social housing point of view this new mechanism of planning policies and agreements seems to be very attractive, experience has thrown up many practical implementation issues. How exactly should the policy be expressed, given the general exhortation not to use planning to prescribe tenure, price or occupancy? In what documents should the policy be set out: regional/strategic plans, local plans, 'supplementary planning guidance'? How are 'affordability' and 'affordable housing' to be defined, and in particular what should be the role for LCHO (e.g., shared ownership) and 'low cost market sale' alongside conventional social renting? How robust are the surveys

Box 5.1 *Different attributes of planning agreements versus taxes*

Planning Agreements	Taxes
Locally determined	Statutory
Discretionary	Universal
Variable	Uniform
In kind	Financial
Hypothecated	Unhypothecated
Re-used locally	Redistributed nationally

of local housing needs and the calculations derived from them (Bramley, Satsangi, Dumore and Cousins 2004)? At what scale of locality should needs be measured and provision specified (the whole district, the individual village, the urban ward)? Up to what minimum size of site should developments be exempted from the policy? This last point generated probably more practical debate in the 1990s than almost any other, and yet arguably this was a red herring since there is no obvious reason in principle for such thresholds and the government itself has (in some documents) recommended having no thresholds in pressured rural communities. Commuted payments have been controversial in some cases and there are certainly issues about how they should be calculated and accounted for. Viability assessments remain an area for further development and guidance to local practitioners. Whether or not public subsidy is available on planning gain sites, and at what rates, has been a very grey area and needs to be clarified. The practical issue of when and how to involve RSLs has been a source of concern (e.g., if they come in too late, they may be saddled with a development which is inappropriate in management terms).

The approach described in this section has developed in the particular context of British land-use planning law and policy. Nevertheless, there are some examples in other countries of policies and practices which may be somewhat similar in effect. Particularly significant in this regard are attempts in parts of the USA to apply 'inclusionary zoning': that is, to ensure that new areas of housing development do include a range of house types/densities/price levels/tenures, in some cases explicitly including housing specifically targeted at low income groups (Danielsen, Lang and Fulton 1999; Bogdon 2001).

It is reasonable to question how effective these policies have actually been in practice at delivering affordable housing. Because of the many implementation problems and issues identified above, it would not be surprising if the actual performance of the policy fell well short of its theoretical potential. Bramley, Bartlett and Lambert (1995, p.164) made an estimate based on a mixture of theoretical assumptions and modelling results, suggesting that planning could deliver an extra 16–22,000 affordable units per year in England, an increase of between 30 and 45 per cent on then current programme volumes. In fact, actual delivery has built up very slowly from a low level in the early 1990s

(2,000 per annum projected by Barlow and Chambers 1994, and about 3,000 per annum in Barlow, Cocks and Rich 1994) to a level of around 12–15,000 in 1999–2000 (Crook *et al.* 2002) and 18,000 in 2003. It is not surprising that there has been a gradual build-up, because planning agreements could only be applied to sites getting new planning permissions and local plans had first to be revised to incorporate suitable policies backed by evidence of need. The current figures remain confusing because not all of the affordable housing linked to planning agreements is 'additional' in the sense of being fully or substantially funded by land value, rather than by the existing streams of social housing grant. Our own view, backed by various research, is that many local authorities have not applied the policies rigorously up till now, partly because of ambiguities about central government support as well as practical implementation difficulties. Nevertheless, the policies are generally getting stronger over time.

Despite these problems and uncertainties, there is no doubt that planning for affordable housing is a policy framework which has become generally adopted, both locally and nationally. There is growing reliance upon it and rising expectations about what it should be able to achieve (e.g., the Mayor of London's well-publicized target of 50 per cent affordable housing across much of London). It is certainly here to stay for the foreseeable future. Among its various broadly beneficial side-effects are the greater emphasis on systematic assessments of need, market monitoring, the collaboration of housing and planning professionals at local level, more awareness of issues of development viability, and a greater emphasis on mixed tenure developments.

Ideas for better planning

We conclude this chapter by looking forward in a positive way at what planning might achieve, for housing and urban development more generally, in the future. In the 1980s, planning was in the doldrums, deeply unfashionable with the then government and pretty low profile at the local level. The 1990s have seen planning gradually emerging from these shadows, re-energized by the ESD agenda and more recently by the kind of links to housing just described. Planning reform has come to the top of the policy agenda, and it has been realized that to be effective planning must be adequately resourced and have the right tools to do its job (ODPM 2003b).

There has been some reformulation and broadening of the goals of planning. In the 1980s, government saw the role of planning as relatively limited, confined to narrowly-conceived land-use matters. There was an emphasis on the negative regulatory role and its administration, and on promoting economic and property development. Overarching national guidance now envisages a more balanced emphasis on a triumvirate of broad goals: economic growth, ESD and social justice (the latter featuring more significantly since 1997).

There is a new interest in longer-term spatial strategies. This stems partly from the EU, which has promulgated a European Spatial Development Framework in part to guide its own investment through structural funds. It also stems from a critique of actual planning practice, where plans have tended to be relatively short term, reactive and opportunistic (Bramley *et al.* 2001; School of Planning and Housing 2001). This situation has arisen partly from the procedural delays plaguing plan approval and updating, and partly from political reticence about major urban settlement extensions in the face of NIMBYist politics. Only if plans look further ahead are the real options for major directions of development and possible major new settlements or urban extensions placed firmly on the agenda. It is interesting that the US growth controls movement tends to focus on longer time horizons (20–25 years) than have been characteristic in British planning (Knaap 2001). Recent government decisions on planning guidance for the South East have, after some delay and dithering, come out in favour of major areas for expansion (ODPM 2003b).

Strategic planning at sub-regional level is a new focus of attention. It has been realized that the key spatial scale for planning housing, employment and transport infrastructure is really the city region or functional urban region. This does not fit very well with the current institutional arrangements, particularly in conurbations, where planning has become rather 'balkanized' on the basis of unitary local authorities, with a weaker regional tier set at too broad a scale. The problem of competing overprovision of new housing land in low demand regions is an example of the consequences of this situation (Urban Task Force 1999; Bramley, Pawson and Third 2000). Proposals for a new approach to strategic planning in Scotland (Scottish Executive 2001b) focus on city regions as the key basis, although there are ongoing uncertainties about exactly where the boundaries should be drawn (e.g., Edinburgh's housing market area extends through the Lothians and into parts of Fife and the Borders). Future institutional arrangements in England remain unclear, with proposals to abolish county-level structure plans and the possibility of Regional Development Agencies (and ultimately elected regional authorities) taking over more of this role.

It has long been recognized that implementation is a weakness in British planning, particularly where the direction and coordination of investment in infrastructure and urban regeneration is involved (Healey *et al.* 1985, 1988). Planning is better at regulating new development than at positively promoting it. What is needed is a framework within which all the major public and infra-structural investments required to give effect to a longer-term spatial strategy are brought together in a common programme, with all the major players signed up to the plan and programme. Official proposals for strategic planning go some way towards this idea (Scottish Executive 2001b). There are examples in other countries of such co-ordinated development programmes: for example, in New South Wales, Australia.

We described earlier how there is something of a structural problem in the British system, whereby local planning authorities tend to be more restrictive in their approach to new housing development than towards other economic developments. This reflects the crude politics of NIMBYism, even though it may be dressed up in a rhetoric of ESD. Can we find ways of incentivizing local decision-makers to support housing development in a more positive way? This may be partly a matter of fiscal and grant mechanisms, and of making these more transparently able to support the investment and other service provision which new housing and population growth require. It may be partly achieved through measures to raise the environmental quality of new developments, as discussed further below. It may also be a pragmatic argument for reinforcing the responsible use of planning agreements to secure both general planning gain and also specific provision of affordable housing for local people in need.

Planning tends to operate through a set of rules and norms, and it may be worth trying to review some of the rules of the planning game. For example, over recent decades, as we saw above, household projections have been used as a basis for planning new housing provision. There is a logic for doing this, and notwithstanding their shortcomings it would be a mistake to ignore this relatively systematic evidence of housing needs and requirements, particularly at the sub-regional level and above. However, we believe that plan-making and plan-monitoring should pay more attention to other evidence of demand in local and sub-regional markets. In particular, house prices provide a readily-available barometer of the balance between supply and demand and of affordability conditions, whilst evidence on employment levels and changes, relative to workforce projections, provide further evidence of potential supply–demand imbalances. We would favour these indicators being given a more formal role in the assessment of the adequacy of planned housing provision. This could include the development of new indicators of the job–housing balance, and the inclusion of rules of thumb to reflect these in future housing allocations. Doing this would arguably contribute to all of the meta-goals of planning, supporting economic growth in dynamic regions, promoting ESD by limiting the extent of unnecessary commuting, and promoting affordability and access to housing by lower income groups. Conversely, use of these economic indicators would help plans to better reflect the problems of low demand in some sub-regions, as described in Chapter 4.

Maintaining an effective supply of land which is actually available for development in the short term (5–7 years) remains an important responsibility of planning authorities. This has been recognized and strengthened in the draft revisions to planning policy guidance in Scotland (Scottish Executive 2003b). Unfortunately, in England this role has been neglected as a consequence of the excessive focus on brownfield development and 'urban capacity'.

Promoting ESD and 'smart urban growth', to use the American term, has come to pervade planning policy in theory, but actual practice is very patchy and at times contradictory. The key relevant ideas here focus on urban consolidation, increasing density to recreate or reinforce the 'compact city', and orienting development to transportation links, particularly public transport

(Jencks, Burton and Williams 1996; Williams, Burton and Jencks 2000). Actual achievements are more mixed. City-centre living has become fashionable and feasible, and there are many successes in brownfield redevelopment and centrally-located high density housing developments promoted in the market. However, this caters for only part of the market, single people and childless households; for many others the lower density suburb and the small town/village setting remain very attractive, and such locations tend to be associated with a more car-dependent lifestyle (Bramley and Morgan 2003).

There are ideas around about smarter urban form, although these tend not to have been subject to rigorous testing. A central feature of British planning has been the green belt ring around major cities, but this is being increasingly questioned (Royal Town Planning Institute 2000). There is a considerable body of opinion which argues for the reformulation of green belts as green wedges beside corridors of urban development well-served by public transport. This would arguably be more sustainable in terms of travel patterns and also offer more effective, accessible green space for city dwellers, as well as more ecological benefits.

Another key issue for the future is the role and sustainability of the suburbs, many of which are now distinctly 'middle aged'. There is currently considerable investment in 'urban capacity' assessments which seem to be primarily driven by the search for more housing land which is not open countryside. There is a significant role of GIS techniques in these studies. But such assessments also need to consider the social and environmental sustainability of restructured suburbs and the quality of living environment which they present.

Another fashionable idea which features strongly in the Urban Task Force report (Urban Task Force 1999) and elsewhere is the concept of 'mixed use'. This means specifically the deliberate creation or fostering of areas which contain a mixture of urban land uses, including both housing and business activities. This is a change from the traditional approach of both the planning and property development industry of emphasizing zoning and separation of land uses. Mixed use is alleged to offer a number of benefits, including shorter journeys to work and leisure, more of which may be made on foot, and a more vibrant 'public realm' which fosters more interaction between people and a greater sense of life and personal security across different times of the day and the week. Images of 'urban villages' are conjured up and portrayed as idealized zones of creativity and communal interaction (Jacobs 1969; Aldous 1992). Such areas undoubtedly do exist and can be supported, but they are relatively rare in the areas where major new urban development is taking place, whether in the new housing estates or the business parks and shopping malls which proliferate around the edge of our cities. Applying planning for affordable housing to commercial developments, and getting employers to engage more with the housing needs of their workers, are two ways in which such desirable patterns of development might be indirectly promoted.

Lastly, there is an agenda about raising the general quality of urban and housing design. Part of the objection of people to new housing developments is that they fear more monotonous or mediocre 'same-looking' housing estates. There are no grounds for complacency in relation to either consumers' views of the quality of new housing or professionally-based assessments of its sustainability or design. Raising the quality of the product should therefore be part of the agenda of planning and regulation of new housing, and there is government support for aspiring to better design (e.g., Scottish Executive 1999; ODPM 2003b). A part of this is about promoting diversity. The demographic trends discussed earlier indicate that the traditional family is in decline and a wider range of household types, including many single person households, will play an ever-larger part in the housing market. Planning should not make highly prescriptive assumptions about the size and type of housing which such households will require, but it can encourage the development industry to provide a wider range. There is evidence that consumers welcome a greater diversity of housing types and styles within developments. While there is a role for regulation, there is also a task of educating and informing consumers, and the public consultation exercises sponsored by the planning system provide one vehicle for doing this.

Guide to further reading

The standard introductory text on the British town and country planning system is Cullingworth and Nadin (1999). Cullingworth (1997) has also written an interesting review of planning in the USA, to provide an international comparative contrast. Good general discussions of planning and housebuilding issues are Bramley, Bartlett and Lambert (1995) and Adams and Watkins (2002).

The demographic and policy issues around household growth are discussed in Department of the Environment (1996), Bramley and Lancaster (1998), Breheny and Hall (1996) and Bate (1999). Migration is particularly important in this respect and this aspect of the debate is reviewed in Bate, Best and Holmans (2000). Fuller discussion of the urban–rural shift of population and reviews of what determines migration are contained in Champion *et al.* (1998).

Arguments about sustainability and its implications for planning for housing development and urban form are developed in the useful collection by Jencks, Burton and Williams (1996). Official policy documents relating to this debate include the Urban Task Force report, *Towards an Urban Renaissance* (Urban Task Force 1999), *Planning for the Communities of the Future* (DETR 1998c), the official planning policy guidance (DETR 2000b), and the parallel documents relating to transport (Department of the Environment 1994b; Royal Commission on Environmental Pollution 1995; DETR 1998a). Good practice guidance on applying sustainable development principles is increasingly available, as for example in DETR (1998e), Ove

Arup and others (1998), or Barton (2000). The most recent English policy statement is the *Sustainable Communities* plan (ODPM 2003b).

The American debate about 'smart urban growth versus sprawl' is reviewed in Downs (1997), Danielsen, Lang and Fulton (1999), Dear and others (2001) and US Dept of Housing and Urban Development (1999).

Bramley, Bartlett and Lambert (1995) provides a general review and analysis of the relationship between planning, the housing market and the house-building industry, from a mainly economic perspective. Some of the empirical modelling findings are updated a bit in Bramley and Watkins (1996a and 1996b) and Bramley (1999 and 2002). Other key British studies include Cheshire and Sheppard (1989, 1997) and Monk and Whitehead (1996, 1999); Jones and Watkins (1999) provide a general perspective. US evidence on the economic impact of land use controls is reviewed in Fischel (1990), Monk, Pearce and Whitehead (1991), Pdogzinski and Sass (1991) and Malpezzi (1996). Needham and Lie (1994) analyse the contrasting European case of the Netherlands.

6

The Development Perspective

Introduction: the role of development

In this chapter we examine the development of housing in Britain in the early 21st century. Development is the process whereby new housing comes to be built and existing housing is improved or adapted to meet changing needs and demands. Although in any one year the proportion of the housing stock which is newly constructed or modified is relatively small, typically 1–2 per cent of the total, in the medium term this is the key process by which the housing stock changes and adapts. Today's development investment creates the housing stock and the wider urban structure of the future, an important legacy for future generations, and this is an opportunity to learn from past mistakes and anticipate future requirements in an intelligent way.

One particularly important and pervasive phenomenon within the development process is that of risk. Development is subject to many uncertainties and risks. Will it be possible to get planning permission, and with what strings attached? Will there be a market for the houses when they are finished? Will it be possible to get them built at an acceptable cost? The central task of the developer is to 'manage' those risks, which entails some combination of anticipating problems, discounting their probability, taking preventative measures, setting contingency plans, and so forth. So risk, and coping with it, is of the essence of development.

Risk is a dominant theme in analysis of the private housebuilding industry (see Bramley, Bartlett and Lambert 1995; Gibb, Munro and McGregor 1995; Ball 1996a and 1996b). However, it would be a mistake to assume that none of the same issues apply to the social housing development sector. Many of the sources of risk and uncertainty in development can apply to RSLs, and in one respect social landlords face greater risk than private housebuilders: they will maintain an interest in the properties they procure over a much longer period than a developer, whose interest ceases once they have sold to the first occupier. It is probably fair to say, however, that awareness of the issue of risk and the need to manage or price for risk is a relatively recent phenomenon in social housing development (dating essentially from reforms associated with the 1988 Housing Act: see Hills 1991). To take an obvious example, the emergence of low demand for social rented housing exposes social landlords to a previously virtually unknown risk of there being no demand for their product, rather than facing a demand perpetually rationed by queues.

Private housebuilders

Structure of the industry

Most new private housing in Britain is built 'speculatively'. In other words, a specialist housebuilding development company undertakes all the processes from identification of the site through to marketing of the finished product, usually in the form of estates or blocks of similar-looking houses which are sold to individual buyers. Clearly, speculative housebuilding is different from the procurement methods by which mass public housing was produced, in Britain and elsewhere, up to the 1970s or a little later.

It is also worth noting that this speculative process is different from that found in some other countries, even where 'private' development predominates. In particular, some countries make much more use of the model where individuals buy a plot of land and then separately procure a house to place upon it, whether this be a bespoke design or a 'kit' or 'catalogue' house from a specialist supplier (Barlow and King 1992; Bramley 1997a). This approach is particularly prevalent in more rural regions, and can be found in the most rural parts of UK such as the Scottish Highlands and Islands.

The British housebuilding industry is not just dominated by the speculative model but it is also increasingly concentrated, with a limited number of large companies dominant. Historically, the industry was quite fragmented. A marked process of concentration was noted in the 1970s by Ball (1983), while a further recent phase of consolidation is noted by Adams and Watkins (2002). Firms building more than 500 units per year accounted for 39 per cent of output in 1980, 41 per cent in 1987–90, 44 per cent in 1992, but no less than 71 per cent in 2000 (Bramley, Bartlett and Lambert 1995, p.89; Nicol and Hooper 1999; Wellings 2001). In 2000 there were 14 companies building 2,000 units or more per year, compared with only four in 1980 (Adams and Watkins 2002). Reasons for this greater concentration include access to finance, enhancing market share, diversifying risks across regions, and acquiring land banks (Ball 1983; Adams and Watkins 2002).

Despite the concentration trend just discussed, housebuilding remains a relatively competitive sector of business when compared with many other sectors, particularly in manufacturing and production, where dominance by a very few companies is quite common. The costs of entry to the sector by new companies are not necessarily prohibitive, and it has been common for new firms to enter the market, particularly in periods of market boom when the returns appear to be high (Lambert 1990).

Housebuilders' business environment and strategy

The overall business environment of housebuilding is characterized by competition, pervasive risk/uncertainty, and dependence upon a very cyclical economic market. Chapter 3 documented the extreme fluctuations in house prices exhibited in Britain over the last 30 years, a key indicator of a volatile market. Housebuilders have adopted a number of strategies to cope with this difficult market environment. Concentration, combined with diversification of location across regions, represents one kind of response. Another typical response has been to seek flexibility in the construction process and supply chain, so enabling a quick response to changing demand conditions, without having too much capital tied up in a development. This is a major reason why sub-contracting has become such a dominant feature of the industry. Sub-contracting has in turn had other, much-criticized consequences for the industry, including a lack of support for apprenticeship training and a technical conservatism. Traditional building techniques are more amenable to a flexible, start-stop approach to assembly on site than are approaches making more use of factory building techniques (Ball 1983 and 1996a).

While this perspective portrays an industry seeking to vary its output flexibly in response to demand, Bramley, Bartlett and Lambert (1995, p.96) observed an interesting tendency for housebuilders to be quite cautious about varying their quantitative output. In other words, they might respond to stronger demand by making higher profits or shifting the product more 'up-market', and vice versa, but remain focused on a particular numerical output target. It has been suggested that the way firms are monitored by City performance analysts reinforces this emphasis on numbers. Other reasons for not varying output dramatically with levels of demand include the need to maintain continuity of work for key, valued sub-contractors, the difficulty of recruiting labour in the upswing, and the desire not to run out of land with planning permission. Somewhat paradoxically, this leads to a picture of an industry which is geared up to cope with fluctuating demand but which actually is relatively unresponsive to demand when it changes. Other evidence cited in Chapter 5, on the supply inelasticity of new housebuilding in Britain, tends to confirm this picture.

It is clear that land is a key resource and strategies to ensure land supply are central to the business of housebuilding. The relatively tight land-use planning system in Britain, and the ways in which it has become in some respects tighter since around 1990, reinforce this. Land is the 'oxygen' the industry needs to survive, and it is no coincidence that much of the lobbying and public pronouncements of the industry relate to land supply. For individual firms there are a number of ways in which they can try to manage their land supply. These include land banking, the use of options (conditional purchase contracts), acquisitions/mergers, and trying to influence the planning system locally.

Recent studies show that use of options (purchase contracts conditional on obtaining planning permission) is widespread (Bramley, Bartlett and Lambert 1995; Adams and Watkins 2002). These reduce the amount of capital tied up in land until the point when planning permission is granted. However, it is also clear that housebuilders are expending ever greater resources, in terms of specialist staff and consultants, on trying to influence the planning system so as to get favourable planning decisions on the sites in which they have an interest (Adams, May and Pope 1992; Farthing 1995). A paradoxical by-product of this effort is that the planning process is slowing down, as local plan inquiries become overloaded with expensive legal representations from a myriad of competing housebuilders and landowners trying to get their particular sites allocated (School of Planning and Housing 2001).

The other key aspect of acquiring land is paying the right price for it. Housebuilders typically undertake a 'residual valuation' calculation when deciding what to bid for a site. This looks at the likely selling price of houses on a site, and deducts the cost of building them plus other development costs, marketing and other overheads, and an acceptable profit margin. This would normally be the maximum they would be willing to bid for the site. Leishman, Jones and Fraser's (2000) analysis of this process suggests a degree of under-bidding relative to the theoretical maximum, probably relating to risk and uncertainty.

While the land side of housebuilding is clearly critical, there are other aspects to success in this business. As in any business, marketing to potential customers is important. In the case of housing, this is typically by far the largest purchase which most households will ever make. Yet what is being marketed is not just the house as a physical structure; equally important are the aspects of location and more intangible factors associated with location, such as an image of a lifestyle. The traditional marketing images of the housebuilding industry do play to deep-rooted wishes and dreams of a wide public, relating to notions of peace and quiet, attractive semi-rural environments and traditional-looking houses. People buying new homes are often trying to 'better themselves', and part of that process is selecting 'better neighbours'.

Whatever the difficulties facing the industry, it is clear that housebuilding remains a profitable activity most of the time. Reported profits of the major housebuilders are high, although this does currently reflect boom conditions and the gains made on land value appreciation. Also, it should be remembered that, as an inherently risky business, returns would be expected to be higher in this industry than in others.

Involvement in private renting

One other aspect of housebuilding as a business is worthy of comment at this point. In Britain, private sector housebuilders are operating almost exclusively on the basis of selling their product to owner-occupiers, rather than creating a long-term private rental investment product. This means that they generally have a relatively short-term horizon in their involvement with a particular site/neighbourhood/development. This certainly distinguishes the British industry from that found in a number of other countries, where new build for private rental, or a mix of rental and ownership, is quite common (McCrone and Stephens 1995; Freeman, Holmans and Whitehead 1996; Bramley, Satsangi and Pryce 1999). The reasons for the lack of new private development for rental are well known and rehearsed in the literature, although there have been debates in the 1990s about the feasibility of reviving commercial/institutionally-financed private renting. Broadly speaking, a more favourable tax regime would be required to encourage such investment, in addition to the deregulation of rents and security of tenure instituted after 1988.

There have been signs in the 1990s of some renewed investment in private renting, but this has mainly focused on the existing housing stock and involved small-scale investors rather than large companies and institutions. In the late 1990s a 'buy-to-let' market developed, particularly in booming cities such as London and Edinburgh, as well as in city-centre areas throughout the country which have been becoming more fashionable as places to live. Rashes of 'to let' signs on recently-completed blocks of flats have become a common sight. Again, this market is fuelled by individual investors supported by flexible mortgage products, rather than large investors (Joseph Rowntree Foundation 2003). A consequence is that, on certain types of new housing scheme (especially flatted schemes in central cities), it turns out that a significant proportion of housing units end up as privately rented, even though this was not necessarily the intention of the original developer (Forrest and Morie 1993; Bramley and Morgan 2003).

Responding to changing requirements

The nature of the housing product is discussed further later in this chapter. Current policies are seeking to encourage a change in the profile of new housing, with more emphasis on higher density, more varied house types and sizes, more affordable housing, more use of brownfield land, and better designed, more sustainable homes. It is regulatory policy mechanisms which are in the front line in trying to achieve these changes, particularly planning and building control.

Bramley, Bartlett and Lambert (1995, pp.231–3) argued that housing, like other commodities, was moving out of the 'modern' era of mass production and consumption of uniform products into the postmodern era of 'more specialized but flexible production for consumers who exhibit more diversified tastes relating to different lifestyles and ways of using the home'. Adams and Watkins (2002) argue that the shift to brownfield urban provision poses a multiple challenge to traditional housebuilders. They argue that firms may need to add value directly from housing products rather than relying so much on land value appreciation, that standardized solutions may no longer suffice in a diversified urban market, and that developments will have to be acceptable to and integrated with existing urban communities. Partnership with the public sector will be a frequent feature of such urban developments. They go on to suggest that some firms look better adapted to this change than others, and highlight a number of firms who have demonstrated that a specialism in urban redevelopment can be combined with good profits. Heneberry, Guy and Bramley (2003) similarly highlight the significant pathfinder role played by new-style niche developers such as Urban Splash in Manchester and other northern cities. In addition, the emphasis on flatted developments underlines the need to establish structured agreements (e.g., commonhold) to facilitate future management and upkeep of flatted blocks (thus assuring their saleability).

It has also been pointed out (School of Planning and Housing 2001; Bramley and Morgan 2003) that part of the consumer appeal of new housing is that not only is the product predictably reliable but the purchase process is straightforward and hassle-free. In Scotland, developers can trade on the advantage enjoyed by potential purchasers of newly-built homes, who can avoid the risk and uncertainty associated with the 'blind bidding' process involved in transactions in the 'second-hand' market. Currently the process of house purchase is subject to reform and legislation, as discussed in the next chapter. If this reform fulfils its promise, then many of the reasons for delay and uncertainty in the process of buying second-hand houses will disappear. This would reduce the relative advantage of new housing in the market, and weaken the demand for new as opposed to second-hand housing. Housebuilders might have to counter this by offering more real technical improvements in their products, and information to back this up.

Social housing developers

The changing model of social landlord

This traditional public sector housing development model has largely disappeared from the development scene (Cole and Furbey 1994). The reasons for its disappearance include: (a) the ending of generalized shortages of housing (Bramley 1997b); (b) a shift of political sentiment against 'monolithic' public sector housing landlords; and (c) public expenditure crises and constraints. Another possible reason for disenchantment was that local authorities were multi-purpose organizations with competing priorities and consequently might not have had a clear enough managerial focus on being a good landlord, as well as being tempted sometimes to siphon resources off from housing to pay for other activities.

Housing Associations (RSLs) are, by contrast, single-purpose organizations. They have become a favoured vehicle for delivering social housing, not just because they appear to offer a more diverse, responsive and effective set of providers, but also because they provide a possible way around the fiscal straitjacket which governments have placed on the public sector since 1976. In addition, associations' non-profit-making status is seen as attractive because it removes any potential for conflict between shareholders and service users (notwithstanding the need to honour loan repayment obligations). RSLs can borrow against their housing assets (and future rental streams) without this borrowing counting as public borrowing or public expenditure. This advantage has proved to be very attractive to successive governments, and indeed it can be argued that the social housing sector has been the largest and most successful example of 'public–private partnership' (i.e., the use of private capital finance to support public services).

Public or private?

In some ways it seems a little odd, or arbitrary, that this should be so. Housing Associations are treated as 'private sector' bodies for the purposes of national accounting, so when they borrow money, these loans are not counted as part of the public sector's financing requirement. It is true that these loans are not subject to formal government guarantee, and in that sense they are not equivalent to (i.e., not as secure as) loans to local authorities or the government itself. But the government is lurking in the background, (a) through sponsoring a regulatory apparatus (operated through the Housing Corporation/ Communities Scotland), and (b) through providing social housing grants to RSLs, which sit in their balance sheets as a sort of buffer analogous to equity in a normal commercial company. The effect is that a market in loan finance to RSLs has become well established and offers terms which are not a great deal more adverse than traditional public sector borrowing.

During the 1990s there was much debate about whether it was necessary to use a body such as an RSL to achieve this result. Why could not local authority housing departments, if structured as 'arm's-length' trading companies, be eligible for the same access to 'private' borrowing? Proponents of this view suggested that this was effectively the position in some other European countries, and that this would be compatible with European fiscal policy convergence criteria, subject only to some minor redefinition of fiscal policy targets (Hawksworth and Wilcox 1995). The government and/or Treasury has refused to budge on this issue. One can only speculate on the reasons for the Treasury's steadfastness, though these may include reluctance to give the financial markets any reason to question the 'prudence' of fiscal policy, and a fairly deep scepticism about local government's ability to deliver responsive and effective social housing services.

The issue of what kind of body could borrow 'privately' to invest in social housing arose in two distinct circumstances: (a) where investment in new social housing provision was required, and (b) where existing council housing required substantial investment in modernization or improvement. In the first case, RSLs have increasingly been the chosen vehicle, and since 1989 the main funding mechanism has been so-called 'mixed funding', namely a combination of capital grant and private loans. In the second case, the favoured vehicle has been the large-scale voluntary transfer (LSVT) of housing stock from local authorities to RSLs.

The new social housing model

In the development process, the position of RSLs may be contrasted with the old public sector model. RSLs typically:

- operate on a small or medium scale, but often in a number of localities
- produce a diverse range of more specialized housing products
- procure by a mixture of traditional and other contracts, on land which may or may not have been publicly owned, and typically using independent design consultants
- are financed by a mixture of grant, private sector borrowing (over 25–35 years), own capital reserves, and subsidy from land values
- are accountable through appointed boards and regulation
- are subject to private sector accounting rules

This transition is much more profound than it would have been had housing associations remained as they were between 1974 and 1988. At that time associations operated in a very sheltered environment, perhaps deliberately created to enable them to grow from small beginnings. However, the post-1988 financial regime changed this quite sharply, especially in England (Randolph 1993). Associations became responsible for setting their own rents. At the same time they had to take responsibility for present and future major repair liabilities and for balancing their revenue accounts. Grants for new schemes became essentially fixed so that associations had greater responsibility for cost overruns (Hills 1991).

The use of private finance introduced an important new relationship for associations, that with their lender(s), very much akin to the relationship between a business and its bankers. They had to undertake a new discipline, the preparing of long-term financial and business plans, to demonstrate that their proposed developments and other commitments were financially feasible and that loans taken out could be serviced. Year-to-year monitoring of performance against these plans provided a sharper discipline and 'reality check'. Although outright failure and default by housing associations/RSLs has been unknown, protecting the general credit of social housing as a lending sector, individual associations have periodically got into difficulties. This may lead to intervention by the Housing Corporation and, typically, merger with another stronger organization and/or a change of management.

The impact of risk

Part of the new discipline of operating in this environment has been a conscious awareness of the risks associated with different decisions, particularly in the development arena. It would be fair to criticize the old public sector development model as being one which largely ignored risk and provided inadequate mechanisms for its management. Certainly slippage and cost overruns were common on traditional public sector (or pre-1988 housing association) developments (Henney 1984).

Another by-product of this risk-sensitive operating environment has been a general retreat by RSLs from rehabilitation activity. In the 1970s and 1980s this was the major activity of associations in some urban areas. By the mid-1990s, rehabilitation had fallen to a small share of the total development programme. Rehabilitation is generally seen as a much more risky type of development: costs and difficulties are much more difficult to predict accurately, and in some circumstances it can be considerably more expensive than new building.

Both conscious decisions by government and further developments have served to increase the risks facing housing associations, or RSLs as they became generally known during the 1990s. In England, a deliberate policy of fostering competition between different RSLs in a sort of 'quasi-market' for the opportunity to develop was encouraged from the early 1990s (Bramley 1993d). Thus, RSLs faced risks of missing out on development opportunities to keep their development staff employed, or conversely the risk of bidding unwisely for developments which did not stack up very well. Until the mid-1990s, rent levels and Housing Benefit (HB) 'took the strain' of some of this, but more recently government has imposed rent caps on local authorities and rent guidelines on RSLs. In the future, the rents eligible for HB subsidy may become more strictly linked to these guidelines. This places severe constraints on the revenue side of RSL business plans.

Changing market circumstances have also increased risks, with the emergence of serious problems of low demand in some areas from the mid-1990s onwards, as discussed in Chapter 4. The risk of failure to let or re-let property in the future poses an obvious threat to the income stream in an RSL's business plan. Some RSLs, considering their strategic options for the future, have concluded that they are already 'overexposed' in some areas, and would be looking to reduce this rather than increase it further. As argued in Chapter 4, competition between housing providers in low demand areas can be counterproductive, and the Housing Corporation is encouraging both more co-ordination of plans and practices and also (in some cases) stock rationalization 'swaps' or transfers. Some organizations whose original base of operations was in the urban north of England have shifted the locus of their development activity to other parts of the country.

Overall, the environment within which RSLs now operate is much less sheltered than the one they experienced in the mid-1980s. As in other sectors (e.g., higher education), this harsher environment leads to a consideration of economies of scale, and to the possibility of a two-tier or multi-tier sector. To respond adequately to all of the above challenges, an RSL needs strong management and professional skills in a range of areas, including development, finance, and even relatively unfamiliar ones such as marketing. These are an overhead cost which smaller RSLs are decreasingly able to afford. Specialist development teams may not be affordable if there is not a steady flow of developments each year. Two trends are discernible as a result of this. One is towards larger RSLs. This comes about through full and partial mergers often facilitated by group structures (Audit Commission/Housing Corporation 2001) as well as through stock acquisition via transfer from former public sector landlords. The other is towards some smaller RSLs shedding their development function completely, and working in partnership with others for this purpose. These pressures have come later in Scotland, where there is still a large sector of small community-based housing associations (CBHAs), especially in west central Scotland, and where – as the design of the recent Glasgow transfer demonstrates – central government and Communities Scotland maintain a commitment to the CBHA model. The extent to which such organizations can withstand future pressures for scale economies is debatable.

It could be argued that RSLs should pay more attention to management rather than development anyway. RSLs are maturing as organizations and, if they are still growing rapidly, this is most likely to be as a result of stock transfer. The quality of the management and maintenance service offered to these former council tenants will ultimately be a key test of the success of this change. Even where RSLs are still developing, it can be argued that housing management should have a stronger say in development decisions. This might involve issues of affordability, including energy costs, vulnerability to crime and vandalism, locational strategy generally, or the lettability of certain dwelling types.

Working with the private sector

Those RSLs engaged in the provision of low cost home-ownership (LCHO) have been engaged with the private market and acting, in some degree, more like private developers over quite a long period. A number of studies of LCHO have concluded that there are specialist skills involved in this process and that some providers are much better at it than others (Bramley and

Dunmore 1996; Dunmore *et al.* 1997; Bramley and Morgan 1998; Bramley *et al.* 2002). The key elements for success include both marketing and vetting/supporting potential buyers. The best providers are generally relatively larger ones, with a longer-standing commitment to the sector.

Concerns about the efficiency as well as the quality of the housing product secured through traditional procurement have led to experimentation with alternative models. These have typically involved some element of 'design-and-build', on the one hand, and the block procurement of larger numbers of dwellings, possibly for several RSL landlords on several sites.

Growing use of the planning system as a fairly normal way of securing land and subsidy for 'affordable housing', as described in Chapter 5, has further potential implications for the development process and the roles of different bodies within this. Since this is increasingly directed towards mixed communities, RSL developments of 'social housing' will be less commonly planned and designed separately, but more commonly incorporated into a general plan and design for a whole estate, where typically the majority of units will be private. More of the 'affordable housing' is likely to be LCHO or other provision (e.g., mid-market rental) aimed at 'key workers'. In some cases the way contributions are sought from developers, comprising 'cross-subsidy' as well as free or cheap land, will lead naturally to the proposition that the affordable dwellings should be built by the developer and then handed over to the RSL at a 'net' transfer price. Taken in conjunction with the mixed communities argument, this will point towards a common product in terms of house type and standard, as well as a common design process. But this may conflict with RSLs' own standards, which are often higher than bottom-of-the-market private sector standards, allowing for higher occupancy levels, long-term residence, and keeping user costs (e.g., energy costs) down.

It is already apparent (Bramley *et al.* 2003) that ways of getting RSLs involved with private developers in relation to planning agreements for affordable housing are a problem area. The kind of mixed developments described above suggest more of a 'partnering' arrangement between RSLs and housebuilders (see below for further discussion of 'partnering' in context of housing product quality). This of course has implications for RSL strategies, suggesting that in future their partnerships with housebuilders may be as (or more) important than their partnerships with local authorities. But this may cut across the 'management perspective' which, we suggested above, also needs to be taken more seriously. Such approaches may also raise particular difficulties for smaller, locally-based RSLs.

Stock transfer process and options

As discussed in Chapter 2, stock transfer (LSVT) first developed in England from the late 1980s, as a response to the increasingly constrained financial situation facing local housing authorities. Developed under the Housing Act 1985, LSVTs involving the complete handover of a council's stock were initially popular among shire district councils in southern England which had relatively favourable financial prospects, such as low debt, good rental income prospects, and modest disrepair backlogs. Typically these authorities had less political adherence to the public sector housing model anyway. By 2002 well over 100 English authorities had carried out LSVTs involving more than 600,000 homes. In most cases the transfer was to a newly-created housing association based on the former local authority (LA) organization. In Scotland, the main focus of early stock transfers was on Scottish Homes' disposal of its own stock, and on passing some council stock to local community-based housing associations. However, stock transfer has become an even more central feature of housing policy in the last few years.

The 2000 Housing Green Paper confirmed the New Labour commitment to LSVT as an essential measure for dealing with the national backlog of disrepair in the council housing stock, frequently estimated as being of the order of £20 billion in England alone. The Conservative government's 'Estates Renewal Challenge Fund' of 1996 was aimed at facilitating the transfer of at least some of the stock in question (see Chapter 9). In Scotland, the New Housing Partnership (NHP) programme launched in 1998 was mainly intended to facilitate stock transfers. Through NHP funding several large local authorities (notably Glasgow) have been supported in bringing forward transfer proposals. The New Labour government's commitment in the 2000 Comprehensive Spending Review to achieve a 'decent homes' target in England, involving dealing with all of the disrepair backlog by 2010, also assumed a high level of LSVT activity. Other mechanisms, including Arm's Length Management Organizations (ALMOs), the Private Finance Initiative (PFI) and the 'major repairs allowance' within the Housing Revenue Account subsidy system were also involved in contributing towards redeeming this pledge, but stock transfers were expected to play a major role. Unlike the situation in the early 1990s, some of these transfers involved large urban authorities with major stock disrepair problems.

Stock transfer has thus been a major policy and managerial preoccupation in the last few years. Much professional and consultant effort has gone into preparatory work, notably in preparing valuations and assessing different options.

The basic idea behind the LSVT valuation model is to value a bundle of social housing as a going concern in its existing use. The positive value derives primarily from the rents that can be collected from tenants, year-by-year, into the future. However, costs will have to be incurred to achieve those rents, such as the costs of management, of ongoing maintenance, and of major repairs or other improvements required. The value of the stock is the balance between those income and expenditure streams, but modified by when those costs and revenues accrue. Incomes or expenditures accruing in the near future weigh more heavily than those in the more distant future. The discounted cash flow technique used in the stock valuation model gives effect to this key assumption. However, it should be noted that it is equivalent to answering the question: if you had to borrow money to run this business, how much could you pay for it now and still break even in the long run? Partly because of the expectation that future rents will be maintained at sub-market levels, this is quite different from open market valuation.

Most transfer proposals involve a set of specific commitments to tenants to make good backlogs of disrepair and to undertake specified improvements within a finite period (typically five years). Increasingly, these repairs and improvements have been geared to achieving the government's 'decent homes' target. Catch-up repairs have been a key factor in persuading both tenants and local elected councils to support stock transfer, because they have seen that such improvements could not be achieved under the traditional public sector housing financial regime. However, estimating the true value of backlog repair bills is quite a difficult technical task for local authorities, generally involving the commissioning of a specialist house condition survey.

The higher the valuation, the greater the chance that this will be sufficient to pay off outstanding debt. Over the 1990s local authorities in England which achieved the status of being 'debt free' enjoyed rather more freedom in their use of capital resources. Even if they did not achieve this outcome, many transferring authorities were able to pay off their housing debt and reinvest some of the surplus receipt in new social housing provision, although in some years central government collected a levy (to reflect the extra HB costs falling on the national exchequer). If the valuation is insufficient to pay off the debt, then the transfer is unlikely to be feasible or attractive without some injection of subsidy from central government.

Local authorities considering transfers have generally engaged in some form of stock options appraisal, usually involving external consultants (Pawson 2002b). This will certainly have involved some provisional stock transfer valuation exercise, as well as some comparison with the 'carry on as LA housing' option, and typically some other possible options, including partial stock transfer, 'trickle transfer' of vacant properties, local housing company/ ALMO, Tenant Management Organization, or PFI.

Throughout the 1990s there was ongoing debate about the possibility of 'local housing companies' as an alternative to LSVT. Wilcox *et al.* (1993) provided a thorough review of these options, suggesting that in general such options would not be financially superior to the LSVT model in most circumstances. One of the motives for promoting alternatives to LSVT in the early 1990s was concern that the private sector would not be able to provide enough funds for lending to new as well as existing social landlords. This concern has subsequently evaporated as the social housing lending sector has grown and matured. Additionally, there was a need for an organizational form which addressed local authority anxieties about loss of accountability and/or reduction of council influence over social housing.

The need for alternatives to LSVT, and particularly alternatives which might look more familiar to a council tenant, has been underlined by the very uncertain and unpredictable history of tenant ballots on LSVTs. About a quarter of LSVT ballots have failed to secure the necessary majority of tenant votes. What has been particularly embarrassing for government has been the extent to which political opposition to stock transfer has grown, with active campaigns in some areas culminating in negative votes in flagship urban transfers which have significantly interrupted the momentum of the transfer programme overall. Particular examples included Sandwell in 1999 and then Birmingham in 2002.

PFI has been used much more (though not uncontroversially) in the areas of transport, health and education than it has been so far in housing. There have been many teething troubles in getting workable models in the housing field. Since 2000 English ministers seem to have warmed somewhat to the local housing company idea, in the guise of the ALMO model. But it should be emphasized that there has been no relaxation of the rules on what counts as public borrowing. This means that, although a number of such organizations may be set up, the overall size of this programme could face resource limitations.

There are also changes afoot in the way local authority borrowing in general is controlled under the so-called 'prudential borrowing' regime. Basically, local authorities would be free to borrow if they could demonstrate through their financial planning that they could service and repay their debts. While superficially attractive to local authorities, it is not clear what difference this will make to the ability of authorities to invest more in dealing with backlogs of defects where this does not generate savings in running costs or additional rent revenues.

Consequences of stock transfer

Since 1988 stock transfers have levered £11.6 billion of private finance into social housing in England alone. Of this, £5.4 billion has been used to purchase the stock, with the remaining £6.2 billion representing finance that housing associations can 'draw down', mainly to fund the renovation of the transferred housing (National Audit Office 2003). The vast majority of stock transferred in England and Scotland (more than 90 per cent) has been passed to housing associations newly created for the purpose (Pawson and Fancy 2003). In this way, more than 180 transfer housing associations (HAs) have been established since the end of the 1980s.

Whilst transfer landlords operate under a common regulatory regime with 'traditional' associations, their tenant- and councillor-influenced governance arrangements, their financial profiles and their strong relationships with local authorities tend to mark them out as a distinct category of organization within the HA sector (Pawson and Fancy 2003).

In general, English transfer HAs have met their 'ballot prospectus' undertakings to tenants in relation to upgrading transferred stock and restraining rent increases (National Audit Office 2003). Commitments on the development of new housing have been slightly less reliable; for example, 15 per cent of transfer HAs have failed to deliver promises on construction of new homes within timescales originally stipulated. The reasons for this have included 'financial or regulatory problems, planning delays or insufficient grant funding from local authorities' (National Audit Office 2003, p.3). Nevertheless, transfer HAs in England and Scotland have developed around 50,000 new homes since 1988, some 80 per cent of which have been for social rent (Pawson and Fancy 2003).

More broadly, transfer HAs tend to have delivered improved housing management services by comparison with their predecessor landlords, and this has been reflected in rising rates of tenant satisfaction after transfer (Cobbold and Dean 2000). However, whilst transfer HAs tend to outperform their 'traditional HA' counterparts in relation to performance measures such as rent collection and void management, there is little evidence that their standards are better than those of comparable local authorities which have retained a landlord role (Pawson and Fancy 2003). Increasingly, with transfers of sometimes problematic urban housing becoming more common, transfer HAs are invested with 'community regeneration' undertakings which may broaden their role beyond the traditional landlord model (see Chapter 9).

Under the usual financial model adopted for stock transfer, the new landlord's early years involve a state of high – and increasing – indebtedness. In the longer term, however, provided that their business plans do not come completely unstuck, most transfer HAs can look forward to developing a very strong financial position as they pass their 'peak debt year' and begin to generate revenue surpluses. Concerns have been raised at the likelihood that the accrual of such surpluses is unlikely to mirror the distribution of housing need and that public policy has little leverage over their application (Malpass and Mullins 2002; National Audit Office 2003).

This point could be linked to the observation that most transfers up to the late 1990s were in non-metropolitan districts in southern England, areas not seen traditionally as having such great housing problems. There is indeed a 'two-speed Britain' feel about the LSVT phenomenon, up until the beginning of the 2000s. The benefits described above have been felt most in these southern districts. However, it can be argued that it is in these areas now where there is often a great shortage of affordable housing and a need for additional provision.

The housing product

The construction process

There has long been dissatisfaction with the performance of the construction industry, in housing and in other sectors, in terms of its ability to deliver buildings of adequate quality, embracing the best technology, on time and at a reasonable, predictable cost (Ball 1996a; Harvey and Ashworth 1997). There has also been criticism of the smaller scale repair and maintenance end of the industry associated with so-called 'cowboy builders'. One of the major areas of concern has been the level of skills and training in the industry (Ball 1996a), a problem arguably exacerbated by cyclical instability, the decline of the public sector role, and the growth of sub-contracting.

Much of this criticism of the industry has focused on the procurement process, particularly traditional contractual relationships, which have been seen as confrontational and stifling, as well as the structure of the industry. The Latham Report (1994) reviewed the field and argued that major clients, particularly the government, had a key role in driving improvements in performance, efficiency, fairness, teamwork, and good design. This led to a further report generally referred to as Egan (DETR 1998d), ambitiously entitled *Rethinking Construction*, which identified more closely the sources of problems in the industry. These included the fragmentation partly associated with sub-contracting, the lack of co-ordination between design and construction under traditional contracting, low profitability and lack of investment in R&D, a general crisis in training within the industry, and too narrow a focus on cost by clients. Egan sought a new structure and approach, emphasizing leadership, customer focus, integrated processes and teams, a quality-driven agenda, and a greater commitment to people whether expressed through on-site supervision, safety, pay, conditions or training. A central idea emerging from Latham and Egan is that contractual relationships should move from an adversarial one towards one based on 'partnering': 'Partnering involves two or more organisations working together to improve performance through agreed mutual objectives, devising ways for resolving any disputes and committing themselves to continuous improvement, measuring progress and sharing the gains' (DETR 1998d p.9).

There is some evidence from case studies and demonstration projects that partnering can achieve significant benefits in terms of cost, delivery time, quality of work, working relationships (fewer disputes) and innovation (both incremental and more radical: see Barlow *et al.* 1997). These gains were achieved at some cost in terms of more time spent communicating, some blurring/ambiguity over where responsibilities lay, and some concerns by contractors that clients could be overdemanding or that competition might be undermined.

It is probably worth emphasizing that some features of the Latham/Egan agenda are not new, and have been sought by previous innovations and movements in the industry. Major 'system-building' techniques used in the 1960s and 1970s were promoted jointly by government, contractors and component suppliers. More recently, the practice of combining design and construction expertise within the contractor's team under 'Design and Build' contracts has become widespread, particularly in relation to commercial buildings but also, in the public sector context, in relation to new hospitals and schools, including when packaged as part of a wider PFI process. Here part of the client role, that of 'facilities management', goes over to the contractor as well, so that longer-term management considerations receive due weight in design. The basic argument for Design and Build is that builders have a much better awareness of 'buildability' – what can be done practically and efficiently on a site – than architects do; and that architects who work in integrated teams with construction managers and engineers will gain a much better awareness of these issues. Design and Build has a more mixed record and reputation in housing. It has sometimes been seen as a route to more standardized, lower cost housing over which the client RSLs have less control.

Both Latham and Egan saw government as having significant leverage over construction through its role as the (indirect) client for social housing, placing social housing in the front line in this battle to achieve change in the industry. The Housing Forum was sponsored by the Housing Corporation to sponsor demonstration projects and to monitor the achievement of Egan targets, and the Corporation is expecting all RSLs receiving grants to be 'Egan compliant' by 2004. While understandable, this emphasis may be questioned from a number of viewpoints:

1 Smaller RSLs may not be able to engage in these processes, further undermining their role as developers.
2 RSL development will continue to account for only a small minority of total housing output so that the major issue of private sector housing is not directly addressed.
3 Some aspects and assumptions of the Egan-driven agenda do not necessarily fit with the changing pattern of procurement, particularly the role of private developers linking with RSLs on mixed planning agreement sites.
4 When Egan is allied to current urban policy preoccupations with raising housing output and density through prefabrication methods, inevitably nagging doubts arise based on the experience with 1960s' system building.
5 Partnering involving trust-based relationships is indeed the negation of traditional models of competitive tendering; but the industry and its clients still need competition to ensure efficiency and prevent cost inflation, so there will always be tensions and compromises.

To what extent is the Latham–Egan agenda applicable to private sector housebuilding? Some of the negative criticism of the organization of the industry – fragmentation, sub-contracting, lack of training, lack of innovation – fits this sector of the industry rather clearly. Issues of cost-effectiveness are rather obscured by the massive role played by land values in the economics of private housing. Issues of design and quality are picked up below. However, it can be argued that in some respects the industry is closer to the Egan model than other sectors: in particular, the integration of design within the overall development and construction team is consistent with the Egan philosophy.

Sustainable homes

In Chapter 5 we drew attention to the way in which the concept of environmentally sustainable development (ESD) had become a central theme of planning policy, and also an important cross-cutting theme of all areas of government policy during the 1990s. It is therefore apposite to ask how 'sustainable' are the homes which were being built in the 1990s and the early 2000s, particularly in view of the long prospective life of this housing and its importance in shaping future urban form.

Proponents of ESD, while drawing particular attention to certain environmental impacts (for instance, in terms of non-renewable energy use, air and water pollution, waste recycling and disposal), have moved beyond an exclusive focus on environmental and ecological perspectives. Sustainability has economic and social dimensions to it as well. People need jobs and incomes, for example, and want to live in communities where they feel secure and not threatened. In some instances, of course, economic and environmental considerations work together: for example, a low energy house has less environmental impact but also saves on annual energy bills.

New housing is a major long-term investment that utilizes a lot of materials and production processes which themselves embody a great deal of energy and have other environmental impacts (e.g., quarrying). There are considerable opportunities through design and technical specifications to reduce the use of embodied energy and to increase the use of recycled materials in construction. Nevertheless, there has been relatively little research or mainstream product development in this respect (Stevenson and Williams 2000). Rather more common have been attempts to look at the energy consumption of different kinds of housing in everyday use. One aspect is the issue of housing type/urban form, since flats and terraced/semi-detached houses are generally more energy-efficient than detached houses/bungalows (fewer external walls/surfaces). This may need to be set against the possibly more complex construction techniques or services (e.g., lifts) required for flats, and the greater possibilities for environmentally-friendly features (e.g., solar panels, conservatories) on detached houses. Construction and ongoing costs may be traded off in 'lifetime costing' exercises (Morgan and Talbot 2000; Newton 2000).

One positive virtue of the PFI procurement system for public service buildings such as schools and hospitals is that there is a stronger incentive to apply these techniques, and to choose design and construction features that tend to reduce both future maintenance liabilities and ongoing energy use (Bramley and Russell 2000). Social landlord housing clients can to some extent seek to achieve the same balancing of capital and running costs that a contemporary PFI 'facilities manager' would seek. Post-1988 responsibility for future major repairs, allied to insurance mechanisms, may reinforce this.

In the private housing market, this kind of balancing of capital and lifetime costs is a more difficult goal to achieve. There is no long-term professional manager involved in owner-occupation: just millions of amateur do-it-yourself managers, who are generally not very interested in or aware of the more technical aspects of their homes. Surveys of owners-occupiers have shown a tendency to ignore or underestimate the structural disrepair in their home, to prioritize cosmetic over structural work, and to 'make do and mend' (Leather, Munro and Littlewood 1999). These problems are obviously particularly acute in the older housing stock, and proponents of the reform of the house purchase process see this as a prime target. People buy new homes because they assume these will be 'state of the art' and problem-free, although practical experience often shows people are sadly disappointed by the level of defects experienced. New house buyers may be given some more information about the technical performance of their home, such as its energy rating (SAP rating), but how interested they are in these details is unclear. However, they appear to be somewhat more likely to take account of energy efficiency than other aspects of dwelling sustainability (School of Planning and Housing 2001).

Underlying consumer attitudes is the knowledge, based on experience over recent decades, that the most important influence on the costs and benefits of owner-occupation for them will be the future capital appreciation in the value of their house. They know that this will be little influenced by technical aspects of the house. Far more important will be national and regional economic cycles, and the general social and environmental character of the neighbourhood.

Higher density living in 'compact cities' is often taken as a key aspect of ESD, and so as noted in Chapter 5 has become part of planning orthodoxy. The key issue here is how acceptable higher densities will be to individual households (an issue also touched on in Chapter 9). The School of Planning and Housing (2001) sound a number of warning notes on this. Many households display a clear preference for detached houses or bungalows rather than flats, with more space inside and outside the home (Scottish Homes 1997, p.285), and even one-person households often share these preferences (Hooper, Dunmore and Hughes 1998). A wider perspective on residential choice is presented by Schoon (2001) in his book *The Chosen City*.

Design quality

Many aspects of sustainability and quality can be defined according to technical standards and measures or benchmarks of performance. Much more difficult to monitor in this way is the issue of design, where there is a good deal of subjective preference involved and a lack of a common language or metric. Among the criticisms of recent private sector housing design are charges of repetitiveness/sameness, use of standard house types and materials in a way which is insensitive to local styles, a general nostalgia for older styles and forms, the use of fake external features to give an appearance of age and distinction ('mock-Tudor'), and the failure to utilize good modern designs. Governments are giving more attention to improving standards of design, through the work of the Commission on Architecture and the Built Environment (CABE) and the Scottish Executive (1999) policy on architecture, and this is further reflected in planning policy guidance (Scottish Executive 2002).

Focus group evidence suggests widespread public support for diversity within estates, both in terms of house types and appearance (School of Planning and Housing 2001). However, housebuilders argue that housebuyers themselves are conservative, and are notably resistant to modern design (which is argued to affect resale value adversely). Others have argued that broadly the speculative housebuilders have consistently produced suburban style housing which was what buyers wanted, despite continuing criticism from elite architectural opinion (Sim 1993).

Associated local services

Housing should never be seen as a discrete product divorced from its context. The old surveyor's maxim about the three things which matter most when choosing or valuing a house reminds us of that: 'location, location and location'. Location comprises a bundle of attributes, including the immediate physical environment, the appearance of neighbouring properties, accessibility to city centres, transport networks and other nodal points, the socio-economic and demographic profile of potential neighbours, and the nature of services provided in the locality. Failure to address some of these associated dimensions has contributed to problematic or unsuccessful housing developments in the past, including examples promoted by the private as well as the public sector. New communities have less informal and organic infrastructures and 'social capital', and may need to be planned and organized more by the developers or the local public authority, if new neighbourhoods are to function successfully. Since local authorities are generally strapped for cash, they will (as explained in Chapter 5) increasingly look to developers themselves to provide these facilities and services.

At the top end of the market, developers expect to provide a range of additional services, relating to security, grounds maintenance, recreation, telecommunications, and so forth. In up-market city-centre or waterfront flatted developments, for example, it is not uncommon to find swimming pools and leisure clubs included in the package. However, these up-market developments tend to be exclusive and excluding, classically labelled 'gated communities', and as such are not necessarily an ideal model for community development.

At the other end of the scale, RSLs have been involving themselves in a wider variety of activities going beyond traditional housing management, generally under the banners of the 'wider role' of housing organizations and 'housing plus' (see also Chapters 8–9). This may involve local security and maintenance activities (e.g., neighbourhood wardens), environmental improvements, employment and training initiatives, child care, financial services, community centres, and so on. As RSLs have become the main providers of new social housing and have tackled the development of larger schemes, the taking of responsibility for the wider social functioning of the neighbourhood has become a function which they are less able to ignore (Page 1993). It seems likely that these activities will develop further, although ongoing funding is often a problem as there is a tendency to rely on time-limited and area-specific special funds and it is not considered appropriate to cross-subsidize these from the basic landlord activities.

Private developers need to think carefully about the package of services they are offering when they are marketing new housing, and will increasingly have to put in place arrangements to supplement the basic local public service offer; these arrangements will endure after the developer has completed the site and moved on. This has already spawned new business opportunities for bodies which, for example, maintain landscaped areas.

Summary and conclusion

In the introduction to this chapter we focused on the risk perspective that is crucial to understanding the structure and strategies of housing development agencies, in the social as well as the private sector. In a British housing market characterized by instability and deepening regional differences, as well as greater diversity, the range of risks confronting housing developers is increasing.

The private housebuilding industry remains based on the speculative model, but has seen growing concentration since the early 1990s as a product of strategies to manage the risks identified above. The industry is locked in a close and difficult relationship with the planning system, and faces new challenges from the policy agendas of environmental sustainability, urban regeneration and building for mixed, diverse communities.

The traditional public sector has been transformed into a new model centred on non-profit, non-state organizations (RSLs) operating increasingly in partnership with each other, with public authorities, with private lenders, and with private developers. This sector has responded to a more overtly risky environment through a degree of concentration and a withdrawal from rehabilitation activity. Regulation has become more pervasive and issues of accountability more pressing in a large-scale sector, expanding chiefly through stock transfers from the public sector. The future role of RSLs in development is unclear, with some perhaps taking a lead role but thereby becoming more market-oriented, whilst others may end up with less of a lead developer role and more of a specialism in management. Social landlords are all adopting a more explicit medium-term 'business planning' approach, allied to systematic asset management, with the LSVT option appraisals and valuations a major exemplar.

Government has addressed the deep-rooted problems of the construction industry and is seeking reform in the construction process, centred around ideas of 'partnering', quality and skills. The social housing sector is expected to pick up on this agenda, and while in many respects it is willing and able to do so it is difficult to see how this agenda applies to an industry which is increasingly dominated by private sector development.

Policy is also seeking to encourage new housing which is more sustainable and better designed. This reflects concerns not just about the individual housing product but also about its location and neighbourhood setting, reflected in the frequent rhetoric about planning for 'communities' as opposed to just 'housing'. Again, these are difficult issues to legislate for and deliver, particularly through a private-sector dominated system. Nevertheless, these issues are changing the market for new housing, as well as its planning and regulatory framework, and to that extent the industry must respond in some way.

Guide to further reading

Bramley, Bartlett and Lambert (1995) looks at both the planning system and the housebuilding industry from a mainly economic perspective, including much data on development in England up to the early 1990s. Adams and Watkins (2002) provide an up-to-date appraisal of the housing development industry, paying particular attention to the implications of the government's drive to emphasize 'brownfield' development in urban areas. The School of Planning and Housing (2001) reviews most of the key issues in a Scottish context.

Wilcox *et al.* (1993) review the financial arguments around different stock transfer options. Updates and evidence on the actual performance of LSVT associations are provided in National Audit Office (2003), Cobbold and Dean (2000) and Pawson and Fancy (2003).

Ball (1996a) and Harvey and Ashworth (1997) provide general, critical overviews of the construction industry, while Gibb, Munro and McGregor (1995) provide a Scottish perspective on this.

Sustainability issues are well summarized in Barton (2000), whilst the collections edited by Jencks, Burton and Williams (1996) and Williams, Burton and Jencks (2000) provide a range of more specific insights.

7

The Consumer's Perspective

What do people want from housing?

This chapter provides an overview of key aspects of the consumer perspective with respect to housing. First it reflects on the meaning and function of home and how this is shaped by rising 'consumerism'. Second, it argues that the experience of owner-occupation has become increasingly fragmented and considers the differentiation within owner-occupation, particularly highlighting the growth in the numbers of marginal and vulnerable owners. Next, it examines the changes that have occurred in the financial services sector and the effects of these on consumers and their choices. We then consider the perspective of social sector tenants: examining the various mechanisms that have attempted to institute tenants as active consumers rather than passive recipients of state/municipal benevolence. Finally the chapter evaluates the mechanisms to help households who find themselves in financial difficulty.

It has become almost a cliché of housing research to assert the central importance of the home to most people. Yet the research evidence confirms that people value their homes in deep and subtle ways (Depres 1991). The home fulfils a range of associated, fundamental needs: affording privacy and escape from the public world and work, where the greatest relaxation and security may be experienced; being a place in which the strongest emotional relationships of family life and child rearing are central, and where personal possessions are stored and displayed and where friends and family are entertained (Saunders 1989; Ravetz with Turkington 1995).

The notion that the home is a place where people can most truly 'be themselves' also connects to a broader range of functions whereby the home can provide important opportunities for self-expression. The choice of decor, furnishing and objects can be used to express status and wealth, or project desired personal qualities (such as being warm and welcoming, or signalling taste and discrimination). The upset that attends disruption to the home, whether from intrusions such as burglary or from the extreme experiences of repossession or homelessness, bears witness to the extent to which the loss of a home is felt much more keenly than other goods (Kearns *et al.* 2000; Nettleton and Burrows 2000). Similarly, the long-term illness or stress associated with poor housing conditions, whether arising from dampness and mould or intrusive noise, also signals the importance of home (Ellaway and MacIntyre 1998).

Housing is also distinctive in being fixed in space, so that choice of housing is inextricably bound up with choice of location, both neighbourhood and broader community. This then determines ease of access to a range of local services, schools, shops, public transport, general practitioners and other local medical services, which in Britain are also of highly variable quality.

The 1980s and 1990s were strongly associated with a rise in an individualistic, consumerist society and saw an increasing focus on individuals as consumers rather than in traditional 'class' terms. Choices, exercised through markets, have become increasingly significant for self-expression and how people are perceived by others. Some have argued that consumption is an essentially postmodern activity, allowing people to experiment with identity (Featherstone 1991). Home, and particularly owner-occupation, embodies and symbolizes these ideas (Forrest 1983). Home-owners' ability to exercise choices of house type and location is also to make a statement about self-image (trendy loft dweller, suburban family). This individualized choice is additionally, in the UK context, seen as providing access to almost inevitable wealth accumulation (see Chapter 3). And for owner and tenant alike, the ability to transform the interior and exterior of the home is encouraged ever more strongly with design featuring strongly in magazines and newspaper supplements and endless permutations of entertainment programmes showing both *how* to make changes and also providing aspirations and ideas as to *what* should be done, and how life should be lived (*Changing Rooms*; *DIY SOS*; *Groundforce*; *House Doctor*, etc.). As in other sectors of public policy, this consumerist trend implies that people will increasingly expect and value choices, and will not be content to accept passively and gratefully what is offered (Carter 1998; Petersen *et al.* 1999).

It is, however, clear that different households want and value different types of house and different features within those houses, and that the demand for housing is affected by broader social, economic and lifestyle changes. But such effects are difficult to predict. For example, households have been getting smaller for many years: the combined effects of an ageing population, increased divorce rates, later marriage and lower fertility rates led to a reduction in average household size to 2.34 in 2001, down from 2.67 in 1981 (see Chapter 2). It might have been anticipated that this would be allied to a demand for ever-smaller houses, but this trend has not been evident. The Communities Plan (ODPM 2003b) implicitly blames the housebuilding industry for failing to recognize this change, wilfully continuing to build four-bedroomed houses. It talks about encouraging the development of smaller houses, as part of the concurrent policy drive to make new housing more affordable. But declining household size may not translate simply into reduced demand for space: increasing affluence generates an ever-increasing number of consumer goods needing to be accommodated. Many children have come to expect separate space equipped with their own games, computers, televisions and so on and where they can have friends in to play (Munro and Madigan 1993).

Increased availability of communications technology and the evolution of more flexible working patterns have increased the demand for home working, which also needs to be accommodated. Changing patterns of marriage and re-marriage have boosted the number of families with children who routinely spend time in both parents' houses, either of whom may be in a new relationship with a new partner and more children. This means that even a separated parent living alone may 'need' enough space to accommodate his or her children when they visit. Older people may resist a 'trading down' move from their family home if this disrupts access to local support networks as well as removing them from familiar surroundings (see Chapter 8). Arguably, then, while affordability inevitably constrains the amount of housing that can be consumed, the contemporary small household may have a range of demands for extra space.

A more 'consumerist' housing system does not necessarily ensure universally desirable outcomes. Systematic inequalities are still found comparing households from the black and minority ethnic (BME) communities and the majority white population, for instance. BME households are still disproportionately likely to live in poor quality accommodation, in overcrowded conditions and in poor quality neighbourhoods. The fear of harassment and violence in predominantly white areas, and the support available when people of the same ethnic background live in 'clusters', tends to restrict the housing type, tenure and neighbourhood choices available and acceptable for many BME households. Other households with specialized needs – for instance, requiring wheelchair-adapted houses, or having particular support needs – also experience significantly constrained choices.

Tenure choice and the experience of home

There is nothing in the preceding discussion to imply any functional superiority of either rented or owned housing. Certainly, in principle, either tenure can deliver the benefits of a home which fosters the range of personal and familial benefits outlined above. The rights, obligations and financial arrangements of available tenures are different (and not inevitable, but shaped by law and regulation, financial institutions and so on: see Kemeny 1981). Logically, different tenures might be perceived as more advantageous at different points in the lifecycle and depending on households' priorities (their relative preference for mobility, responsibility for property upkeep and so on).

In Britain, however, there is an overwhelming preference for owner-occupation which is of long standing (DoE 1994a). The Survey of English Housing (2001/2) found that over 70 per cent of social renters and over

80 per cent of private renters would like to buy. Chapter 1 charted the increasing dominance of home-ownership over the last 20 years. There can be no doubt that this is partly because residualized social housing and a generally poor quality private rented sector offer largely unattractive alternatives. But equally, the perceived advantages of owner-occupation for an increasingly affluent population also drive demand upwards.

There are many explanations for this strong preference. Although owner-occupation may typically be regarded as expensive, generally requiring occupiers to borrow more than their income over a long period of time, it is also seen as offering good, relatively low risk investment returns (see Chapter 3). And, while there is great variety in the quality of houses and neighbourhoods available within owner-occupation, it is also seen as offering the opportunity of trading up to access ever better conditions (Forrest and Murie 1987). Arguably owner-occupation has been 'normalized' (Gurney 1999) to become a part of attaining 'normal' citizenship. To choose to rent in this context is then 'abnormal' or 'deviant', associated with failure and irrational choices (renting as 'money down the drain').

The rising dominance of home-ownership has, though, created a very diverse sector. Countering the commonly held belief that poverty is largely synonymous with social renting, Burrows' recent work (Burrows and Wilcox 2000; Burrows 2003a and 2003b) has established that 'half the poor' now live in the owner-occupied sector. But home-ownership is not accessible to all, and there are still some who make a positive choice to be in other tenures. Private renting is perhaps typically a short-term, easy access choice, most suitable for those who do not intend to live in the same place for very long. Such people include students and those moving to employment or following relationship breakdown (Crook and Kemp 1996). There is also evidence that the private rented sector is increasingly providing an attractive alternative to social housing for some households, perhaps driven chiefly by dislike of estate conditions (Pawson and Bramley 2000). And although social renting is now undoubtedly a residualized sector (Forrest and Murie 1990; Cole and Furbey 1994), this should not overlook its real value and role as (sometimes good quality) housing for those in low paid, insecure or intermittent work, or those who are not participating in the labour market at all (including those with long-term health problems: see Smith and Mallinson 1997). In addition, new tenure forms have been created in the last 20 years, such as shared ownership, driven by an aspiration to increase the accessibility of owner-occupation to those on the margins of affordability.

In both the private and the social rented sectors there have been changes consistent with the 'consumerist' trend. This can be seen in policy measures to increase owner-occupation, particularly through the Right to Buy, and is also witnessed in the burgeoning choice of mortgage products now available. Equally, there has been a major shift within social housing, where it is increasingly seen as unacceptable (and perhaps inefficient) to treat tenants as passive 'clients' in receipt of services. Instead tenants are increasingly seen as customers who can exercise effective choice within the sector and whose voices are valuable both in shaping and evaluating the level of service that is provided (see Chapter 8). Greater empowerment of tenants as consumers was part of the rationale for seeking to dismantle local landlord monopolies to create a diversity of providers. It is also reflected in the requirement to keep tenants informed of key aspects of council landlords' performance through publication of performance indicators (initiated under John Major's 1992 Citizen's Charter). Most strikingly, the primacy of tenants' preferences is recognized in current moves towards 'choice-based' lettings schemes (see Box 8.1 in Chapter 8). The risks within the tenures are also differentiated and mediated by the state which plays an important role for all households who find themselves in financial difficulty, through the rules governing access to benefit assistance with housing costs (see pp. 148–9).

Differentiation within the owner-occupied sector

As nearly 70 per cent of all households in the UK are now owner-occupiers, it is inevitable that the sector contains a differentiated mix of households. Thus, while most data analysis would suggest that owner-occupation is the most advantaged tenure (in both socio-economic terms, such as in relation to income, wealth and health, and in housing terms, such as quality, state of repair, location), it is wrong to assume that this implies that all owner-occupiers are part of the affluent, protected middle classes (Forrest, Murie and Williams 1990; Lee and Murie 1997).

An early recognition of the issue arose from the recognition that outright owners were rather outside the policy frame as they were eligible for very little state financial assistance. In the context of the then available mortgage interest tax relief as a major subsidy to home buyers, this was argued to be clearly inequitable. Whilst, for many, housing costs will have been relatively low, the key concern was that some of the poorest owners owned outright and that some of the poorest house conditions were experienced by this – disproportionately elderly – group. The difficulty that they had in mobilizing resources to improve their conditions was summed up as being 'cash poor, asset rich' (Leather 2000).

The successive boom and slump of the late 1980s and 1990s crystallized concerns around 'marginal' buyers. This was a broader term used to capture the fragility of the position of those who found owner-occupation difficult to access or sustain. With negative equity and house possession having become a serious and widespread problem, the plight of marginal buyers became politically salient. What emerged was that although (mis)fortune affected the incidence of risks for home-owners, particularly depending on the timing of purchase, structural factors were also important. In particular, it was found that poorer owners were also most at risk in the downturn (Dorling and Cornford 1995).

More recently, Burrows (2003a and 2003b; Burrows and Wilcox 2000) has helped give the issue new focus by examining evidence from the Survey of English Housing (SEH). Captured in the title 'Half the Poor', this analysis notes that while 12 per cent of owners are poor, considering the population of all households who are poor in Britain, half were buying their homes or owned them outright. This phenomenon is argued to result partly from measures to widen access to the tenure, but also the increased risk exposure of owners. These risks include marital breakdown and separation as well as job insecurity. Consequently, the population of poor owners is made up of a group who were poor when they entered the tenure and others who become poor because of such transitions. Burrows argues that it is the latter group that is more numerous.

In this context the inequity between the help available to poor home-owners as compared to poor tenants is particularly striking: 'tenant households receive 92 per cent of the state's help with housing costs to low income households while owner-occupiers receive only 8 per cent' (Burrows 2003b, p. vii; and see also pp. 146–8 below).

As noted above, BME households have been identified as a particular group for whom owner-occupation may not always be advantageous. Some research has suggested that the choice of owner-occupation may be a constrained one, resulting from an absence of alternatives (Third, Wainwright and Pawson 1997). Harrison with Phillips (2003) draws together extensive research evidence which starkly reveals the inequalities both when comparing BME households to the majority and also between different BME communities in the UK. Communities from Pakistan and Bangladesh are particularly concentrated in poor quality owner-occupation. While there is evidence of a general preference for private sector housing in these communities, this may in part result from perceived entry barriers, including the fear of racist harassment, in relation to social rented housing.

Changing financial services and mortgage finance

Most households entering owner-occupation in Britain need to secure long-term mortgage finance. This immediately creates a set of barriers, as households intending to buy must demonstrate their creditworthiness to a potential lender. As the loan is secured against the value of the property bought, the lender also has to be convinced that it is a sound purchase. At first sight, this may seem a neutral set of conditions, but there is evidence to show that this can work in discriminatory ways. For instance, Karn, Kemeny and Williams (1985) found evidence that some inner-city communities were concentrated in the poorest quality housing, considered unmortgageable by lenders, so that they disproportionately had to rely on family and informal support, or less conventional and more expensive forms of credit.

Some dwellings bought under the Right to Buy have subsequently been found to be unmortgageable, particularly flats in blocks built using unconventional construction systems. Smith *et al.* (2003) have found that, in dealing with people with health problems, mortgage lenders sometimes treat income derived from benefits differently from other forms of income. This reduces access to loan finance and hence owner-occupation. Other inequalities are created through insurance mechanisms: a particularly controversial development has been the industry's growing reluctance to provide cover for flood risk, potentially rendering many geographically clustered groups of houses unmortgageable and therefore unsaleable. The main point is that these rules can create systematic differences in the treatment of different types of household, which largely serve to reinforce existing structures of disadvantage.

There have been tremendous changes in the financial services industries through the 1980s and 1990s, reflecting growing interlender competition for what has traditionally been a relatively low risk and lucrative business. To a large extent this has eliminated the more overt forms of discrimination that existed when mortgage finance was in short supply and rationed by lenders (Stephens 1993). The fact that it is a commercial relationship between borrower and lender has, perhaps surprisingly, not always seemed apparent to borrowers. This may perhaps partly result from an overhang from the pre-1980 era when mortgage lending was a more tightly regulated business, with interest rates centrally determined so as to balance the interests of borrowers and savers. It is also clear though that, even as traditional building societies changed so as to become indistinguishable from other large-scale commercial institutions, they have been happy to trade on their image of being a 'friend and trusted adviser' to owners and aspiring owners.

The mortgage business has changed beyond all recognition in since 1980. Building societies of the 1970s were specialist mortgage lenders, subject to special centralized control and regulation. Importantly, they were mutual organizations: that is to say, the members of the organization (the borrowers and savers) were the owners rather than shareholders. Although they faced some restrictions, in principle mutuality should have allowed some economies within the business and enabled building societies to offer a better deal to savers and borrowers. However, as competition progressed through the 1980s and 1990s, the societies sought increased commercial freedom, allowing them to offer a wider range of consumer financial products. Despite new legislation allowing some increased freedom, the greatest commercial advantage appeared to be offered by transition to commercial bank status and most building societies have opted to convert into public limited companies.

Between 1986 and 2001, the number of building societies declined by 57 per cent (from 151 to 65). The offer of a 'windfall payment' to borrowers and savers as compensation on conversion from mutual status proved persuasive in organizational ballots asking members to agree to conversion. It even spawned a class of so-called 'carpet-baggers', who opened accounts in mutuals considered to be ripe for conversion simply in order to cash in on the change. Where building society managers were resistant to conversion, such individuals were also instrumental in attempting to persuade the Boards and members to endorse the change. As a result, by 2002, only one large building society retains mutual status, the remainder having converted.

Although some might regret the passing of the traditional mutual building society, the strong competition that has developed has encouraged the emergence of a much broader range of mortgage products and has prompted fierce competition for business. There are even niche lenders who particularly seek the business of those who find it difficult to get credit from elsewhere (subprime lenders). Increasingly too, lenders encourage people to move their business (loan) to another provider during the life of an existing mortgage. In 2002, some 46 per cent of all mortgage borrowing was for remortgaging rather than new business. This creates opportunities for equity extraction (see below) and also creates an enormous choice for new and existing borrowers as to their preferred mortgage instrument.

The two main types of mortgage are capital repayment mortgages and interest-only mortgages. The former involve equal monthly payments through the life of the mortgage, consisting of interest on the outstanding debt and an initially small (but growing) repayment of capital, whereas in the latter the equal monthly instalments are only interest on the outstanding debt while another product, traditionally an endowment policy, is used as a savings vehicle to cover the outstanding debt at the end of the mortgage term. Through the 1990s these basic options have fragmented into innumerable variations. For instance, interest rates can simply vary as the lender changes them (typically in response to changes in base rates), or change annually, or be fixed for some term, or be capped so that rate increases do not exceed a certain level, or be discounted for some period (guaranteed to be some percentage below the lenders' standard rate) or track base rates according to some formula, or even combine some of these features. Instruments to repay the debt on interest-only products are at least as diverse and probably harder for most consumers to weigh up, given the longer time period over which risks and returns should be considered.

Such a competitive environment has the potential to deliver real benefits to consumers who can, in principle, find a very competitive deal and select a product that best suits their likely income profile and their attitude to risk. However, the very complicated environment can make it difficult for people to make well-informed choices. People can lack understanding about the characteristics and risks of complex financial products and many do not struggle to read through and assimilate a lot of small print. There are plenty of financial advisers available, but it may be impossible for consumers to judge whether they are going to receive good, impartial advice. There are government regulations, operating through the Financial Services Authority (FSA), designed to ensure the impartiality of financial advice, and to outlaw misleading advertisements. Similarly, there are mechanisms (such as through ombudsman schemes) through which wronged consumers may seek redress. The effectiveness of these mechanisms is hard to judge. For instance, CAT standards (charges, access and terms) were introduced as a voluntary code, as a mechanism for delivering clear and fair mortgage products for consumers. However, only a minority of mortgage products advertise adherence to these standards and it is not clear how much impact this regulatory mechanism has had on consumer confidence or choices.

At the same time, however, there have been clear examples of failure in the protection mechanisms. For instance, endowment policies were strongly promoted by lenders in the late 1980s, with supposedly impartial staff incentivized by the lure of commissions. And although the prospect of a large lump sum at the end of the mortgage term was undoubtedly an attraction for borrowers, it is also clear that the risks of such products were not always fully explained and the financial benefit to the lenders from the sale of these products was not transparent. With the down-turn in stock market returns since the late 1990s, many borrowers with endowment-linked loans face the likelihood of having insufficient funds even to repay their end-of-term mortgage debt and can certainly expect no windfall gain. It has been established that many people were mis-sold these policies (Consumers' Association 2003).

Flexible mortgages

Despite the importance of mortgage finance to individual households and the economy as a whole, there is remarkably little research that examines people's understanding, choices and use of mortgage products. A recent exception was a study into the ways in which people choose and use flexible mortgages (Smith, Ford and Munro 2002; and see also O'Leary and Farquhar 2003). These are a relatively new type of product in the UK and have been growing very fast both in range and take-up. The facility to pay off early is a universal feature of such mortgages, and a good deal of the promotion leant heavily on the great savings that can be made when regular or occasional overpayments reduce the lifetime of the loan. Of course, many standard repayment mortgages allow outstanding capital to be reduced in this way (even if this possibility is not heavily promoted). The main distinguishing feature of flexible mortgages, though, is that they also provide access to housing equity (within pre-agreed limits), by allowing the withdrawal of lump sums, underpaying or taking 'mortgage holidays'. Many such products are now also marketed as 'offset' mortgages, encouraging borrowers to move their savings into the same account to offset interest payments on their outstanding mortgage debt.

The research found that flexible mortgages were held by borrowers who were better off and slightly older than average. Nearly a quarter had only taken the opportunity to get ahead of their repayment schedule through regular overpayments or occasional lump sums, but approaching one in five had only used draw-down facilities, mainly extracting one large lump sum. A mere 10 per cent had used the products in a more sophisticated way, both to overpay and to extract equity. What was most striking in the research though was that, looking forward, many more borrowers expected to make use of the facilities available to them. Only one in seven had no plans to use any flexible features, but two in five planned to both invest into and withdraw from their mortgage account. Around one-third of borrowers planned to change mortgage in the next five years, typically seeking an even more flexible product.

A parallel survey of lenders found that 80 per cent agreed with the proposition that in the future 'most products will have today's flexible features' (Smith, Ford and Munro 2002). What this research suggests, therefore, is that there is a potential sea change in the ease with which people can access and use their housing equity, with potentially huge consequences for the borrowers themselves and the macroeconomy. At present, it is hard to predict what the most significant impacts will be. Where people repay faster than scheduled, a financial cushion is created, enabling mortgage holidays to cover for a period of reduced income. This would, for instance, be a route by which people could avoid the need to take out mortgage payment protection insurance (MPPI: see pp. 147–8). On the other hand, the temptation of equity extraction may lead people into higher indebtedness and a postponement of mortgage repayment.

Tenants as consumers

The traditionally paternalistic style of housing management practised by social landlords positioned tenants as passive supplicants, waiting for welfare help. This powerlessness was reinforced in practices that, echoing the earliest housing management approaches of Octavia Hill, for example, vetted tenants' suitability for particular grades of housing by judging house-keeping skills and cleanliness. It might be argued that current approaches to anti-social behaviour (and other practices designed to weed out 'neighbours from hell') are re-echoing some of these judgemental ideas. Generally, nevertheless, conventional wisdom has shifted decisively in favour of involving tenants in the management of the housing they occupy (though tenants involved in the management of their houses may also advocate strong policies of social control).

Hague (1996) argued that the shift was partly underpinned by economic considerations, as the cost of unsuccessful attempts to regenerate areas was seen to be caused by in part by a failure to create the improvements that really mattered to local people. Certainly tenant participation at the estate level has been a strong focus of attempts to turn around the worst estates since the 1970s (see Chapter 9).

More broadly Carr, Sefton-Green and Tissier (2001) argue that the growing significance of tenant involvement is associated with a shift from local government to *governance*: a loss of confidence in traditional mechanisms of accountability created through the ballot box to attempts to find more direct ways of engaging and responding to local citizens (Daly and Davies 2002). Goodlad (2001) traces the growth of tenant participation from the late 1970s and shows that, while it retained a strong rhetorical support from central government, there was also some ambivalence, particularly from the Left. In particular, the idea that tenants – and particularly tenant activists – could be 'incorporated' into the structures in a way that stifled real opposition and robust criticism informed a perspective which judged only full tenant control as true empowerment. The commonly used heuristic devices, which develop 'ladders' of tenant involvement ranging from 'being given information' to 'tenant control' (Arnstein 1969; Riseborough 1998) grow directly from this perspective. But they have also exposed the shortcomings of analysis that relies on a description of the structures that are in place to facilitate tenant involvement. To know that tenants are given a place on a management board is not sufficient to understand the true extent of the power and influence that they are able to wield (Cairncross, Clapham and Goodlad 1997; Pawson and Fancy 2003).

A similar problem attends the provision of legal rights that are not always exercised in such a way as to create substantive rights. For example, the 1980 Housing Act gave tenants the right to be consulted about management matters but appeared to have little impact on the way in which council housing was managed. This was later supplemented in 1992 by John Major's Citizen's Charter, giving local authority tenants an entitlement to an annual landlord management performance report. Rights for council tenants to choose a different landlord, created by the 1988 Housing Act's 'tenant's choice' measures, were largely unsuccessful and were subsequently (in England) repealed. Attempts to exploit opportunities to 'break free' of council control through large-scale voluntary transfers (LSVTs) have generally required the strong and explicit backing of the local authority concerned to progress (and even in these circumstances, of course, around one-quarter of council-backed ballots have failed to attract majority support). However, the language of tenant involvement and the emphasis on choice is a way of extending the consumerist agenda into social housing where people are to be treated as customers rather than clients in a quasi-market framework of accountability.

The Best Value regime for local authority landlords which replaced Compulsory Competitive Tendering (see Chapter 8) has placed consultation with tenants (and other service users) at the heart of mechanisms to promote management improvement. Importantly, this obligation is backed up by an inspection system intended to ensure compliance. This regime is given force not only by the potential stigma of being labelled as delivering 'failing' services (or, at worst, suffering direct government intervention), but also by the rewards of enhanced resources (such as those being made available under the Arm's Length Management Organizations, or ALMO, regime in England).

Additionally, council landlords in England are required to have in place Tenant Participation Compacts (TPCs) which set out how tenants can get involved in local decisions and what councils and tenants want to achieve locally (DETR 1999a and 1999e). Best Value, though not Tenant Participation Compacts, have been extended to RSLs, increasing the general exhortation across the whole sector to engage with tenants. Nevertheless, an early evaluation of the TPC regime found no evidence to suggest that it had 'actively increased' tenant involvement (Aldbourne Associates 2003).

Arguably, the longest history and strongest commitment to tenant participation has been witnessed in relation to urban regeneration, and it is from research evaluations of such initiatives that much evidence of how difficult it is to make tenant participation effective originates. More recently this has been seen to be part of a broader creation of partnerships which also ideally involve other local stakeholders, as well as landlords. What this emphasis exposes, however, is the inequality – of power, skills and resources – that is available to different partners, and between the community representatives and professional actors in particular. The Joseph Rowntree Foundation's Area Regeneration Programme research review argued that an organizational culture shift was still needed to value residents' role within partnerships (Joseph Rowntree Foundation 2000). While JRF concluded that good practice had refashioned mechanisms to create effective and streamlined partnerships, it was also argued that in the past participation has often been tokenistic and that residents know this and can be disillusioned. This may be a consequence of a possible tension between strategic approaches to regeneration and empowering tenants (see also Chapter 9). In many cases, the community may not share the priorities or even the vision of the overall strategy. Anastacio *et al.* (2000) found tenant participants were pressurized to conform to official agendas even where communities had other priorities. Participants felt that their own 'acceptability' as representatives was judged in relation to how closely their agendas coincided with council agendas and/or private sector interests (such as property development interests).

Much research has also pointed to the difficulty that residents can have in contributing to formal participation bodies. Tenants may need training and other support to make effective contributions at partnership boards and such like. But more fundamentally, community involvement tends to be very underresourced, relying on the efforts of volunteers who can quickly suffer from partnership fatigue and burn-out. Regeneration funding often lacks even small budgets to support voluntary activities (Duncan and Thomas 2000). It has also been observed that 'the community' may well be far from homogeneous, presenting dangers of relying on the 'activists' who may not represent the diversity of community views. This creates a dilemma as to whether to try to foster structures of representative democracy within the tenant body, or to use more consumerist types of mechanisms such as surveys and focus groups to elicit opinions.

Although the commitment to policies of increasing tenants' participation has been consistent over a number of years, it is clear that it is very difficult to achieve in practice. Similar difficulties were found in the Boards of stock transfer housing associations, where it was often found difficult to engage tenant Board members in discussions at the strategic level required (Pawson and Fancy 2003). Empowering tenants as individual consumers, such as in choice-based lettings (see Box 8.1 in Chapter 8), is an alternative way of expanding (individual) consumer influence. This approach also underpins the attractiveness to many commentators of introducing so called 'shopping incentives' into the structure of Housing Benefit. The argument here is that once rents are restructured so as to fairly reflect differences in the overall attractiveness of houses on offer, tenants should not automatically be given the full cost of whatever rent they are paying. Instead, some standard allowance should be given, thereby sensitizing benefit-dependent tenants to considerations of cost and quality (Kemp 1998).

Help with housing costs for households in financial difficulty

Since the 1970s there has been a systematic switch in the subsidy support to housing in all tenures from so-called general or bricks and mortar subsidies to help targeted at those deemed to need it most: that is, person subsidies (Gibb, Munro and Satsangi 1999; Garnett 2000). Given the divided housing system in the UK it is not surprising that this help is delivered differently to owners compared with renters. However, for both, efforts to reduce the overall bill and encourage other behavioural changes have led to the support becoming rather less generous, at least for some households. This section briefly examines the impacts of the way in which help is delivered to each sector.

Owner-occupiers

As argued earlier in this chapter, there are systematic divisions and inequalities within the owner-occupied sector that leave identifiable groups of households more vulnerable to requiring help with mortgage costs. In addition, changing market conditions (outlined in Chapter 3) present further risks for households: the linkage between depressed macroeconomic conditions and depressed housing markets means that there will inevitably be more households losing employment income at the same time as house prices become less buoyant and trading more difficult. The support available for mortgage costs, ISMI (Income Support for Mortgage Interest), has been restricted so that those who have taken their mortgage out after October 1995 have to wait nine months before any contribution to mortgage payments is made. Further, in order to qualify even then, the individual must also be in receipt of Income Support (requiring that there is virtually no other income coming into the household and that household savings do not exceed £8,000). Once eligibility is established interest only is paid (there is an equity argument for the inappropriateness of the state providing money to acquire a household's major asset) and at a standard rate of interest. There is also an upper limit (£100,000) on the mortgage that will be covered. Again, this reflects an equity argument that it is inappropriate for the state to help pay for 'overgenerous' housing provision, though it is arguably a rather crude means of achieving this in the context of a housing market where £100,000 will currently buy far more in some areas than in others, and where the average price of an owner-occupied house across the UK as a whole now exceeds £100,000.

It is immediately obvious that this potentially leaves the owner-occupier who becomes reliant on state help facing an incomplete safety net. It was intended that the nine-month waiting period be covered privately, through MPPI. However, research has established that the coverage afforded by private insurance is very partial (Ford, Burrows and Nettleton 2001). The private market will not provide this sort of insurance universally; for instance, contract and temporary workers are not insurable. Claims are typically allowed on the grounds of accident, sickness or unemployment (although some policies allow insurance for only some of these hazards), but this excludes other circumstances in which people might face difficulty in repaying the mortgage (such as following separation from a partner). It is a market potentially affected by 'adverse selection' (those most likely to become unemployed are more likely to take up the offer of insurance), and 'moral hazard' (people with insurance may be less anxious to avoid the insured-against outcome). Consequently, claims are often subjected to rigorous review, to ensure that the claim is legitimate (e.g., that the person did not have prior knowledge of an illness or is not at fault in becoming employed). Between one-third and one-quarter of all MPPI claims are rejected each year (Ford 2000a).

Take-up of MPPI has been slow. Approximately 19 per cent of all borrowers and 25 per cent of new borrowers had insurance in 2000 (indicating slow progress towards the government's target of 55 per cent). This is no doubt partly to do with cost. The insurance has been criticized as offering relatively poor value for money. Further, people are typically offered it in longer discussions about mortgages, which will often include insurance cover for life, buildings and contents, and many people clearly decide that yet more insurance is unaffordable. In sum, private insurance does not cover the ISMI gap for a great many people.

Other aspects of the ISMI eligibility rules increase the extent to which the coverage for many people is partial. The tightly-drawn eligibility for Income

Support clearly excludes many owner-occupiers who find themselves in difficulty: for instance, if only one partner loses their job. Further restrictions can also result in households slipping ever further into debt. The 'standard' interest rate may be less than the actual rate being charged by lenders. In addition, many owners must continue to pay buildings insurance, and many try to keep up payments on endowment policies or continue to contribute towards the capital element of their mortgage payment.

All these factors mean that households affected can accumulate a good deal of debt. Sometimes lenders will be happy to accept reduced payments, but this can only be a temporary solution. Owners will eventually have to consider selling their house in order to stop debt accumulation. But this can be difficult in times, or areas, of low demand for housing. This option also creates the problem that local authorities may consider a 'voluntary' sale in these circumstances as demonstrating that subsequent homelessness is also 'voluntary', potentially excluding the household from rehousing. For a variety of reasons, then, households with mortgage arrears may ultimately have their house repossessed, which is a very stressful and distressing experience (Nettleton and Burrows 2000). The level of house repossessions varies with the cycle of the housing market, but was just under 12,000 households in 2002 (see Chapter 3).

The government argues that the nine-month ISMI waiting period is justified not only because it is insurable, but also because most owners get back into work within that time. They have also responded to some criticism of the scheme by allowing repeat claims for ISMI, without a second waiting period, within a year (this is intended to encourage people into the labour market, even where the job that they take is perceived as being relatively risky). It may well be the case that many people who experience temporary financial difficulties do manage to negotiate the period, perhaps helped by some lender forbearance, and emerge relatively unscathed. However, the system as it currently exists does not enable that outcome for all, creating significantly worse outcomes for those who find themselves pursued for substantial debts for many years after the initial default.

Tenants in the social rented sector

Arguably in the social rented sector the safety net, created by Housing Benefit (HB), is much less incomplete. Tenants who are in receipt of any of the main, longer-term benefits (Income Support, Job Seeker's Allowance, invalidity benefit) are entitled to Housing Benefit, which normally covers all of their rent. For those with incomes slightly above these levels, the support from HB tapers off so that a progressively greater proportion of rent is paid. A criticism from advocates of shopping incentives is that entitlement to partial HB provides 100 per cent marginal subsidy on rent increases, but this, of course, also makes the safety net more secure for those in receipt of partial benefit. Another longstanding argument is that the taper of benefit is too steep, so that rent burdens fall relatively heavily on low paid workers. There is no waiting time before tenants can claim, so although the repeated bureaucracy is no doubt daunting and time consuming, and tenants often fall into significant 'technical' arrears whilst claims await processing, there is in principle no disincentive to take up unstable or short-term work.

The debate concerning the adequacy of the Housing Benefit safety net has tended to focus on rather different issues from that in the private sector. First, the government has been keen to reduce fraud as far as possible, as part of the drive to minimize the overall benefit bill. Second, there is a broader concern that the scheme's design undermines the moves towards a more 'consumerist' tenant body. There is (largely anecdotal) evidence that HB has created a widespread 'culture of non-payment' where many believe that they do not pay *any* rent. Of course, landlords have preferred and maintained the system in which rents paid through HB are channelled directly to themselves. This is problematic for reforms that hope to create incentives through more rational pricing mechanisms and also for fostering a more engaged, critical tenant body that will hold landlords closely to account to deliver value for money.

Third, a great deal of attention has been paid to the unanticipated consequences of the design of Housing Benefit in undermining incentives to take up work. The argument is that because HB (and Council Tax benefit) are quite sharply withdrawn as income rises above income support levels, people earning modest incomes can find that they are worse off working than on benefit (Wilcox 2002). This is exacerbated as rents become higher in real terms (a consistent trend for much of the past 20 years), because the absolute amount of rent that has to be found from a low weekly wage also becomes higher.

This is a real barrier in the government's aim to promote social inclusion, which is significantly focused on the potential of reconnecting people (and places) to labour markets. It has been partly alleviated by the use of tax credits to help support low income families in work. Under this regime, Wilcox (2002) notes, lone parent households earning over £164 per week (equivalent to 40 hours at the minimum wage) only need to claim HB when their rent exceeds £60 per week and a couple with the same earnings would claim HB only when their rent was greater than £50 per week (depending on exact circumstances, e.g., number and age of children).

Tenants in the private rented sector

Tenants in the private rented sector are also entitled to HB, but a dominant thread of policy towards this sector has been to restrict benefit entitlement. There is a particular possibility of fraud in the private rented sector, whereby landlords and tenants could collude to benefit from a higher than reasonable rent for a property, as underpinned by benefit. And there has been concern that unless benefit is structured to prevent it, private sector tenants could choose to live in a house that is too big or luxurious for their needs. Consequently, the regime has been considerably tightened through the introduction of local reference rents in 1996 (which sets a benchmark rent for property in the local housing market) and, where tenants pay more than this, they can be required to make up the difference from their own income. A further restriction was placed on single benefit claimants under 25, which entitled them only to sufficient rent to pay for a single room (on the argument that this was what most young workers accept). Wilcox (2002) argues that the shortfalls that people must cover under this rule are making it increasingly difficult for young people on benefit to sustain a tenancy and notes that the number of young single people in receipt of HB fell from 116,000 in November 1996 to just 31,000 in May 2001.

Shopping incentives

As noted above, it has long been argued that the system removes the link between changes in rent and what people pay (Hills 1991 and 1997). This undermines the important market-style mechanism that provides incentives for both tenants and landlords to behave in an efficient way (Kemp 2000; Kemp, Wilcox and Rhodes 2002). A key problem of moving towards a more rational system are the irrationalities in existing rent structures, particularly in the social rented sector in England, and the huge regional and local differences in rents in both sectors. The latter problem makes it difficult to design a scheme that is fair to tenants across the whole country; put simply, how can you construct a rent allowance scheme which recognizes that tenants in one place face very high rents and others very low, while still placing more of the decision-making responsibility on to tenants? It is hard for any scheme with a flat rate element to reflect accurately the very complex mosaic of local and national price differences.

The problem of inconsistent rents in the social sector is also a thorny issue to resolve. Two related problems have emerged. First, within a given landlord's stock, rents often have a fairly flat structure so that there is not much price difference between the 'best' and the 'worst' stock. Second, comparable properties in different areas, or with different landlords, may also charge quite different rents, again not related to the relative desirability of the properties, but because of differences in historical funding regimes. However, a major restructuring of rents is under way in England, at the behest of the government, to introduce some consistency, by relating rents to capital values and local earnings (DETR 2000c). The end result of a reform period planned to run for ten years from 2002 is intended to be a pricing structure for social rented housing that is amenable to the introduction of a Housing Benefit scheme incorporating shopping incentives. Some fear that the difficulty which implementing new rent structures is causing to landlords and their business plans is not worth the, as yet unproven, benefits of a reformed Housing Benefit scheme (Pawson and Sinclair 2003).

Tenants in difficulty

Although the debate concerning support for tenants has, as argued above, usually focused on the way in which the structure of the scheme creates unintended consequences, discussion as to whether the safety net can fail tenants in the social sector has tended to be more muted. Certainly, there is evidence that in the private rented sector, HB problems can create great difficulty, including eviction for some tenants.

Whilst the structure of HB is somewhat different for social sector tenants, deficiencies in its operation can lead to arrears putting a tenant at risk of eviction. Changes in the Housing Benefit scheme since 1990 only appear to have worsened existing problems. The Audit Commission (2002) argued that most of these changes were intended to control expenditure or to improve fraud detection and these have made the scheme '*more complex and difficult to administer*'. Evans and Smith (2002) suggested that the voluntary verification framework system, introduced to improve the detection of fraud, had substantially increased staff workloads with no corresponding increase in resources. Consequently, the service to claimants has declined: councils are now processing fewer claims within the statutory 14 day period, despite a fall in the number of claimants (Audit Commission 2002). Evans and Smith (2002) estimated that Housing Benefit problems were responsible for around 40 per cent of the arrears in Welsh housing associations and 13 per cent of arrears in councils.

Particular difficulties result from an unresponsive Housing Benefit administration when tenants move in and out of often low paid employment. A housing association tenant moving into work may experience a lengthy delay in having his or her benefit payment adjusted. This can result in an eventual 'overpayment recovery' by the local authority whereby a sum is deducted direct from the landlord, with the amount being recouped from the tenant's rent account, thereby creating sometimes very substantial arrears for the tenant concerned (Neuberger 2003). Sometimes such a sequence of events can place a tenant on the slippery slope towards eviction.

It is estimated that evictions by social landlords in England totalled 27,000 in 2001/2 (Delargy 2003). And, whilst precisely comparable figures for previous years are unavailable, the number of possession orders granted by to social landlords by the courts rose by 100 per cent between 1996 and 2002 (Phelps and Carter 2003). In the housing association sector it has been estimated that eviction rates rose by 14 per cent from 1998 to 2000 (Pawson and Ford 2002). Problems with the benefits system and interactions with labour market changes may be partly responsible for this substantial increase. However, other policy changes such as the spreading use of (insecure) introductory and starter tenancies by landlords in England and from tougher approaches to rent arrears due to lender and regulatory pressures may also have contributed. Another possibility is that falling demand for social housing in some regions means that a tenant may place a declining value on their tenancy and will, therefore, be less diligent about sustaining it. Suggestions that rising evictions are mainly due to landlords' increasingly assertive policies to 'crack down' on anti-social behaviour are almost certainly wide of the mark, since – as demonstrated by Bryant (2001) in relation to HA evictions – only a tiny percentage result solely from action to tackle nuisance.

Whatever its cause, however, loss of a tenancy through eviction may cause longer-term difficulties for an evicted tenant over and above the obvious immediate problems. In terms of the homelessness legislation, loss of accommodation through repossession can be interpreted as 'intentional homelessness', potentially obviating a local authority's rehousing duty. More broadly, social landlords' increasingly widespread adoption of rehousing eligibility restrictions debarring 'potentially troublesome tenants' – so-called 'exclusion policies' – are frequently targeted on former tenants previously subject to eviction (Pawson *et al.* 2001; Pawson and Mullins 2003).

Conclusion

It can be argued that growing consumerism has been one of the dominant trends affecting the housing system since 1980. This chapter has explored how this trend has impacted on people in the public and the private sector housing stock. There is a mixed picture overall. On the one hand, a growing landscape of choice is apparent, in relation to landlords, mortgage products, and consumption within the home. On the other, where people lose or lack income, and have to rely on state help, the policy imperative of containing and controlling public expenditure has led to limits that can severely restrict the options available. In this increasingly risky context, it is important to bear in mind that the risks are not equally distributed within the population. Those who are most marginal and vulnerable in the labour market are also likely to occupy the most vulnerable housing market position. Just as the gains available from booming housing markets are subject to structured inequalities, so are the risks of losing a tenancy or having an owned home repossessed.

Further reading

There is no single source that brings together the discussion of the rising spread and impact of consumerism in the owner-occupied sector. There is what can sometimes be a fairly theoretical literature in the sociological tradition examining concerning the meaning of home and home-based consumption and interested readers might start with Ravetz with Turkington (1995) or Rybczynski (1987), both of which are very readable and enjoyable accounts that engage with the meaning of the home literature. Burrows (2003a and 2003b) is interesting for an up-to-date account of differentiation within the owner-occupied sector although Forrest, Murie and Williams (1990) shows that the issue has a longer history. The Joseph Rowntree Foundation (2000) provides a good overview of the issues of involvement in sustainable regeneration and Goodlad (2001) considers the evolution of tenant participation. Ford (2000b) reveals the weaknesses of the MPPI safety net and Kemp (2000) covers contemporary debates in Housing Benefit.

8

The Manager's Perspective

Pressures on the managers

This chapter examines how housing managers respond to shifting market conditions and other changes in their external and policy environment. 'Managers', for these purposes, are social landlord organizations: that is, local authorities and housing associations, or registered social landlords (RSLs).

Framing the chapter in this way raises two questions: first, the apparent equating of housing management with social housing. Although housing management activities occur in other tenures, they are undertaken in different ways and, for the most part, do not involve an organized quasi-professional approach to asset stewardship. In owner-occupation, for example, most housing management is 'self-management' and tends to be largely reactive in nature (see Chapter 6); hence this chapter's focus on social landlords' activities and approaches.

A second question raised by the framework is how to interpret 'housing management'. The short answer is that it is defined broadly as all activities connected with the ongoing administration and stewardship of existing housing stock, including the administration of access to this stock. Generally, these are activities involving 'revenue' rather than 'capital' expenditure. It should, however, be acknowledged that the precise scope of 'housing management' is both fiercely contested and shifting territory (Scott *et al.* 2001b). This issue is explored further below (see pp.165–7).

Pressures on social landlords in Britain

Although social housing, broadly defined, is common throughout the developed world, social landlords are unusually important in Britain, where they continue to own and manage over one-fifth of the national housing stock (see Chapter 2). Historically, the great bulk of social rented housing has been controlled by local authorities (Merrett 1979). Only in the last decade of the 20th century did RSLs begin to become more dominant (see Chapter 2).

British social landlords range in scale from the metropolitan councils managing 50,000 homes and more through to a myriad of 'not for profit' housing associations with stockholdings numbered in dozens rather than thousands. Whilst stock transfers are tending to break up the largest local authority holdings, economies of scale are at the same time encouraging agglomeration amongst housing associations (Audit Commission/Housing Corporation 2001). In England's RSL sector, the 250 associations with more than 1,000 homes are now responsible for 90 per cent of total RSL stock and, within this group, over 100 now manage 5,000 dwellings or more. RSLs' diverse origins and organizational forms are explored in Malpass (2000). The general point here is that the size and geographical distribution of a landlord's stockholding has some implications for its management style. In the past (and particularly in Scotland), for example, this has tended to be reflected by a contrast between the more community-focused RSL approach and the more professional yet more bureaucratic local authority style.

The market changes which have buffeted British social landlords since the mid-1990s were described in Chapters 4 and 5. In short, there has been a growing divergence between generally high and rising demand in areas such as London and the south of England and generally lower and falling demand in central and northern England. Similar regional contrasts can be seen within Scotland and Wales. Additionally, the sector as a whole is affected by growing residualization as poverty is increasingly concentrated in social housing (see Chapter 2).

In addition to social trends and housing market changes, local authorities and RSLs have to contend with growing demands to be:

- more consumerist
- more efficient and businesslike
- more socially responsible

The chapter begins by outlining the nature of some of these pressures and the mechanisms through which they are transmitted, and then examines social landlords' responses to those pressures for change which apply irrespective of local housing market conditions. The ways that landlords have been developing more 'businesslike' operational styles are examined, which leads to consideration of the changing roles played by social landlords and their staff. The second half of the chapter then focuses on the ways that landlords have been responding to the changing and/or extreme market conditions of recent years, in terms of both falling and rising demand.

Consumerism

The creation of more customer-focused organizations is a key objective of central government regulation and oversight carried out on its behalf by agencies such as the Housing Inspectorate, the Housing Corporation and Communities Scotland (formerly Scottish Homes). The Best Value (BV) principles which underpin the operation of all these regulatory bodies stress the importance of involving customers in service review and service planning, and encouraging social landlords to adopt a more consumerist outlook.

The BV regime has, since 1997, replaced the previous Compulsory Competitive Tendering (CCT) system which required local authorities to tender out service provision. However, whilst the highly prescriptive housing management CCT framework affected only larger local authorities in England, the somewhat more subtle BV obligations apply much more generally across the sector, throughout Britain. They also apply to RSLs and relate to all housing functions rather than the restricted CCT list. Under BV principles, periodic service reviews must respect the 'four Cs':

- *challenge*: why, how and by whom is a service being provided?
- *compare*: examine performance alongside that of others, taking into account the views of service users and potential suppliers
- *consult*: collect the views of stakeholders in setting of performance targets
- *compete*: use 'fair and open competition wherever practicable as a means of securing efficient and effective services'

Comparison in the Best Value in Housing (BVH) framework is facilitated by statutory performance indicators which have evolved from those first introduced under the Citizen's Charter initiative in 1993 (see Table 8.1).

There is a view that the BV regime differs from its CCT predecessor more in form than in content (Geddes 2001; Vincent-Jones 2001). It has been argued that BV has increasingly become 'an approach which is centrally driven, prescriptive and mechanistic' (Maile and Hoggett 2001) with a growing resemblance to the CCT regime it replaced. It is, however, undeniably distinctive in its emphasis on partnerships, public consultation and service user involvement (Mullins 1999; Bovaird and Halachmi 2001). A specific BVH requirement for local authorities in England has been the development of Tenant Participation Compacts (TPCs), documented agreements specifying a clear role for tenants in their landlord's decision-making processes.

This new requirement for intensified tenant involvement compounds longer-established signals transmitted through the competitive Housing Investment Programme (HIP) system for the allocation of housing capital resources (Cole and Goodchild 1995; Lambert and Malpass 1998). Under this system, as operated since 1991, central government's assessment of an authority's 'performance' in facilitating tenant participation (among other things) influences the authority's housing capital allocation. Whilst housing management 'performance' and resource allocation have never been linked in this way in Scotland, the Housing (Scotland) Act 2001 obliges all social landlords to promote tenant participation.

Table 8.1 *Best Value and statutory housing management performance indicators for LAs in England and Scotland*

Policy area	England 2001/2	Scotland 2002/3
Repairs	BV72. % of 'urgent repairs' done within government time limits BV73. Average time for non-urgent repairs BV71(a). % of dwellings renovated at cost of >£5,000 BV 71(b). % of dwellings renovated at cost of <£5,000	Indicator 1(c). % of repairs completed within the target response time for each priority category Indicator 1(d). % of all repairs due for completion within 24 hours completed within target
Void management	BV68. Average re-let interval	Indicator 3(b). Average re-let interval Indicator 3(a). % of homes re-let in: (i) less than 2 weeks; (ii) between 2 and 4 weeks; (iii) More than 4 weeks
	BV69. Void rent loss due to voids as a % total rent due	Indicator 2. Void rent loss due to voids as a % total rent due
Rent collection	BV66(a). Rent collected as % of rent due BV66(b). Arrears as % of rent due BV66(c). Rent written off as % of rent due	Indicator 4 (a). Current tenant arrears as a % of net rent due Indicator 4(b). % of current tenants 13 weeks in arrears at year end
Housing management costs	BV65(a). Weekly cost of housing management per dwelling BV65(b). Weekly cost of housing repairs per dwelling	None
Homelessness	BV67 % of homelessness applications decided in 33 working days	Indicator 6(a). The number of households assessed as homeless during the year Indicator 6(b). The average time between assessment and completion of duty Indicator 6(c). The number of repeat homelessness cases as a % of all applicants
Council house sales	None	Indicator 5(a). The % of house sales completed within 26 weeks Indicator 5(b). The average time to process council house sales
Tenant satisfaction	BV74. % of tenants very/ fairly satisfied with overall landlord service BV75. % of tenants very/ fairly satisfied with opportunities for participation	None
Energy efficiency	BV63 Average SAP rating of council dwellings	None
Equalities	BV164 Does the authority follow the CRE Code?	None

Note: Indicators for Scotland as proposed in Audit Scotland consultation paper on 2002/3 framework.
Sources: Data from www.audit-commission.gov.uk; www.audit-scotland.gov.uk

Best Value, with its attendant array of inspectorates, is part of a wider trend towards increased central government regulation of public bodies. Hood, James and Scott (2000), for example, estimate that the number of staff employed by regulatory bodies in England rose by 90 per cent in the 20 years to 1995. They also conclude that this growth has accelerated after 1997.

Efficient and business-like operation

Best Value principles require social landlords to demonstrate – through service reviews – that in-house provision can be justified in terms of both cost and quality. For local authorities throughout Britain, the emphasis on operational efficiency has been shown in the requirement to publish a standard set of housing management performance indicators (see Table 8.1). The significance of these indicators for the distribution of capital resources has declined somewhat since 2000, as a new financial framework for English local authorities has partially replaced the (performance-related) HIP allocation with the (formula-driven) Major Repairs Allowance (MRA). At the same time, however, the stress on business efficiency has been emphasized by the introduction of the Arm's Length Management Organization (ALMO) option, under which 'high performing' authorities (as assessed under the Housing Inspectorate's star rating system) have the chance to qualify for additional public investment (DETR 2000c).

For social landlords in England and Wales, additional incentives in favour of efficient operation have also arisen from the increasingly strict central controls on the rents they may charge. A key turning point here came in 1995 when central government explicitly abandoned its previous policy of pushing up social sector rents towards those charged by private landlords (Department of the Environment 1995a). This reflected concerns about the poverty trap (see Chapter 2), and about the public spending consequences of rising rents, both directly through Housing Benefit expenditure, and indirectly through the contribution of council rents to Retail Price Index-triggered increases in Income Support and other benefit payments. Since the mid-1990s local authorities in England have had their rents effectively capped through controls on Housing Benefit subsidy. And in both England and Wales, de facto controls on housing association rents have been imposed through the development finance system. With the government's announcement of a 10-year programme of rent restructuring (DETR 2000c), these pressures are now intensifying for social landlords in England, particularly for those RSLs whose previously adopted business plans envisaged significant real-terms appreciation in rents for the foreseeable future.

RSLs' exposure to a measure of financial risk (see Chapter 2) has created a particular incentive to maximize operational efficiency. Associations are in competition with each other for both public and private funds and, in a competitive environment, their success in attracting such funds will be in part dependent on efficiency considerations. As Lambert and Malpass (1998) argue, the need to minimize risk and to satisfy private funders may influence associations to scale down their involvement in inner-city areas and to bias their activity towards areas offering the best prospects for capital appreciation of the stock. 'At the very least, there is growing tension between the social concerns of housing associations and the pressure on them to behave like businesses' (1998, p.107).

Social responsibility

Arguably, tensions between business and social roles are further exacerbated by government expectations that social landlords should contribute to community regeneration and social inclusion. Expectations of this sort are familiar to local authorities and – in the context of their multi-service role – justifiable, but whether such activities are legitimately part of the housing management task is perhaps questionable. Housing managers may, understandably, see the growing demands for them to provide direct support for vulnerable tenants as substituting for the role of social services or specialist voluntary agencies. Similar doubts apply in relation to tackling anti-social behaviour (see Chapter 4).

Such questions are even sharper for the 'single function' RSLs. Nevertheless, both the Housing Corporation and Communities Scotland encourage associations to develop 'community regeneration' activities (provided that these do not incur undue risk for 'core functions'). RSLs' responses to these signals are discussed below (see pp.165–7).

Building competitive, customer-focused organizations

As discussed above (and in Chapter 1), British social landlords have been facing an array of top-down and bottom-up pressures to transform themselves into leaner, fitter and more consumerist organizations. Top-down pressures are transmitted through regulatory frameworks (e.g., through inspection and grading), and through competitive funding systems. The emphasis on customer empowerment within frameworks such as Best Value compounds bottom-up stresses arising from rising consumer expectations and, in some areas, the need to compete more openly with other social landlords (see Chapter 4, pp.84–5).

New Public Management

Since the 1980s public sector organizations have taken a growing interest in adapting private sector managerial approaches and structures, largely in response to the advocacy of competition within public services by the Thatcher government and its successors. In the field of social housing, this advocacy has been pursued through resource allocation systems (e.g., the Housing Investment Programme framework), through regulation (e.g., under CCT and Best Value) and through legislation to promote ownership transfer of local authority stock (Housing Acts 1985, 1988).

The techniques developed by public sector organizations in response to these pressures are often grouped under the heading New Public Management (NPM). The essence of NPM is an emphasis on 'competition, decentralised units and services, performance measurement ... [and] private sector management practices, including new human resource practices' (Walker 2001, pp.676–7). NPM contrasts with the traditional bureaucratic model of the public sector organization. Whereas a bureaucracy is characterized by a strongly hierarchical structure and centralized decision-making, NPM stresses the value of flatter organizations whose middle managers enjoy greater operational discretion as well as shouldering more responsibility for setting and achieving their own targets (Walsh 1995; Walker, 1998).

NPM approaches also undercut the traditional autonomy of public service professionals 'through the promotion of management to establish a business ethos' (Walker 2000, p.286). This acts to restrict the extent to which professional groupings within public services can maintain discretionary decision-making by reference to a licensed body of knowledge. However, whilst this is clearly significant in fields such as health and education, it is perhaps less relevant in housing where the requirement for senior staff to hold professional qualifications specific to housing is often only weakly enforced. Nevertheless, in housing as in other areas, the NPM emphasis on openness and accountability undermines professional mystique (Pearl 1997).

The contract culture

A key theme of NPM-style techniques to promote 'business efficiency' has been the development of a 'contract culture' whereby previously unified client and contractor functions are split. Service provision is prescribed in detailed specifications which facilitate competitive tendering among potential service providers. Client/contractor separation was a formal requirement of Housing Management Compulsory Competitive Tendering (HMCCT: see Harries and Vincent-Jones, 2001), but such restructuring has also been implemented by landlords not subject to CCT, and since CCT's demise. For example, whilst RSLs were never exposed to CCT, Mullins (1999) found that over one-third of RSLs in England had recently considered out-sourcing functions, and that more than one-quarter had recently bought in services on this basis.

For local authorities, restructuring along client/contractor lines has also been inspired by the contention that the tail of estate management should not wag the dog of housing strategy. Similarly, the DETR argued that stock transfer will enable councils to focus their attention on their strategic and enabling roles rather than their landlord function (DETR 2000c). The view is also reflected in the ODPM rules governing local authority eligibility for ALMO status, which require the separation of housing policy and provision.

Research has shown that there is a continuing impetus towards the 'contract culture' arising, in part, from the emphasis on competition incorporated within the BV regime (Geddes 2001). However, the resulting operational style has attracted growing criticism. Apart from the potentially substantial 'transaction costs' involved in tendering and monitoring contractor service provision, such approaches can generate adversarial relationships, both between potentially competing contractors and between client and contractor. The prescriptive detail required within service provision contracts is also likely to inhibit innovation. An appreciation of such problems is inspiring renewed interest in both 'partnership commissioning' and 'relational' (rather than adversarial) contracting, as promoted by the Egan report on public sector procurement (see also pp.126–8).

Given its endorsement of such activities, Best Value can be seen as a middle course between NPM and the Community and Local Governance (CLG) models of public service reform, rather than entirely embodying 'managerialist' NPM principles (Bovaird and Halachmi 2001). Lending support to this interpretation, more than one-third of English local authorities and nearly half of RSLs believe that the BVH framework has changed 'a lot' their engagement with tenants (Aldbourne Associates 2001).

Developing customer focus and quality assurance mechanisms

The NPM emphasis on developing a 'customer-focused' orientation evolves from the recognition that public services are not delivered in a market context where the consumer is relatively free to pick and choose from competing suppliers, or to consume a higher quality product for a higher price. A degree of shortage of social housing continues to prevail in most parts of the country, meaning that access is restricted largely according to administratively defined 'need'. And for those within the sector, transferring from one landlord to another is generally difficult. Since the tenant or applicant is generally in no position to register dissatisfaction with the service by withdrawing their custom, accountability to service users demands the development of specific mechanisms to monitor customer opinions and to ensure performance of a high standard. An appreciation of this is reflected in many aspects of social landlords' activities. Three of the most important areas involve the development of:

- feedback mechanisms to monitor and evaluate service user responses
- quality assurance techniques

- more flexible service provision frameworks which enhance customer convenience and individual choice

Such approaches are, in any case, formally required under the Best Value regime. At the heart of the BV framework lies the concept of service review. This model emphasizes the need to gauge the opinions of service users and other relevant stakeholders. Even in the late 1990s, however, English RSLs tended to solicit tenant feedback through direct communication with individuals (e.g., circular letters) rather than collectively (e.g., through focus groups, residents' panels, analysis of complaints records, etc.: see Mullins 1999). Since the millennium, however, changing regulatory requirements have fostered a growing reliance on survey-based instruments, supported by developments such as the National Housing Federation's promotion of its standard tenants survey 'STATUS' model.

The aspiration to deliver 'high quality services' is frequently cited in social landlords' annual reports and so on (as one stock transfer RSL mission statement of the early 1990s put it, 'we aspire to provide services which are not just excellent but legendary'). Private sector style techniques increasingly employed by housing associations to enhance quality include 'business process re-engineering', 'zero-based budgeting' and benchmarking (Mullins 1999). As another way round the problem of how to demonstrate the provision of 'high quality services', many landlords have sought to validate or 'kitemark' their activities under programmes such as Investors in People Chartermark and ISO 9000 (International Standards Office). By 2002/3, for example, more than a third of local authorities in Scotland had achieved, or were working towards, Chartermark or Investors in People (IIP) accreditations covering housing activities (Pawson *et al.* 2004).

Pearl (1997) criticizes quality tags of this kind as 'largely process-driven and ... not reflect[ing] the quality of output, or the relationship with consumers' (p.47). Thus, whilst a regime such as BS5750 (now ISO 9000) assesses the extent to which a service is delivered consistent with the organization's documented procedures and service standards, it does not critique the standards themselves (Catterick 1992). Advocates of the European Foundation for Quality Management/Business Excellence approach, however, counter that the emphasis of this model on 'linking managerial effort with organisational processes and actual outcomes appears to offer a significant conceptual step forward' (Lewis and Hartley 2001, p.493).

It should not, of course, be assumed that the managerial reforms and techniques discussed here necessarily impact on services as they are experienced by consumers. This may be because of a lack of commitment to the BVH concept. One recent study, for example, reported that 'for some (social landlords) the implementation of BVH involves doing simply what is necessary to conform rather than fully embracing the principles and spirit of the policies' (Aldbourne Associates 2001, p.3). However, the same study found that 44 per cent of local authorities and 33 per cent of RSLs believed that implementation of BVH had enabled them to improve service delivery 'a lot'. Only one in six landlords believed that the regime had had no impact at all in this respect.

In responding to the 'compare' component of the BV framework, social landlords have also become increasingly committed to 'benchmarking' their activities against each other and, in some cases, against the performance of organizations in other sectors (Mullins 1999). Many landlords are active members of benchmarking clubs through which performance indicator scores are collated and compared. Increasingly, these networks are facilitating 'peer review' exercises, where club members inspect services provided by their 'peer' organizations. The growing volume of 'self-assessment' activity of this sort is argued to illustrate the success of the BVH regulatory inspection regime in changing landlords' behaviour: 'Inspection has been internalised in progressive organisations' (McIntosh 2002, p.27). There is an argument that such good practice 'should be rewarded with light-touch external scrutiny, thereby releasing official capacity to deal with poor and unrepentant organisations' (McIntosh 2002, p.27).

Bureaucracy and consumerism

Social landlords have traditionally operated in a rather paternalistic way, where the interests and choices of individual service users have tended to be given rather little weight by comparison with the 'well-intentioned' decisions of officials and the interests of the workforce. However, such a critique is quickly becoming obsolete. Increasingly services are being reshaped to be more convenient for the customer and to allow some individual choice, such as through the growing tendency for landlords to offer appointments for repairs. Housing Corporation performance indicators show that by 2000/1 some 36 per cent of RSLs operated such systems, up from 29 per cent in 1999/2000. Another example involves lettings systems (see Box 8.1) and tenant involvement in policymaking (Chapter 7).

The ministerial push for choice-based lettings in England is symptomatic of a broader official commitment to greater consumerism in public services (see Chapter 10). At the same time, however, central government is expanding 'citizen's rights' to social housing by widening the range of homeless applicants to whom local authorities owe a rehousing duty (e.g., in the Homelessness Act 2002 and the Homelessness (Scotland) Act 2002). There are tensions between this 'rights based' agenda and the consumerist CBL ethic, with one stressing empowerment and independence and the other the need for a more comprehensive welfare safety net.

Box 8.1 *Consumerist reforms to lettings systems*

In the last quarter of the 20th century the dominant trends in social landlords' approaches to lettings tended towards the closer alignment of rehousing priority with assessed housing need and eliminating the scope for unfair discrimination (Pawson *et al.* 2001). In implementing these objectives allocation systems became increasingly bureaucratic, rule-bound and complex. Whilst applicants were generally offered some opportunity to express rehousing preferences (e.g., on property type and location) in general terms, house seekers were largely excluded from any direct say in the selection of vacancies, this power being retained by officials. Such a framework, of course, differs markedly from the private market where house seekers make their own choices, selecting from among various available properties by trading off priorities (e.g., price versus location) against one another.

Since the late 1990s, however, Britain has seen the beginnings of a sea change in social landlords' approaches to lettings. Partly prompted by the challenge of falling demand for social housing in some areas (see below and Chapter 4), there has been growing disillusionment with mechanistic, needs-based allocations systems. This has been fuelled by the dawning realization that the bureaucratic nature of such methods has significant negative connotations. Not only are systems of this kind highly staff-intensive, but their typically opaque nature makes them hard for consumers to understand, thus undermining their legitimacy.

A major stimulus to reform in this area came with the 2000 Housing Green Paper (DETR 2000c) which called for far-reaching reforms to lettings systems in favour of greater consumer choice and enhanced transparency, even if re-let times increased: this reduced efficiency might be 'a price worth paying' (DETR 2000c, para 9.35). Ministerial thinking in this area was clearly inspired by the 'social market' approach to lettings originating in the Netherlands and now practised by over 80 per cent of Dutch social landlords (Westra 2001). Systems of this kind are often referred to 'Delft model' approaches (Kullberg 1997 and 2002).

The hallmarks of the Delft model are the open advertising of vacancies, and a relatively simple system of applicant prioritization, less focused on assessed need and more on straightforward queuing (e.g., date order priority). Rather than being largely passive actors in the process, applicants play an active role in finding a home. Whilst their primary emphasis is 'individualist', some of the 'choice-based' approaches inspired by the Green Paper also reflect the government's more communitarian objectives: that is, using allocations systems to influence the social and demographic mix within a block or neighbourhood (Somerville 2001).

Following up the Green Paper's clarion call for 'choice-based lettings' (CBL), ministers provided additional impetus by establishing a £13 million challenge fund for local authorities piloting 'customer focused' approaches. That more than 90 of England's 354 local authorities submitted proposals illustrates the widespread interest in reshaping allocations systems in a more consumerist mould. Many of the 27 funded initiatives, which ran from 2001 to 2003, involved a number of landlords in addition to the lead local authority (Pawson 2001). It is also significant that interest in CBL-style reforms has been shown by landlords in Scotland and Wales even though the devolved administrations have shown less interest in (and have exerted no pressure to develop) such approaches (Pawson 2002a; Stirling and Smith 2003).

Cultural change and stock transfer

The growing importance of stock transfer landlords also has implications for the spread of a more 'consumerist ethic' in social housing. In the fifteen years to 2003, the transfer programme had spawned more than 180 new landlord organizations – the vast majority of them registered housing associations – in England and Scotland. By 2003 transfer landlords were managing almost half of all properties in the HA sector (Pawson and Fancy 2003). As noted in Chapters 2 and 6, the main motivation for transfers has been financial: as a means of realizing the asset value of the housing stock and/or accessing private finance to fund stock refurbishment. For some local authorities planning transfers, however, cultural change is an explicit objective. And all housing departments morphing into transfer HAs are entering a world where the overriding importance of the organization's business plan income targets implies a central concern with tenants as 'customers'.

Similarly, transfer housing associations commonly emphasize the need to secure widespread employee ownership of business plan objectives and targets. The success of such strategies is exemplified in the research finding that 69 per cent of transfer HA staff at all levels say they understand their organization's objectives, as compared with the local authority norm of only 38 per cent (Taper, Walker and Skinner 2003). Such 'ownership' forms an essential foundation for the development of a performance culture. The authors' own research shows that, from the viewpoint of transferring staff, the post-transfer regime is widely seen as replacing a bureaucratic, hierarchical work environment with one which is more egalitarian, inclusive and encouraging of initiative (Pawson and Fancy 2003).

The changing role of social landlords and their staff

The emphases on combating social exclusion, on community regeneration and on holistic, 'joined-up' responses (see, e.g., SEU 1998) have encouraged landlords to embrace a broader definition of 'housing management' and to develop greater linkages with other agencies. A related line of thinking has advocated the concept of 'on-the-spot housing management' (DETR 1999b; Cole, Hickman and Reeve 2001): see below.

To some extent, these policy trends predate the Labour government: as early as 1995 the Housing Corporation encouraged 'housing plus' (R. Evans 1998). This term (or its Scottish equivalent, 'wider role') refers to '[activities] undertaken by RSLs, in addition to the provision and management of social housing to build sustainable communities' (Scottish Homes 2000, p.1). More recently the term 'community regeneration activities' has tended to be used in place of 'housing plus'. These activities include those 'which aim to tackle economic and social exclusion and to improve the economic, social and environmental circumstances of the communities where RSLs work' (2000, p.1). To some extent, the impetus here can be traced back to concerns raised by David Page about the failure of some new RSL estates to operate as 'balanced and sustainable communities' (Page 1993).

The Corporation urged RSLs to include relevant proposals for what are now termed 'diverse activities' within development funding bids, arguing that they are essential to achieve core objectives (Bacon and Davis 1996). Since 2000, the Scottish Homes (now Communities Scotland) stance on wider action has also become more bullish and this is reflected in the setting-up of the agency's Wider Action Fund (see below).

Furbey, Reid and Cole (2001) argue that another catalyst for 'community-oriented housing practice' has been the emergence of low demand and the realization by the social landlords affected that a 'self contained housing-focused strategy might not be an adequate response to the diverse causes of neighbourhood unpopularity' (p.46). As noted in Chapter 4, responding to the emergence of a 'buyers' market' in rented homes calls for skills in marketing and promotion quite alien to traditional housing management practice.

RSLs have responded to official encouragement to engage in non-housing or wider role activities with initiatives aimed at countering poverty and exclusion, such as:

- the development of workspace for community businesses
- the establishment of training programmes for tenants
- the setting-up of credit unions

In some cases, these activities have been pursued through the creation of subsidiary agencies, linked to the parent association through a group structure (Scottish Homes 1998; Audit Commission/Housing Corporation 2001). This insulates tenants from financial risk associated with a landlord's 'non-housing' business. Even so, some RSLs remain highly reluctant to become involved in activities outside their 'core business'.

In part, scepticism about community regeneration activities reflects the minimal public funding made available for such schemes. In Scotland, for example, the Wider Action Fund (established in 2000) involved only £2 million in its first year. Additionally, the agency has an annual budget of some £6 million for environmental improvements, and there are small sums potentially available from specific central government programmes such as the Working for Communities fund (similar to the New Deal for Communities in England). Community regeneration initiatives may also be eligible for finance from sources such as the European Union (Social Fund and Regional Development Fund) and the National Lottery Charities Board, and may charge users.

Overall, the changing policy context has potentially far-reaching implications for 'housing work' and for the housing profession. The daily duties of social landlords' staff are increasingly likely to include activities such as community development and multi-agency working. Analogous to the view that housing policy is being increasingly subsumed under different disciplinary headings (Bramley 1997b), these changes are seen by Furbey, Reid and Cole (2001) as having 'made the delineation of the housing domain more ... difficult' (p.45).

The housing management task is also being reshaped by the replacement of 'council estates' by mixed tenure neighbourhoods, with the Right to Buy's penetration of all but the most problematic estates. Increasing numbers of flatted blocks in mixed ownership make organizing and funding planned maintenance and major repairs difficult (Leather and Anderson 1999).

These factors are tending to lead to a more generic role for housing managers, requiring a broader knowledge base and a wider range of skills than under the traditional centralized framework (Cole, Hickman and Reeve 2001). Greater accountability to tenants and more thorough-going multi-agency working are driving forces for the staff involved. At the same time, however, the Cole *et al.* research revealed a countervailing trend towards greater specialization within the same organizations where some locally-based staff were adopting a more generic posture. Some of those responsible for tasks such as arrears control and repairs specification were being charged with a more – rather than less – specific remit.

These changes pose a challenge to the existing model of housing professionalism. Rather than 'specific knowledge', Furbey, Reid and Cole argue that the housing staff of the future will be more in need of generic skills and competencies. They argue that there will be 'a growing emphasis, characteristic of managerialism, on personal skills and qualities before domain knowledge' (Furbey, Reid and Cole 2001, p.45).

Managerial responses to low demand

Moving from types of change affecting social landlords across Britain to those specific to particular market circumstances, this section and the next examine local authorities' and RSLs' reaction to changing local demand for housing.

Classifying responses to low demand

It is clear from Chapter 4 that low demand for housing has major implications for social landlords. Variations in the scale and nature of the associated problems, and in their housing market context, clearly call for different combinations of responses. Broadly, such responses may be classed as managerial, physical and structural (see Table 8.2).

Table 8.2   *Classifying social landlords' responses to low demand*

Managerial responses	Physical responses	Structural responses
• Marketing, allocations and pricing policies	• Physical security measures	• Change of use and/or ownership (tenure diversification)
• More intensive housing management	• Dwelling conversions	• Demolition and redevelopment
• Community development and multi-agency working	• Block rehabilitation • Environmental improvements	

Physical and structural responses may be distinguished from managerial initiatives because they usually involve capital expenditure and/or 'downsizing' of the social housing stock, possibly in response to an assessment that local problems reflect more general oversupply or fundamental tenure imbalance. (Because these may be carried out within the context of a broader area regeneration project, such responses are covered in Chapter 9.) The remainder of this section draws substantially on the authors' study of low demand housing carried out for DETR in 1999–2000 (Bramley, Pawson and Third 2000; Bramley and Pawson 2002).

Selecting appropriate responses to low demand problems in a specific area or neighbourhood clearly requires that the phenomenon is thoroughly analysed and understood. Monitoring can pick up early warning signs of weakening demand so that responsive action can be implemented before a spiral of decline sets in (Cole, Kane and Robinson 1999). The advice here is that demand monitoring frameworks should avoid overreliance on any single indicator (e.g., vacancy or void rate).

Particularly where weak demand applies only at the neighbourhood (rather than the HMA) level, managerial responses may offer a realistic chance of success in arresting the problem. Managerial responses – particularly those involving changes in allocations policies – are, in any case, likely to be adopted by landlords as an initial step in tackling low demand, if only because they do not (necessarily) involve substantial expenditure. This is illustrated by Table 8.3, which shows the widespread use of 'managerial' actions. Figure 8.1, however, suggests that such responses are perceived as having a low success rate. As further discussed in Bramley, Pawson and Third (2000), however, there is a noticeable regional contrast between North and South in terms of the extent to which these measures are accompanied by other responses. This reflects the differing nature of the phenomenon: not only is the proportion of social housing stock affected by low demand much higher in the North, but the problems involved tend to be deeper and more intractable in this part of the country. Hence, 'structural' responses were much more common in the north than elsewhere.

Figure 8.1 *Perceived success rates of responses to low demand by LAs and RSLs*

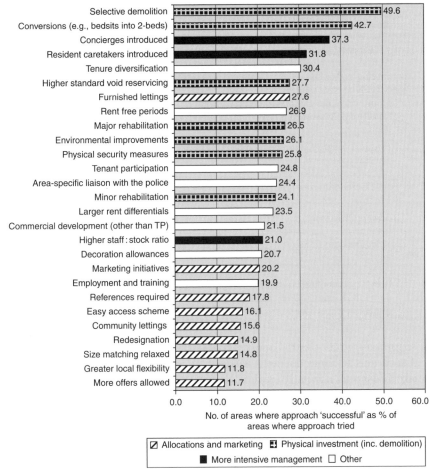

Source: Chart reproduced from Bramley, Pawson and Third (2000).

Managerial responses: allocations, marketing and pricing policies

Table 8.3 shows that the commonest response to low demand is to alter allocations policies. Among both local authorities and RSLs, the commonest allocations policy response to low demand is *underletting* – the practice of allowing 'extra bedrooms' to applicants accepting 'low demand' tenancy offers (see Table 8.4) – instead of the normal tight match between household and house size. Typically applicants may be allowed one 'extra' bedroom so that a childless couple, for example, might be offered a two-bedroom property.

Table 8.3   *Responses to low demand by social landlords in England, 1996–9 (%)*

Response type	Local authorities	RSLs
Managerial responses		
Marketing or allocations policies	97	91
Pricing policies	77	63
More intensive management	48	37
Community development and/or multi-agency working	78	63
Physical responses		
Physical security improvements	46	39
Dwelling conversions (e.g. bedsits converted into 1-beds)	14	9
Stock rehabilitation	48	37
Environmental improvements	45	28
Structural responses		
Change of use or change of ownership	9	4
Selective demolition	24	7
No. of cases (low demand areas)	507	261

Note: percentage figures represent the proportion of identified low demand areas where each action was being/had recently been implemented in 1999.
Source: Postal survey carried out by Bramley, Pawson and Third (2000).

Allocations schemes dubbed *easy access* generally remove or lower housing needs thresholds normally applied to applicants for social housing. Under recently-adopted terminology, such schemes might fall under the heading 'choice-based lettings' in that they often involve the open advertising of specific vacancies. Choice-based lettings approaches are now being attempted in areas where demand remains strong; this is a new development, largely brought about through central government encouragement (DETR 2000c) and pump-priming funding (see Box 8.1). Easy access schemes in low demand areas, by contrast, have been operated by local authorities such as Dundee, Mansfield, Rochdale and Salford for a number of years.

Easy access schemes aim to compete with private landlords by offering ready access housing at comparatively affordable rents. In advertising vacancies alongside privately owned properties, social landlords seek to widen their customer base to those who might assume that they would not qualify for public housing.

'*Community lettings*' policies are sometimes presented as a response to low demand, though they may be motivated by broader concerns of the type identified by David Page (Page 1993). 'Community lettings' take special account of the potential contribution an applicant can make to the 'community' (block or estate) where a vacancy is located (Griffiths *et al.* 1996). They seek to achieve 'community balance' or, at least, to avoid gross imbalance. It can be seen

Table 8.4 *Managerial responses to low demand implemented by social landlords in England 1996–9 (%)*

Broad category	Specific policy or action	LAs	RSLs
Pricing incentives	Decoration allowances for new tenants	74	57
Allocations and marketing	Relaxation of size-matching criteria (allowing 'extra bedrooms')	67	52
Allocations and marketing	Greater flexibility for local interpretation of lettings policies	59	48
Allocations and marketing	Easy access schemes	58	50
Community development etc.	Tenant participation initiatives	56	46
Community development etc.	Area-specific liaison arrangements with police/other agencies	56	45
Allocations and marketing	Marketing the estate or area/vacancies in the estate or area	50	47
Allocations and marketing	Relax normal offer limits	44	35
Community development etc.	Community development initiatives other than tenant participation	42	29
Community development etc.	Employment or training initiatives	25	13
More intensive management	Introduction of higher staff:stock ratio (i.e., smaller 'patches')	24	13
Allocations and marketing	Stock re-designation (e.g., re-classification of sheltered housing)	22	9
Allocations and marketing	Higher standards of void repair/redecoration	21	17
More intensive management	Introduction of resident caretakers	19	18
Allocations and marketing	Introduction of furnished tenancies scheme	18	11
Pricing incentives	Rent-free periods for new tenants	14	7
Allocations and marketing	Applicants required to provide references	14	16
Allocations and marketing	Community lettings policies	11	13
More intensive management	Introduction of concierges	8	3
Pricing incentives	Introduction of greater rent differentials related to area (un)popularity	1	10
No. of cases (low demand areas)		507	261

Note: percentage figures represent the proportion of identified low demand areas where each action was being/had recently been implemented in 1999.

Source: Postal survey carried out by Bramley, Pawson and Third (2000).

from Table 8.4, however, that schemes of this type are fairly rare among local authorities, though somewhat commoner among RSLs.

Marketing initiatives to promote low demand housing often involve advertising specific vacancies in association with easy access lettings schemes (see above and Box 8.1). Other marketing may attempt to re-brand particular areas – or social housing in a more general sense – through direct mail, bus or poster advertising. Landlords 're-branding the social housing product' may emphasize:

- availability of 24 hour repair services
- no deposit required
- decoration allowances for new tenants
- freedom from risk associated with a mortgage

However, whilst this kind of pitch is clearly aimed at (would-be) private sector tenants, most social landlords believe that their main competitors are others of their own kind.

The *re-designation* of housing as a response to low demand typically involves re-categorizing formerly sheltered housing so that it can be offered to applicants of any age. Less commonly, re-designation transforms unpopular high rise blocks into popular sheltered housing (though such solutions are likely to prove costly), or the earmarking of former mainstream housing for 'middle market' (i.e., unsubsidized) letting.

Introducing a *higher than normal standard for void repairs and/or redecoration* on low demand estates might involve higher decoration standards or the installation of new kitchen and bathroom fittings, garden clearance, fence repair and similar activities.

Pricing incentives to boost demand for unpopular homes are represented at both the top and the bottom of the ranking shown in Table 8.4. Whilst the offer of decoration allowances was very widespread in 1999, hardly any local authorities, and only a few RSLs, reduced rents to reflect (un)popularity. Under the government's national rent restructuring programme, of course, rents across the whole of social housing are intended to become more closely aligned with market variations by 2010 (DETR 2000c).

Managerial responses: more intensive housing management

'More intensive housing management' involves additional revenue expenditure for the landlord and includes initiatives such as:

- the introduction of resident caretakers
- the installation of concierges
- the application of higher staff : stock ratios

Table 8.3 shows that these are more common among local authorities than RSLs but this is because associations manage few of the larger blocks most physically suitable for the installation of concierges.

Moves to instate or reinstate *caretakers and concierges* on housing estates respond to concerns about crime and anti-social behaviour and are believed to be generally popular with tenants. This is consistent with the ethos of decentralized management promoted by the Priority Estates Project (PEP: see Power 1987) and by the Social Exclusion Unit's Policy Action Team (PAT5) on housing management (DETR 1999b). This has become known as 'on the spot housing management', a style of operation which typically includes:

- local presence
- proximity to tenants
- local offices
- surgeries
- local staff
- accessibility to users
- decentralized housing services
- concierge and warden services
- local lettings
- links to other providers and agencies
- tenant and resident involvement (Cole, Hickman and Reeve 2001)

Measures to combat anti-social behaviour (ASB) by social landlords often apply most particularly, though by no means solely, to areas affected by low demand. This problem has become increasingly high profile. As noted in Chapter 4, the effectiveness of landlords' usual sanctions (e.g., the threat of eviction) tends to be weakened in a slack housing market. In this sense, falling demand for housing may be a contributory factor in bringing this situation about.

Traditionally, the legal tools available to local authorities in combating ASB focused on social landlords' powers over their own tenants and access to their stock. The Housing Act 1996, for example, encouraged councils to vet housing applicants in terms of their previous tenancy record and to offer insecure Introductory Tenancies so that unruly action during the first year could lead to their swift removal.

Approaches emphasizing the deployment of landlord powers have, however, become less viable because in mixed tenure localities perpetrators may well be property owners or private tenants. Attention is now focused on remedies such as injunctions (or interdicts) and, since their creation by the Criminal Justice Act 1998, Anti-Social Behaviour Orders (ASBOs).

Managerial responses: community development and multi-agency working

Many low-demand areas could be described as concentrations of the socially excluded. For some commentators the alienation of residents underpins many of the difficulties. Creating or restoring some sense of ownership of the area among residents is thus seen as essential to 'turning the area round'. Given the multiplicity of organizations involved in low demand neighbourhoods, there is also a need for 'joined-up action' as well as joined-up thinking. Such work, classed under the 'community development and multi-agency working' heading, includes:

- tenant participation initiatives
- area-specific liaison arrangements with police/other agencies
- community development initiatives other than tenant participation
- employment or training initiatives

As far as *tenant participation* is concerned it has already been noted that all social landlords have, since the 1980s, been obliged to promote tenant involvement more generally (see p.156). Hence, whilst Table 8.4 suggests that 'promotion of tenant participation' has been a response to low demand attempted by local authorities on over half the estates affected, it may not be specifically related to market conditions.

Commonly, tenant participation accompanies a physical investment programme including in low demand areas. There is also an increasing tendency for *crime prevention* to serve as an effective focus for participation. In particular, the development of area-specific community safety plans (CSPs) can generate resident involvement and involve interagency liaison between the landlord and the local police. Some CSP recommendations may provide a further impetus to community involvement.

Generally, it is clear that the past few years has seen increasing communication between police forces and social landlords. Police forces often send representatives to residents' committee meetings set up in low demand areas, though these delegates are not always seen as making a useful contribution to the work of such groups (Bramley *et al.* 2001).

Managerial responses to booming demand

Whilst the need to cope with low and falling demand has dominated the agenda for many British social landlords since the mid-1990s, it is clear from Chapters 4 and 5 that some others have experienced quite different pressures. In London and many parts of southern England, with post-1995 house price inflation running well ahead of earnings, growing numbers of households have been priced out of the private sector. This has been reflected since 1997 in rising homelessness statistics and housing waiting list applications. And, as the scope for social sector tenants to enter home-ownership has dwindled, so the continuing contraction in the social housing stock in these areas has been compounded by falling tenancy turnover (see Figure 4.2).

Social landlords in high demand areas have responded in a variety of ways. Refinements to allocations policies, for example, have sought to:

- ration available supply in a more 'targeted' way
- make more efficient use of existing social housing stock
- preserve some access to social housing for low paid workers in 'essential services'

Policies of this kind typically run alongside strenuous efforts to boost the overall supply of 'affordable housing' through a variety of measures including, most importantly, the creative use of the land-use planning system (see Chapter 5).

Refining rationing

Traditional housing allocations policies evolved where demand always exceeded supply; hence the need to operate a system which rationed available vacancies in an orderly and systematic way. A simple date-order queue could, of course, serve such a purpose and the term 'waiting list' reflects this. However, partly stimulated by the Cullingworth Report (Council Housing Advisory Committee (CHAC) 1969), the dominant tendency during the past 30 years has been towards 'needs-based' systems. Such arrangements have been generally well-suited to the growing shortage of social housing seen in certain parts of the country over the past few years.

Social landlords have never been required to include formal means-testing for rehousing eligibility. Nevertheless, those landlords facing the greatest demand pressures have increasingly adopted such assessments. By 2000, nearly one-third of local authorities in London and the south of England were operating across-the-board eligibility restrictions in relation to the income and/or savings of housing applicants (Pawson *et al.* 2001), with thresholds set at a level considered to be the minimum required to access home-ownership for a property of an appropriate size. The means-testing principle also underpins the policies of many landlords who disqualify home-owners from qualifying for social housing.

Such means-testing is consistent with the 'welfare targeting' principle which has gained increasing hold across the public services since the 1980s. Recent official guidance (ODPM 2002a) has reinforced the Housing Green Paper's emphasis on the continuing obligation on social landlords to prioritize applicants according to housing need (DETR 2000c).

As discussed above (see pp.159–65 and Box 8.1), however, these Green Paper messages sat alongside strident calls for a more market-style approach to social housing allocations (i.e., choice-based lettings). It might, however, be supposed that this would be impractical in housing shortage areas and would unjustifiably raise expectations as predicted by Cowan (2001). In practice, the take-up of choice-based lettings systems has so far been at least as great among landlords operating in high demand areas as in other regions. Whilst the reconciliation of needs and consumer choice is certainly more challenging in such contexts, emerging evidence refutes the belief that CBL systems are irrelevant or unworkable here (Pollhammer and Grainger 2003).

Making more efficient use of the housing stock

Stock may be used more efficiently either by maximizing the proportion of the stock occupied by tenants at any one time or, alternatively, by achieving a 'best fit' between households and dwellings so that the available space is used in the most efficient way.

Squeezing down the vacancy or 'void' rate is a priority for all landlords, since empty homes represent lost rent. For local authorities operating in high demand areas, the opportunity cost of vacant homes also often includes additional expenditure on expensive temporary accommodation (such as bed and breakfast hotels) for homeless households. One contributor to 'excess' void rates is the rejection of tenancy offers by applicants, as rejected vacancies remain empty while they are successively matched to the queue of house seekers. To discourage the refusal of offers, landlords tend to impose restrictions on the numbers of offers allowed; if an applicant rejects their *n*th offer they are typically penalized by being 'suspended' from the waiting list for a set period (often six or 12 months). Whilst such sanctions were being applied by most English local authorities in 2000, the precise rules tended to be much stricter in the high demand regions of London and the south of England than elsewhere (Pawson *et al.* 2001).

Given central government's recently-voiced aspiration for 'less coercive' allocations policies (DETR 2000c), the use of such restrictions may fall in the future. In a sense, such restrictions are superfluous within the 'choice-based' approaches to lettings now spreading across Britain, since the refusal of tenancy offers should be minimal within a system where applicants select vacancies directly rather than having this done on their behalf by an official (Pawson *et al.* 2001). (These approaches are further discussed in Box 8.1, earlier.)

In seeking to achieve 'best fit' between households and dwellings, social landlords generally attempt to facilitate 'trading down' moves by 'underoccupying' tenants: that is, households living in homes larger than their 'needs' (typically older people whose adult children have left home). In 1998/9, for example, 12 per cent of tenants in the social rented sector in England were living in homes containing two or more bedrooms 'in excess of their needs' (Barelli and Pawson 2001). The housing case for minimizing 'underoccupation' of this kind is strongest where:

- there is an overall shortage of social housing
- the shortage of larger homes is particularly acute

The economic incentives to trade down in social housing are weak, first because rent differentials between properties of different sizes are relatively 'flat' (Walker and Marsh 1998) and, second, the 100 per cent subsidy offered by Housing Benefit means that those qualifying for full benefit derive no immediate financial advantage from moving to a cheaper home.

Since the early 1990s, central government has generally encouraged local authorities in England to actively encourage trading down moves by underoccupiers. With the post-1995 intensifying shortage of social housing in London and the South, however, policies to this end were at a particular premium and many landlords operating in these regions have developed underoccupation strategies (see Table 8.5). Typically, these involved three components:

- allocations policies and practices favouring underoccupiers
- cash incentive payments to underoccupiers trading down
- services provided to underoccupiers

Notwithstanding their widespread application, the effectiveness of cash incentive schemes in generating genuinely additional 'trading down' moves

Table 8.5 *Operation of policies to combat underoccupation by (landlord) LAs in England, 1997*

Region	% of local authorities operating/employing ...		
	Priority transfers for underoccupiers	Cash incentive payments to underoccupiers	Designated underoccupation officer
East Midlands	90	47	10
East	82	75	10
London	100	78	25
Merseyside	20	40	0
North East	61	26	0
North West	83	53	8
South East	98	71	20
South West	86	76	16
West Midlands	71	46	7
Yorks & Humberside	89	26	16
England	85	59	13

Source: Reproduced from Barelli and Pawson (2001), reproduced with the permission of The Stationery Office.

has no strong research basis (Barelli 1992; Barelli and Pawson 2001). A recent pilot project instigated by the Department for Work and Pensions which provided additional financial incentive for Housing Benefit claimants to trade down was also shown to have little if any effect (Pawson and Sinclair 2003).

Key worker allocations policies

The booming housing markets of London and south-east England during the late 1990s triggered concerns that employees responsible for 'vital services' were being increasingly priced out of private accommodation. The problem was highlighted by the housing Green Paper (DETR 2000c), which proposed a 'starter home' initiative to assist eligible households in accessing home-ownership in areas where it would otherwise be unaffordable (see Chapter 6).

Prioritizing key workers' access to social housing has a longer history, though the incidence of such policies was probably in decline until recently. By 2000, less than one-third of local authorities in England awarded any additional priority to key workers. In London and the South East, however, it was clear from an unpublished survey carried out in 2000 for DETR that this was reversing: half of all the social landlords in this part of the country which accorded key worker priority had adopted this policy since 1997. Nevertheless, given the demand pressures in London and the South East, the practical impact of policies facilitating key worker access to social housing is likely to remain fairly marginal. In quantitative terms, the provision of key worker housing through the starter home initiative and the land-use planning system (Chapter 5) will prove more significant.

Conclusion

As local authorities and RSLs have struggled to respond to the rapidly changing housing market conditions of recent years, they have faced pressures of many other kinds. In the main, these have been top-down initiatives, transmitted through funding and regulatory systems such as Best Value. Housing associations, exposed to private sector risk, also need to reassure their financial backers that their investments are sound and that changes in the business environment do not threaten organizational viability.

While the rather crude tendering framework of HMCCT has been replaced by the more flexible Best Value regime, central government's emphasis on the benefits of competition remains strong. Moreover, in its all-encompassing scope, as well as in its stress on customer and stakeholder involvement, BV presents a major challenge for social landlords just as it does for other local authority services within its remit. Housing associations, who were previously exempt from CCT, have faced a particularly steep learning curve. Local authorities, having been brought within a formal regulatory and inspection regime only since 2000 (and 2003 in Scotland), are also confronted by a taxing challenge.

However, whilst they involve market-style elements, regimes such as HMCCT, BV and 'choice-based lettings' are not markets in the true sense. Landlords compete for public resources and for the right to manage their housing directly; housing applicants may be afforded greater opportunities for trading off their rehousing priorities. Nevertheless, such competition among landlords is highly structured and regulated and involves direct competition for customers only in relatively unusual circumstances. And even the purest 'Delft-style' lettings systems do not make it possible for housing applicants to outbid one another financially. As Pearl (1997) points out, such 'markets' tend to be provider- rather than consumer-led. And, given their highly limited scope for 'shopping around', the appropriateness of the term 'customer' to describe housing applicants or tenants is somewhat debatable. In reality, the 'competitive' systems described here at best create quasi-markets (Bramley 1993d; Le Grand and Bartlett 1993).

The recent pace and extent of change in the external environment has forced social landlords to adapt their strategies, structures and activities in sometimes quite radical ways. Managerial responses to low demand have, in some cases, turned on their head long-established management orthodoxies developed in an era of seemingly endless housing shortage. Landlords operating in weak housing markets have found themselves needing to adopt more consumerist perspectives to avoid more drastic responses such as large-scale demolition, or even (in the case of RSLs) potential bankruptcy. Top-down regulatory pressures, rather than self-interest, have ensured that those working in higher demand areas have also had to confront the challenge of re-fashioning themselves in a less bureaucratic mould.

Further reading

More detailed discussion of the application of Best Value to the activities of social landlords is explored in detail by Mullins (1999), who reports survey evidence on RSLs in England. Mullins and Riseborough (2000) adopt a more longitudinal perspective on the changing managerial approaches and organizational structures being developed by English RSLs in the late 1990s. The nature of the BVH regime and its likely longer-term impact is discussed by Vincent-Jones (2001). Walker (2001) draws together evidence from a variety of sources on the spread of NPM approaches within social housing. Hood, James and Scott (2001) provide background on the broader evolving framework of regulation of public services following the 1998 Modernising Government White Paper.

The changing expectations on social landlords and the impact of their changing roles on staff activities are considered by Furbey, Reid and Cole (2001), who reflect on the implications of these changes for housing as a profession.

More in-depth analysis of the impact of low demand on social landlords, together with the national policy implications of the phenomenon, can be found in Cole, Kane and Robinson (1999), Bramley, Pawson and Third (2000) and Bramley and Pawson (2002). Scott *et al.* (2001b) look at the issue in the Scottish context. Measures to promote better use of the social housing stock in high demand areas through reducing underoccupation are discussed in detail in Barelli and Pawson (2001).

9

The Challenge of Regeneration

The role and significance of 'regeneration' programmes

Throughout the UK housing policy is increasingly seen as subordinate to a regeneration agenda. This is reflected in the substantial proportion of public housing investment earmarked for regeneration projects, and in the influential role of regeneration objectives on the activities of housing organizations. Key messages contained in regeneration policy statements such as the Social Exclusion Unit's *National Strategy for Neighbourhood Renewal* (SEU 2000) have assumed central importance in the activities of many social landlords, as well as shaping local authority housing-related activity in the land-use planning field.

The term 'regeneration' has, of course, come to be used in increasingly flexible ways. At its most basic level, it implies the recovery or renewal of lost vitality, whether physical or social. The impact of 'community regeneration' objectives on the modern conception of 'housing management' has been alluded to in Chapter 8. More broadly, the adoption of increasingly all-embracing definitions of 'regeneration' during the 1990s is an important theme of this chapter.

The significance of the 'regeneration' concept for housing organizations derives partly from the increasing need to tackle neighbourhood decline in many parts of the country, which is often linked with falling demand for housing, and especially social housing. As discussed in Chapter 4, this scenario has in recent years become particularly common in parts of the Midlands and northern England, west central Scotland and South Wales. Where there is a deeply entrenched dynamic of declining population it may be that the kinds of managerial solution discussed in Chapter 8 are insufficient. Reversing, or at least managing, decline in these sorts of circumstances requires more fundamental (and probably more expensive) interventions in local housing systems. Such interventions may also be required in localities experiencing acute physical, social or reputational problems in spite of relatively favourable regional economic or housing market area contexts. This would apply, for example, to many large council estates in cities such as London, Bristol or Leeds, particularly those of system-built or other non-traditional construction.

Nevertheless, whilst regeneration practitioners may subscribe to common principles irrespective of the local conditions they face, the precise nature of the appropriate intervention in any locality will, of course, depend in part on local housing market conditions. In particular, this will have implications for the extent to which any major (re)investment in the physical fabric of an area incorporates a net reduction in overall housing stock or a restructuring of housing tenure (see pp.195–201).

Increased interest in broad-based approaches to neighbourhood regeneration since the early 1990s also reflects concerns that large-scale investment in the physical upgrading of existing public sector housing estates in the 1970s and 1980s has failed the test of sustainability. This is clear in that certain localities have been subject to repeated rounds of 'special programme' intervention (Carley and Kirk 1998). In part, at least, this is often seen as a result of overemphasis on 'housing renewal'. In value for money terms alone there is clearly a need to develop area improvement strategies which can bring more pervasive benefits in relation to both the physical fabric and the socio-economic character (e.g., in terms of benefit dependency, employment rates) of the areas concerned. As the established consensus now has it, only by tackling a neighbourhood's problems in a comprehensive way is there a chance that investment will bring lasting improvements. Herein lie some of the challenges of regeneration (see Box 8.1).

Urban regeneration at the turn of the millennium has been made more challenging by the decentralizing dynamic of population and economic activity affecting cities throughout Britain. One important facet of this 'urban exodus' has been the shift of employment from urban to out-of-town and rural locations. During the decade to 1991, for example, English metropolitan districts involving 'principal cities' experienced a jobs contraction of 8.5 per cent. 'Resort and retirement' districts, on the other hand, saw an increase of 9.5 per cent, whilst 'remote, largely rural' districts recorded expansion of 13.3 per cent (Breheny 1999). Similarly, in the retail sector one-third of national sales shifted from town centres to suburban and urban fringe locations in the 15 years to 1998 (Carley and Kirk 1998). Underlying these changes has been the broader tendency for income polarization and growing poverty (see pp.32–3).

In common with preceding chapters, this one focuses on the ways that housing and regeneration practice are responding to change; in particular, changes resulting from market patterns, from changing official thinking on regeneration and from changing expectations among residents and other stakeholders as to their involvement in policymaking. In discussing these issues we draw on a range of practical examples, some from our own research and some from elsewhere.

The evolution of urban regeneration policy and the role of housing

The concept of area-based initiatives

Within British urban policy, area-based initiatives (ABIs) are a long-established approach to the targeting of public resources to tackle deprivation. In the housing field, today's ABI programmes are descended from the slum clearance initiatives of the interwar and immediate postwar years. These programmes tended to involve the demolition of densely built-up, privately owned inner-city terraces and multi-occupied blocks, with displaced populations being rehoused both locally and remotely (e.g., in suburban or New Town locations).

The current generation of ABI-style housing programmes, however, dates from the creation of General Improvement Areas (GIAs) under the Housing Act 1969 (Carley and Kirk 1998). GIAs were distinguished from their slum clearance predecessors not only by a preference for rehabilitation rather than redevelopment, but also by their emphasis on addressing the problems of run-down areas within those areas themselves (rather than through the remote rehousing of displaced households). The Housing Action Area (HAA) programme initiated by the Housing Act 1974 confirmed the official preference for area-based approaches and resulted in the channelling of substantial public funds into housing renewal in defined localities (Bailey and Robertson 1996). Much of this involved the purchase and rehabilitation of run-down privately owned housing by housing associations, a role from which associations have more recently tended to withdraw.

Part of the rationale for ABIs is that, both historically and currently, geographical concentrations of poverty and poor housing have been all too obvious (though most poor people do not live in poor areas: see Glennerster *et al.* 1999). G.R. Smith (1999, p.4) lists a number of other arguments in support of area-based intervention.

1   Problems overlap in particular localities and they are often made worse when they co-exist; the sheer scale of the difficulties means that locally-targeted action is needed.
2   Growing polarization between deprived and more affluent areas calls for special action for people living in deprived areas.
3   Where problems are geographically concentrated, a greater number of deprived people are captured if resources are geographically targeted than if they are spread more evenly.
4   Focusing activity on small areas within tight boundaries can, potentially, make a greater impact than if resources are dissipated.
5   An effective 'bottom-up' approach underpinned by partnership working is more easily achieved through area-based policies than through national mainstream programmes.
6   Locally-focused programmes may boost community confidence and capacity to participate.
7   Successful area-based programmes may act as pilots and ultimately lead to changes in the delivery of mainstream policies.

The locally specific focus of urban policy has often tended to place housing – and the improvement of housing – in a central role. Before discussing

---

Box 9.1   *The multi-faceted problems of run-down neighbourhoods*

The multi-faceted problems faced by residents of declining neighbourhoods were well illustrated by Power and Mumford's study of inner-city Manchester and Newcastle (Power and Mumford 1999). A prolonged contraction of local employment (particularly manufacturing jobs) had contributed to very high rates of poverty and joblessness (see table below), of which a large proportion was of a hard core, long-term nature. The knock-on consequences of falling property values in these areas included rapid population turnover and dwelling abandonment, with reactive local authority (and housing association) demolition proposals seen by the authors as tending to undermine confidence among property owners and other residents and consequently 'destabilizing communities'.

Whilst the design and condition of much of the local housing stock in the study areas was seen as not inherently problematic, the 'disorderly neighbourhood environment' was seen as a factor undermining housing demand.

In a study of people defined as 'vulnerable to social exclusion' on three housing estates, Page (2000, p.1) found that, whilst they formed only a minority of local residents, 'the norms and values of this group defined an estate culture which dominated the common areas of each estate, and coloured its reputation in the neighbourhood'. Overwhelmingly the most significant problem identified by local residents was the anti-social behaviour of young people (e.g., involving vandalism and drug abuse). The young people themselves described an *estate culture* which:

- tolerated crime, drugs and anti-social behaviour
- accepted low personal achievement and educational attainment
- had low aspirations and expectations
- held estate norms that were different from mainstream society
- exerted strong pressure from peers to conform to them

The young unemployed people interviewed in Page's study tended to adopt a rather ambivalent attitude towards employment, with few appreciating its potential benefits in terms of personal independence, self-esteem and social contact. Until members of this group can be re-engaged with wider society, the outlook for their neighbourhoods is bleak.

$\longrightarrow$

---

this further it ought to be acknowledged that the ABI approach is not without its critics. It is, for example, argued that 'concentrating resources on a small number of neighbourhoods is both administratively and politically convenient, masking the widespread nature of the deprivation within society and allowing us to feel that the problem is being dealt with', and that such approaches 'deflect our attention from ... the causes of ... problems and their potential solutions as lying outside the deprived areas' (Oatley 2000, p.89). Indeed, there is a view that an area-based approach 'only further stigmatises these places as "problem areas" to be set apart from the rest of society [and] fosters the idea of a "culture of poverty" and an "urban underclass" who are responsible for the conditions they are surrounded by' (Chatterton and Bradley 2000, p.100).

→

Characteristics of city and neighbourhood population (%)

Indicator	Nationally	Manchester	Newcastle	Neighbourhoods			
				M1	M2	N3	N4
Deprived working households	18	34	30	41	41	39	46
Those of working age without work nor studying, 1991	24	37	31	46	48	49	50
Long-term unemployed (of all unemployed)	27	39	34	40	38	45	42
Male manual employees, 1991 (% of all male employees)	49	56	50	73	70	76	82

Note: M1 and M2 – Manchester neighbourhoods N3 and N4 – Newcastle neighbourhoods.

Source: Reproduced by permission of the Joseph Rowntree Foundation from *The Slow Death of Great Cities? Urban Abandonment or Urban Rennaissance* by Anne Power and Katherine Mumford, published 1999 by the Joseph Rowntree Foundation.

Whatever the merits of these arguments, it is clear from the official emphasis placed on recent Social Exclusion Unit reports (SEU 1998, 2000) that 'area-based' or 'neighbourhood' explanations of deprivation have gained new momentum under New Labour (Chatterton and Bradley 2000, p.98).

The role of housing in area-based approaches to regeneration

Housing investment has formed a key element within a succession of ABI programmes implemented since 1988 (see Table 9.1). With hindsight, however, many of these programmes are now regarded as having been flawed by an overemphasis on remedying the physical condition of the housing stock at the expense of specific measures aimed at social, economic or community revival.

This view is encapsulated in Tony Blair's introduction to the Social Exclusion Unit's National Strategy for Neighbourhood Renewal report where he writes: 'Often huge sums have been spent on repairing buildings and giving

estates a new coat of paint, but without the matching investment in skills, education and opportunities for the people who live there' (SEU 2000, p.7). This
is not a new theme. By the early 1990s it was already clear that 'fixing up
housing', the primary aim of most area regeneration projects in the 1970s and
early 1980s, had been supplanted by an aspiration to achieve area or neighbourhood regeneration, and that contemporary initiatives were inspired by an
interest in wider urban policy objectives (McGregor and MacLennan 1992).

Official recognition of the need for 'comprehensive' solutions to urban
deprivation can, in fact, be traced back as far as the mid-1970s: for example,
in the form of the Community Development Projects (CDPs) set up in a number of inner-city areas at this time. However, these were largely experimental
in nature. Only since the late 1980s have more mainstream area-based regeneration programmes explicitly rejected the assumption that renewal of physical infrastructure would bring about an automatic improvement in social,
economic and health indicators. Instead, there has been an attempt to target
intervention on these issues directly. In an early example, the Scottish Office's
New Life Partnerships (NLPs) channelled resources into employment, training and community development as well as housing. Even so, housing
absorbed two-thirds of the total NLP expenditure: £321 million as compared
with £55 million on enterprise, employment and training (Cambridge Policy
Consultants 1999). Similarly, the Housing Action Trust and Estate Action programmes in England paid some attention to community capacity building and
to social, economic and environmental initiatives. As in the NLP case, however, these programmes remained largely focused on the need for physical
upgrading (and/or replacement) of housing stock.

With the New Life Partnerships having been wound up, the Scottish
Executive's most recent area-based regeneration programmes have included
the 40-plus Social Inclusion Partnerships (SIPs). This initiative, launched in
1996 under the title Priority Partnership Areas (PPAs), derives its main funding from the spatial concentration of Urban Programme (UP) resources. As
Table 9.1 illustrates, its core activities reflected pre-existing urban programme
priorities, particularly community development, training and health projects.

SIPs were intended to promote multi-agency partnership approaches to the
regeneration of designated areas. Through this means it was hoped that partner agencies would 'bend main programmes' so that non-UP resources would
also be concentrated within PPAs. This is powerfully reflected in the fact that
Scottish Homes, the (then) national housing agency for Scotland, planned to
direct 44 per cent of its total 2001/2 investment budget to projects within SIP
areas (Scottish Homes 2001), a set of areas encompassing only a fraction of
Scotland's population. The extent to which local authorities 'bend' mainstream expenditure in this way is, however, unknown.

In England, the replacement of Estate Action by the Single Regeneration
Budget (SRB) in the mid-1990s signalled a move away from a housing-led
approach. And whilst the SRB was, for a few years, complemented by the
housing-focused Estate Regeneration Challenge Fund, or ERCF (see Table 9.1
and pp.195–201), this was wound up in 1999.

Table 9.1 *Main post-1988 housing-related area regeneration programmes in England and Scotland*

Programme	Dates[a]	Public investment (£m)[b]	Brief details
England			
Housing Action Trusts	1988–92	1,091	Involved ownership transfer of large council housing estates identified by central government to facilitate (mainly publicly funded) housing refurbishment.
Estate Action	1986–95	3,002	Focus on large council estates with emphasis on tenure diversification and tenant involvement.
City Challenge	1991–5	546	Mainly concerned with economic regeneration across defined neighbourhoods but including some housing investment funding.
Single Regeneration Budget	1994–2000	c.5,500	Successor to a range of predecessor programmes including Estate Action but largely focused on social and economic regeneration rather than housing renewal.
Estates Renewal Challenge Fund	1996–9	488	Explicitly a housing programme to facilitate ownership transfer of council estates with highly negative values through debt write-off. Limited focus on wider regeneration objectives.
New Deal for Communities	1999–	c.2,000	Designed as a more bottom-up approach to regeneration, with local programmes and budgets governed by Boards constituted from the local community. Primary focus on social and economic rather than housing regeneration.
Housing Market Renewal Package	2003–	500	Programme intended to help underpin and restructure housing markets seen as 'vulnerable' to low demand, especially across the Midlands and the north of England.
Scotland			
New Life Partnerships	1988–95	321	Programme focused on four large local authority estates designated by central government. Partnership ethic informed constitution of local Boards under civil service leadership. Aspiration for a comprehensive rather than housing-dominated approach.
Smaller Urban Renewal Initiatives	1991–6	155	Explicitly housing-led programme co-ordinated by Scottish Homes and targeted largely on council housing estates in smaller towns and cities. Key aim of facilitating tenure diversification.

Table 9.1   *Continued*

Programme	Dates[a]	Public investment (£m)[b]	Brief details
Social Inclusion Partnerships	1999–	315	Successor to Urban Programme/Priority Partnership Areas with an emphasis on community development, social and economic regeneration led by local authorities in partnership with community groups. Primarily revenue rather than capital expenditure.
New Housing Partnerships	1998–	183	Housing-led programme mainly aimed at facilitating local authority stock transfer (partly through the relief of housing debt on negative value stock).

[a] dates spanning period when new funds approved under specified programme
[b] designated public expenditure (cash figures) up until 2003/4 (except New Housing Partnerships figure which relates to the period to 2002).
Sources: Data from Wilcox (2002); ODPM, Scottish Executive, Communities Scotland.

Most recently, the New Deal for Communities (NDC) has attempted to operationalize a substantially 'bottom-up', community-centred approach to regeneration. In the government's own terms, the NDC programme's key ingredients are:

- community involvement and ownership
- joined-up thinking and solutions (action based on evidence about 'what works')
- long-term commitment to deliver real change, with communities at the heart of this, in partnership with key agencies

Under the programme, partnerships have been set up in 39 'clearly defined neighbourhoods' of fewer than 4,000 households, a scale intended to be 'small enough to put the community at the heart of the renewal process'. NDC funds totalling £35–60 million per area are channelled through these partnerships rather than through local authorities as is more conventional (e.g., under the Estate Action, SRB and ERCF programmes). NDC Partnership Boards are elected by local residents.

Like its SIP counterpart, NDC is explicitly not a housing-led programme. Nevertheless, NDCs may choose to focus some of their resources on housing investment. In addition, NDC and SIP areas benefit from the 'bending of main programmes' in terms of the distribution of housing association invest-ment by the Housing Corporation and Communities Scotland. This ambition, though widely shared among post-1988 regeneration programmes, is not always achieved. The experience of Scotland's SURIs (Smaller Urban Renewal Initiatives) is symptomatic. Here, local authorities signally failed to 'bend' their mainstream housing investment as hoped. In part, at least, this can be traced to the 'top-down' nature of the SURI approach, with the leading role assigned to Scottish Homes rather than to councils and area designations being determined centrally rather than locally. Local authorities, therefore, felt little ownership of the programme and, indeed, may have wanted to correct a perceived imbalance in spending (Pawson *et al.* 1998).

Whilst there are strong arguments underpinning the swing towards a more comprehensive rather than a housing-led approach to regeneration, there is a view that the pendulum has now swung too far. MacLennan, for example, has described as 'throwing the baby out with the bath water' the view that 'as a nation, because we have wasted so much public capital on poor housing systems... housing investment and systems have, at best, minor roles to play in remaking [some] neighbourhoods' (MacLennan 2000, p.14).

Partnership working

'... only a joined-up response will be effective in tackling the problems of deprived neighbourhoods'. (Social Exclusion Unit, Policy Action Team 17, DETR 2000a, p.7)

Alongside the generally growing emphasis on 'holistic' approaches to area-based regeneration there has developed a strong consensus in favour of 'partnership working'. A particular aspect of this is the stress on community participation, an issue further discussed below (see pp.201–3).

Under challenge-funded programmes such as Estate Action and Scotland's Social Inclusion Partnerships, credible commitment to the partnership principle was a key criterion in the selection of successful bids. In drawing up plans in keeping with this principle, therefore, local authorities and other stakeholders have been – in part, at least – responding to a 'top-down' national policy imperative. Until 1997 or thereabouts, it can be argued that this was partly motivated by a political aspiration to limit the role of local government in controlling the funds distributed through regeneration programmes and a general view that the private sector 'does things better'.

There is, however, a broader body of thinking which underpins the importance of a partnership approach in this context. Part of the reasoning here is that 'Whilst the problems of deprived neighbourhoods and their residents are interconnected, the public sector is organised on a fragmented and usually functional basis ... different local authority departments ... [tend to operate] as "silos" – long vertical towers delivering services independently of one another' (DETR 2000a, p.21). Only through genuine cross-department and cross-disciplinary collaboration, it is argued, can an area's problems be tackled in a sufficiently holistic way.

An additional dimension is the involvement of local business interests, again seen as important in ensuring broad-based local commitment to the success of a regeneration strategy. This may be achieved in practice through the engagement of an existing organization such as the local Chamber of Commerce.

Implementing area regeneration in a true spirit of 'partnership' is not, however, easy. As Carley *et al.* (2000) point out, for example, there is a tension between the partnership principle of 'inclusiveness' and the need for efficient, streamlined decision-making. Partnership boards which are overambitious in encompassing the diversity of local stakeholders risk becoming completely unwieldy. According appropriate weight to the views of partnership members is also a frequently problematic area. In particular, there is often a tendency for real power to reside with the organization 'bringing most to the table' in terms of resources. In the case of Scotland's SURI programme, for example, what were presented as partnerships were in practice seen by most of the participants as creations of Scottish Homes, within which Scottish Homes – as the main funder – held most of the real power. Perhaps partly because most stakeholders doubted the reality of the SURI partnerships there was a tendency for 'partner' bodies to be represented by staff of insufficient seniority so that they were unable to commit their organizations to decisions proposed. This only further weakened genuine partnership operation (Pawson *et al.* 1998).

Sustainable regeneration

The growing consensus in favour of 'comprehensive' rather than 'housing-led' approaches to area regeneration has been informed partly by the recognition that some areas subject to often expensive housing renewal in the 1970s and 1980s failed to shake off a stigmatized image or otherwise subsequently 'slipped back' into physical and/or social decay. Avoiding the repetition of such 'unsustainable' regeneration is seen as an overwhelmingly important objective, not least in terms of securing value for money.

'Sustainable regeneration' is, of course, a frequently invoked but rarely defined phrase. Drawing on a range of other work, Fordham (2002) summarized the varied conceptions implicit in the use of the term into three broad categories:

- sustainability in a quasi-ecological sense (e.g., areas as 'stable and self-generating environments': Stewart and Taylor 1995)
- sustainability as permanence or durability (e.g., 'housing which enjoys a continued healthy demand for letting throughout its projected lifetime': Housing Corporation 1998)
- no longer requiring special funding

Partly based on these insights, Fordham (2002) categorized individual estates in terms of their 'sustainability' according to a range of indicators:

- durability of physical improvements
- stability of population (e.g., as measured through turnover)
- popularity among actual and prospective tenants (as indicated by voids, waiting lists and offer acceptance rates)
- 'manageability' from the landlords' perspective

Carley and Kirk (1998) identify the origins of the 'sustainable regeneration' concept within the 'sustainable development' philosophy which has emerged mainly as a response to environmental concerns (see Chapter 5). The two key pillars of this philosophy are the potential for beneficial interaction of economy, environment and social development, and the possibility of inter-generational equity: 'ensuring that whatever we do now leaves future generations better off' (Carley and Kirk 1998, p.3). Following from this, sustainable urban regeneration involves (pp.4–5):

- robust long-term solutions of benefit to the next generation whilst being cost-effective for the current generation
- steady strategic processes of urban development which can weather unforeseen intervening variables such as global economic change
- the generation of positive reinforcement in development or investment sectors
- activities facilitating the physical, economic and social re-integration of hitherto disadvantaged communities

This last point hints at the need for the re-connection of areas disconnected from mainstream society (i.e., subject to social exclusion). This issue is further discussed below (see pp.195–201).

Learning from experience

Again, partly inspired by the view that regeneration initiatives have often 'repeated the mistakes of previous programmes', the government has become increasingly committed to active 'learning from experience'. This is exemplified by the initial designation of 'pathfinder' projects under both the New Deal for Communities and the Housing Market Renewal programme (see below), and by official encouragement for experimentation and innovation by the bodies involved. Likewise, evaluation studies are being set up to shadow the implementation of these programmes as they take shape, rather than to assess their impact after the event. In this way, it is hoped that 'early lessons' can be drawn and that these can inform the design of the subject programmes themselves.

Housing renewal within wider urban strategies

The role of housing within urban regeneration in the new millennium needs to be seen in the context of contemporary urban policy thinking more broadly. This has been strongly influenced by the 'urban intensification' philosophy advocated by Lord Rogers through his Urban Task Force report (Urban Task Force 1999) and the subsequent Urban White Paper (the arguments have already been alluded to in Chapter 5). The Task Force report argued that 'increasing the intensity of activities and people within an area is central to the idea of creating sustainable neighbourhoods' (1999, p.60). 'Sustainability' is used here to refer to both environmental and social objectives, in particular the aspiration to ensure the viability of public transport and other local services through discouraging low-density sprawl. Implicit here is a preference for 'brownfield' redevelopment over construction on 'greenfield' sites. As Chapter 5 explains, recent planning guidance has strengthened the emphasis of official policy accordingly.

In terms of the inner-city areas containing 'obsolete' (mainly private sector) housing described in Chapter 4, the Urban Task Force vision would see 'renaissance' coming about through clearance and high density (possibly mixed-use) redevelopment. As is the case for any planning policy, however, it will be difficult to sustain such an approach if it is inconsistent with existing market trends. Proponents of the Urban Task Force philosophy can point to the strong revival of interest in city-centre living which has boosted central populations in places such as Manchester, Leeds, Liverpool and Glasgow since the early 1990s. Much of this has been characterized by high quality, 'up-market' flatted developments, often in waterfront locations and sometimes involving the conversion of disused warehousing. The saleability of such housing has been enhanced by the successful promotion of loft living as a fashionable lifestyle choice, especially for young childless professional adults.

It is, nevertheless, questionable whether the 'urban intensification' model represents a realistic way forward for the non-central inner areas which surround some of these booming city quarters. In regions where economic performance is generally weak it may be impossible to maintain existing population levels in such areas, particularly in the face of fairly deeply embedded consumer preferences for lower density (car dependent) living. The evidence is that neighbourhood depopulation in parts of inner Manchester and Liverpool, for example, is partly attributable to resident dissatisfaction with cramped Victorian terraced housing and aspirations for houses with private gardens and off-street parking (Bramley, Pawson and Third 2000). In practice, it may be possible to retain population in these areas only through 'thinning out' the existing housing stock – focusing on less popular dwelling types in poor condition – and redeveloping at *lower* densities.

Regardless of which of these approaches is adopted, there will be an unavoidable need to confront the question of how obsolete and unwanted stock is to be decommissioned. The fact that much of the Victorian housing stock in the kinds of areas mentioned above is in private ownership raises particular difficulties for any clearance programme (the rather distinct issues connected with demolition of council housing are discussed below: see pp.201–3). The Compulsory Purchase Order (CPO) procedures needed to acquire dwellings scheduled for clearance are complex and time-consuming. Conversely, the problems in some low demand areas can escalate rapidly. A review by (the then) DETR in 2000 concluded that, perhaps because of a lack of experience in using them, local authorities had a poor understanding of how to make CPOs work. Particular difficulties arise when housing – though unwanted – is not, in fact, physically unfit for human habitation from a technical viewpoint. And there is, in any case, a new nervousness about the implications of the Human Rights Act for CPO powers and other aspects of planning.

Perhaps more importantly, clearance programmes covering private sector housing are inherently expensive. Existing owner-occupiers, in particular, need to be compensated financially to enable them to move to another home without involving capital loss or additional outlay. Market values for compensation therefore often look suspiciously higher than market values actually achieved in other sales (through auctions or in the local pub). And relocation grants as well as Home Loss and Disturbance payments also need to be factored into the cost. Experimental schemes for facilitating such decanting through the constructive involvement of mortgage lenders are as yet in their infancy.

In order to meet the kinds of challenges discussed here, the government has recently launched its Housing Market Renewal (HMR) pathfinder initiative (see Table 9.1). The programme is in part a response to research focusing on large conurbations across the Midlands and the north of England and which identified substantial areas as vulnerable to housing market collapse (Nevin *et al.* 2001). Unlike most of its predecessor programmes (see Table 9.1), the HMR initiative is focused on large areas, sometimes including entire conurbations, and generally involving two or more local authorities as well as other partner agencies. The aim is to encourage the formation of housing market renewal partnerships which will develop strategic responses to low demand by:

- bringing together key stakeholders
- informing investment priorities
- testing out new and innovative approaches (ODPM, *Housing Signpost*, November 2002)

Whilst the HMR partnerships are to be established at sub-regional level, it can be anticipated that much of the action agreed by the partners (e.g., CPO and demolition) will bear on well-defined localities. In this way, it is argued, the programme has the capacity to make the link between the government's neighbourhood and regional strategies (Nevin and Battle 2002).

The impact of population change on regeneration outcomes

Intrinsic to the current enthusiasm for evidence-based policy (as discussed earlier) is an enhanced commitment to evaluating regeneration investment outcomes. Such assessments are, however, complicated by the difficulty of measuring 'displacement' and 'spillover' effects. Displacement effects might include, for example, a local reduction in crime rates through 'target hardening', but this might simply shift criminal activity into a neighbouring area. Displacement and spillover often result from population change. This might involve, for instance, an apparent reduction in local unemployment achieved purely by replacing social housing with privately owned homes, with former social sector residents (with a relatively high propensity for unemployment) 'displaced' outside the neighbourhood.

More problematic for those seeking to revive specific localities is where the beneficiaries of area-based training and/or employment initiatives may move away from the neighbourhood as a result of being 'reconnected' with the labour market. In principle, therefore, selective outmigration can frustrate the positive impact of regeneration investment focused on a particular locality.

MacLennan (2000, p.17) noted that '[over] the last five years... neighbourhood abandonment has risen as employment of city residents has grown... it may be that less affluent city workers, on getting back to work, are simply rejecting the tenure and housing quality offers available in the social rental neighbourhoods they inhabited whilst unemployed'. It should, however, be acknowledged that whilst some regeneration evaluations (e.g., Kintrea *et al.* 1995; Cambridge Policy Consultants 1999) have speculated about the impact of selective outmigration as discussed above, little conclusive research evidence has been published to demonstrate its significance.

Role of social housing allocation systems

Another key component in the 'selective outmigration' hypothesis as described above is the filtering effect of social housing allocations systems. In general, it can be assumed that these systems tend to replace (possibly 'upwardly mobile') households moving out of regeneration areas with new tenants who are highly disadvantaged in an economic and/or social sense. In 2001/2, for example, less than 30 per cent of households entering the RSL sector from outside social housing contained anyone in full-time employment. For every household leaving a social rented tenancy, therefore, there is an odds-on chance that they will be replaced by a workless household. This process was the explanation put forward in the New Life Partnership evaluations for the observation that the large numbers of local residents trained and/or placed in employment did not seem to have fed through into improved local employment profiles (McGregor *et al.* 1995).

This brings us to the role of social housing management policies in urban regeneration, and in particular the effect of allocations policies. Partly because of the impact of the Right to Buy, we have seen the nature of social housing change markedly since 1980 (see Chapter 2). Social housing has become increasingly equated with welfare housing (housing of last resort for those with no other option). As demonstrated by Figure 4.4, the age structure of the sector has become increasingly dominated by the old and the young: the middle aged groups have been dramatically eroded not only by the Right to Buy, but also through the growing tendency of younger tenants buy on the open market or even switch into private renting (Pawson and Bramley 2000).

The allocation policies and practices adopted by particular landlords may accentuate or moderate the tendency for new tenants rehoused in a particular area to contribute to existing social and/or demographic imbalances. Research in the 1980s (e.g., Clapham and Kintrea 1986; Henderson and Karn 1987) informed the still-widely held view that the systems used by social landlords tend to filter the most deprived and/or vulnerable people into the least desirable areas (though a recent study of housing association lettings in England found no clear evidence of this: see Pawson and Mullins 2003).

Local authorities and housing associations are increasingly aware of the impact of allocations policies on the social characteristics of areas. As Chapter 8 describes more fully, some have experimented with novel methods in an attempt to use allocations policies to strengthen rather than undermine local communities affected by low demand.

Reshaping and restructuring public housing estates

The problems of social rented estates affected by serious disrepair in combination with low demand for housing are unlikely to be amenable to the kinds of 'managerial responses' to housing market weakness described in Chapter 8. Only through more fundamental 'structural' responses is there a chance that such difficulties may be adequately addressed. As shown in Table 8.2, structural responses to low demand can be seen as encompassing:

- change of ownership (tenure diversification)
- demolition and redevelopment

Tenure diversification

By comparison with the limited scope for engineering social mix through allocations policies, altering the tenure mix of an area holds out greater prospects for changing the neighbourhood's profile. In principle, the diversification of tenure can involve simply reducing the common dominance of local authority renting in an area. This could mean simply increasing the share of one type of social landlord (RSL) at the expense of another.

Tenure diversification is well established as a key element of official policy on the regeneration of local authority estates (although it has not only been advocated within this context). It formed a key objective of both the Estate Action and New Life Partnerships programmes (see Table 9.1) and hence the increased share of non-local authority housing achieved during the Wester Hailes New Life Partnership project – up from 5 per cent to 36 per cent – was regarded as a major achievement in itself (Cambridge Policy Consultants 1999). Similarly, in Niddrie House/Niddrie Marischal, another Edinburgh estate subject to major regeneration investment during the 1980s and 1990s, the reduced share of local authority stock from 95 per cent in 1981 to only one-third by 1998 was also seen as a substantial feat (Pawson, Kirk and McIntosh 2000).

However, whilst diversifying tenure has remained an important policy objective for some time, the emphasis of the policy has changed. In the early 1990s, the reduction in local authority stockholding was seen as desirable in itself. One argument was that the problems of such estates were partly a product of 'monopoly landlordism' and that shifting stock from local authorities to housing associations would, in some way, encourage 'healthy competition'. The extent to which housing applicants generally see social landlords as competing for their custom, however, is open to question. A second argument in favour of replacing local authority with housing association ownership relates to governance. Through the creation of community-based housing associations (CBHAs), it is contended that local residents can be empowered and a stronger sense of local policy ownership can be engendered (Kintrea and Clapham 2000). Community regeneration '[will] only work if the community itself [is] in the driving seat' (Perry 2002, p.34). A third, more practical, consideration is that the 'independent' status of housing associations allows them to access private finance secured against the value of stockholdings so that they can fund substantial repairs and improvements and/or new construction (see the broader discussion of stock transfer in Chapter 6).

Numerous small-scale CBHA stock transfers by Glasgow City Council and other Scottish local authorities during the 1980s and 1990s were motivated by these sorts of considerations (as well as the expectation of substantial public funding which would not otherwise have been made available). Since 1996 a wave of such estate or 'partial' transfers have taken place in England, mainly primed by the creation of the Estate Regeneration Challenge Fund. By 2001, more than 50,000 homes had been handed over in this way through over 40 separate transfer transactions. In the main, these were inner-city estates often involving stock in substantial disrepair. ERCF funding helped to pay off residual debt resulting from negative valuations (i.e., where the cost of repairs and modernization exceeded the future rental value of the housing concerned: see HACAS Chapman Hendy 2002).

In the main this generation of partial transfers has involved the creation of special purpose housing associations, some set up as subsidiaries of larger established RSLs, managed by Boards constituted according to the 'local housing company' model: one-third tenants, one-third local councillors and one-third 'independents'. As noted above, ERCF is primarily a housing regeneration programme and the main function of the transfer landlords is the upgrading and managing of housing stock. However, a number of these landlords have been set up with specific obligations to promote 'community regeneration' with respect to the transferred stock. Activities undertaken in pursuit of these objectives have included the provision of after-school clubs, employment training and crime prevention (Perry 2002).

Although housing associations are often seen as playing a key role, the emphasis of tenure diversification policy in the regeneration context has shifted during the 1990s in favour of increasing the share of owner-occupiers within deprived communities. This is often achieved by replacing demolished council housing with newly constructed homes for sale (DTZ Pieda 2000). In Scotland such construction can be subsidized under the Communities Scotland GRO (Grants for Renting and Ownership) programme which, through bridging the gap between construction costs and sale costs, is partly intended to attract mainstream private developers into what would otherwise be considered risky or unprofitable areas. Analogous programmes operated in England during the 1990s included Citygrant and English Partnerships' Gap Funding, though all schemes of this nature have had to be reviewed in the light of the EU's competition rules. These proscribe the payment of 'unfair subsidies' to firms where these could, in theory, help recipients to undercut competitors. The aim of such programmes is both to draw into the area better-off, employed people, and to retain upwardly mobile people within the area who would otherwise move away as a means of accessing home-ownership.

There is 'no clear statement of the precise connection which is intended between [the introduction or expansion of] owner occupation and the regeneration of communities' (Atkinson and Kintrea 2000, p.95). However, McGregor and MacLennan (1992) summarized the arguments underlying the policy as:

- boosting local spending
- introducing local leadership
- providing a market to bring about improvement in the quality of local services
- stabilizing population

Nearly a decade on, the relative importance of these contentions may have changed, but the case continues to rest on the view that it is 'area effects' which define and reinforce deprivation in deprived neighbourhoods. In other words, 'deprived people who live in deprived areas may have their life chances reduced compared to their counterparts in more socially-mixed neighbourhoods ... living in a neighbourhood which is predominantly poor is itself a source of disadvantage' (Atkinson and Kintrea 2001, pp.3–4).

Such disadvantage may stem from the poor reputation and negative stigma attached to living there. It is, for example, sometimes claimed that citation of a home address in such an area can result in direct discrimination against residents in relation to credit, education and employment. Certainly, an entrenched 'negative image' attached to a neighbourhood or estate is often found to be highly pervasive, even in the wake of substantial regeneration investment (Dean and Hastings 2000).

The prescription of mixed tenures also stems from the diagnosis of social exclusion which attributes significance to restricted social networks. Proponents of this view argue that 'the social dynamics of deprived areas can promote inward-looking attitudes, stigmatisation and weak social capital and an acceptance of unconventional social norms' (Atkinson and Kintrea 2001, p.3). Also, in terms of obtaining employment, informal networks may be equally (or more) important as formal channels such as contacts with the local job-centre (Perri 6, 1997). To the extent that physical proximity improves the chances of developing networks, bringing better-off, better-connected people into an area where deprived people were previously concentrated ought to help to reconnect excluded individuals.

Research in Scotland by Atkinson and Kintrea (2000), and in England by Jupp (1999), concluded that:

- there is only a limited amount of contact between owners and renters living on mixed tenure estates
- owners play only a small part in the community life of mixed tenure estates
- there is, in any case, little sign that intertenure contacts bring direct benefits to renters

At the same time, however, both studies found that the physical layout of estates had a significant influence on the extent of cross-tenure contacts. The Jupp study compared responses from people living on mixed streets with those from people whose estates were effectively zoned. The former were no more likely to perceive problems with mixing tenures than the latter. However, cross-tenure contacts were much more likely among people living in mixed streets.

The two studies both concluded that the best chance of fostering communities is to reduce residential turnover. It was also argued that thought needs to be given to where social networks between owners and tenants develop. The role of schools is important but, for childless households, local shops or pubs could be crucial. Other evidence (e.g., Bramley and Morgan 2002) demonstrates that developing owner-occupied housing in deprived estates can lead to reduced residential turnover.

Demolition

As noted above, demolition of social housing in the context of area regeneration may be part and parcel of a broader tenure diversification strategy. Alternatively, in particularly weak housing markets, demolition may be a rational response to the gross oversupply of accommodation such that overall downsizing – rather than clearance *and replacement* – is the selected option. In England, rising council housing demolition rates during the 1990s have been seen by some as an indication of the growing problem of low demand at the national scale. The overall volume of demolitions rose three-fold in the decade to 2002 (see Figure 9.1). The doubling of clearance seen in the North over the past four years probably does reflect intensifying problems of low demand in this part of the country (see Chapter 4). In addition, however, the numbers are affected by changes in funding regimes. For example, the upsurge of clearance activity in London during the mid-1990s was largely attributable to the creation of the Estate Action programme in 1992; hence this trend was directly linked with area regeneration activity.

Figure 9.1 *Demolitions of LA housing in England, 1990/1–2001/2*

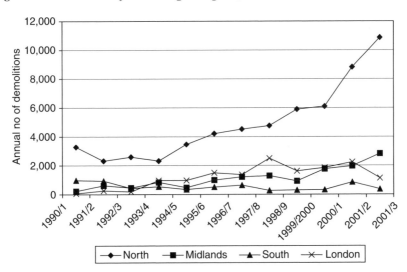

Source: Data from ODPM (LA Housing Investment Programme/Housing Strategy Statistical Annex/HRA Business Plan Statistical Annex returns).

Across England as a whole demolition rates in 2001/2 remained fairly modest, amounting to only around 0.6 per cent of the total local authority housing stock (1.1 per cent in the North). In some individual local authorities clearance rates are, of course, considerably higher: Liverpool, for example, demolished 2.5 per cent of its council housing in 2000/1.

In Scotland the annual incidence of demolition during the 1990s was considerably higher than in England, tending to account for around 1 per cent of the national stock of council housing (the figure for Glasgow has averaged around twice this value). There is, on the other hand, less evidence of any clear upward trend in recent years (see Figure 9.2).

Commentators such as Cole, Kane and Robinson (1999) have argued that social landlords operating in de-industrialized areas of northern England, for example, have tended to shy away from facing up to the need for more aggressive demolition strategies rather than continuing in sometimes vain attempts at area revival through new housing development. 'Planning for decline' is seen as presenting a particular challenge to a sector accustomed to growth and development.

Part of the problem here is that, whilst a regeneration programme may be planned to involve a phased series of investments over a long period, the fickleness of housing demand can undermine the case for the programme's continuation even whilst it remains ongoing. A case in point concerns a large

Figure 9.2   *Demolitions in Scotland, 1991–2001*

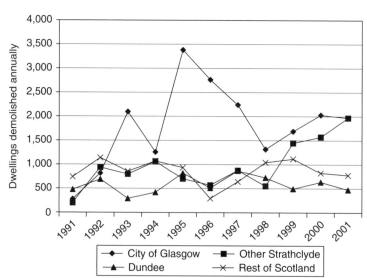

Note: Figures represent total dwellings demolished or closed, annually. The vast majority of these will involve LA housing.
Source: Data form Scottish Executive (LA returns – unpublished).

city-fringe estate in northern England studied by the authors. In this instance, a 10-year sequence of renovation funded under the Estate Action programme (see Table 9.1) was only half completed when the continuing decline in the area's popularity – and consequent rising void rates – became impossible to ignore. Even some of the expensively refurbished homes had become difficult to let. Belatedly, the programme had to be reconfigured to incorporate the demolition of hundreds of homes originally earmarked for upgrading, together with the diversion of resources into environmental and security work in an attempt to stem the rising tide of crime and anti-social behaviour. Examples of this kind also illustrate the general reluctance to designate areas as 'irredeemable'. This adds to the perception of wasted resources if money is invested in the refurbishment of houses that are then – sometimes quite quickly – demolished.

One attraction of demolition from a national policy perspective is that, to the extent that it involves stock with disproportionate repair costs, it will help to reduce the national price tag attached to remedying disrepair in council housing (Bramley and Pawson 2002). Also, demolition of local authority stock is, in itself, relatively cheap (£1,000–3,000 per unit) and may be relatively easy to manage if demand is so low that decanting options are plentiful (and provided that problems associated with pepper-potted – i.e. scattered – ex-RTB flats do not arise).

Arguments for a presumption against demolition as an element within a strategy aimed at managing decline include the concerns that it may be seen as symbolizing, accepting and accentuating neighbourhood decline and can leave unsightly and unmanaged open spaces (Power and Mumford 1999).

Public participation in regeneration strategies

An aspect of the consensus favouring 'partnership working' is the commitment to community involvement of regeneration strategies. As Atkinson and Kintrea (2001, p.27) observe, 'All area regeneration programmes now have a faith that involving "the community" will give rise to more effective and sustainable ... solutions, help local people exert control over social problems, assist the improvement of mainstream services, as well as contribute to democratic renewal.' In part, this thinking follows from the critique of 'old style' (pre-1988) approaches to area renewal, which are often seen to have failed the test of sustainability in part at least because of the paternalistic, 'top-down' way that they were planned and executed. Part of this critique is that where plans are conceived by remote bureaucrats and not informed by the day-to-day experience of local people, they will inevitably incorporate 'wrong decisions'. An allied, though slightly distinct, argument is that only where local residents 'assume ownership' of plans for reviving their area can there be any chance of achieving 'regeneration that lasts' (Taylor 1995).

These practical justifications for community participation are consistent with the broader dynamic in favour of more consumerist and participative approaches to planning and public service delivery which, as other chapters in this book demonstrate, are having a major impact on housing practice in Britain. As noted above, this philosophy is exemplified particularly strongly within the New Deal for Communities framework where the local agencies responsible for planning and co-ordinating regeneration are community partnerships rather than local authorities.

Whilst the imperative for resident participation in regeneration is well established, the need for community capacity building as a pre-condition for the effectiveness of such an approach has been recognized only recently. Current thinking stresses that, for community involvement to produce 'a real transfer of power to those currently powerless', regeneration programmes should budget for such activities right from the start, and that programmes' success should be measured partly in terms of the community confidence and skills acquired through the process (Carley *et al.* 2000).

Particularly where urban decay is serious enough to imply a need for widespread housing system restructuring, however, community involvement in planning for regeneration can be more problematic than is generally assumed. In cities where falling demand for housing and/or poor housing conditions call for a strategically planned clearance programme, for example, it may be extremely difficult to secure consensus support across affected neighbourhoods. In the US context, referring to Baltimore's efforts to tackle such difficulties, Cohen (2001, p.432) argues that there can be a serious clash between the generally accepted twin necessities of strategic planning and resident participation: 'There is an inherent tension between the city's commitment to helping local neighbourhoods develop their own revitalisation plans and the need to have [a] citywide strategy for assembling and disposing of large parcels [of run-down housing] to serve redevelopment goals affecting an area larger than a single neighbourhood.' Cohen goes on to argue that 'grass roots, community-based planning ... is not a reasonable way to devise revitalisation strategies that include large-scale initiatives transcending individual neighbourhoods' (2001, p.442).

The unquestioned prime role generally accorded to resident involvement in area regeneration is queried from a different angle by Atkinson and Kintrea (2001). From their 'neighbourhood effects' perspective, they argue (p.28) that deprived communities tend to 'embody an inward-looking set of values which play a key role in socialising residents in ways which reinforce their exclusion'. Unless the social base of such communities is broadened, therefore, 'attempts to strengthen the[ir] voice ... [are] not going to be helpful for the social inclusion of their members'.

Among a number of examples illustrating their case, Atkinson and Kintrea cite the early 1990s experience of the Wester Hailes Representative Council in Edinburgh, 'a rare example of a body which did actually wield some power within a major regeneration scheme'. The Council, established under the Scottish Office's New Life Partnerships programme (see Table 9.1), resisted and ultimately defeated a proposed housing strategy which would have seen a substantial diversification of tenure. Implementation of the plan would have seen the area's social base being considerably broadened, arguably aiding its 'desegregation'. For the 'community', on the other hand, the priority was the improvement of existing social housing. A similar train of events has recently been played out in the Shoreditch New Deal for Communities project where residents have strongly rejected proposals for local authority stock transfer.

As seen by Atkinson and Kintrea, citizen involvement in area regeneration can effectively invite residents 'to put the needs of their own [unreconstructed] communities first'. The policies favoured by such communities may, therefore, 'only contribute further to their introspection'. Consequently, 'any extension of real power for deprived communities, which is what most commentators want to see, almost certainly will mean more effective resistance to opening up and diversifying estates' (Atkinson and Kintrea 2001, p.29).

Future directions for housing and area regeneration policy

As this chapter has argued, there is a strong consensus around a small body of urban regeneration principles. Theoretically, at least, official and academic thinking has solidified in favour of regeneration approaches which incorporate:

- the targeting of regeneration activity and investment on areas subject to concentrations of deprivation
- a broad-based, joined-up approach embracing social and economic development as well as environmental and housing improvement
- partnership working, incorporating resident participation (or leadership)

These are the directions in which regeneration policy has been travelling and probably indicate the route likely to be followed in at least the medium-term future. Some of these shibboleths are, however, beginning to attract a degree of scepticism, particularly from critics of area-based strategies (as cited above: see p.184), and from advocates of the 'neighbourhood effects' thesis. Atkinson and Kintrea (2001), for example, contend that there is an overwhelming need to 'desegregate' deprived neighbourhoods and that current policies do not give this objective a sufficiently high priority. Measures to promote home-ownership in regeneration areas are regarded as too timid, particularly in the context of the continuing presumption in favour of targeting social housing investment into such areas (Atkinson and Kintrea 2001). Bearing in mind the residualized status of social housing, additions to the existing social rented stock in deprived areas may simply be seen as simply confirming a locality's status as a poor neighbourhood.

An example of the scenario being described here can be seen in the regeneration of Niddrie House/Niddrie Marischal, Edinburgh. Here, during the period 1988–98, some 148 owner-occupied homes were built under the Scottish Homes GRO programme. This helped to boost the level of owner-occupation in what had previously been seen as a highly marginal area. At the end of the period, however, the rate of home-ownership remained only 21 per cent. The number of rented homes built by housing associations over the same period – 157 – was actually greater than the number constructed for sale. The conclusion of the Niddrie evaluation that tenure diversification had failed to produce significant spin-off benefits for remaining social sector tenants is consistent with the argument that it was too small in scale to result in a decisive change in the area's social composition and reputation (Pawson, Kirk and McIntosh 2000).

Atkinson and Kintrea discuss two alternative approaches which could follow from their critique. First, they suggest that social housing investment should be redirected *away from* regeneration areas except where it is part of a genuinely mixed development with private housing in the majority. It is recognized that this may add to development costs, given that land values in other areas are generally likely to be higher than in deprived neighbourhoods. However, in contrast with schemes in such areas, the market value of homes developed in less marginal areas is more likely to equal or exceed development costs, and therefore will be less of an investment risk. The latter is an important consideration for housing associations, some of which are increasingly alarmed by the decline in the asset value of their stock due to the spread of low demand (Bramley, Pawson and Third 2000).

A different approach would be to 'de-link subsidy from place' by giving individuals (residents of run-down social housing estates) the opportunity to find their own home which would be purchased on their behalf by a social landlord. Such an approach is inspired by the apparent success of the US Moving to Opportunity programme which aims to improve the lot of poor people living in deprived areas. It is also similar to the Do it Yourself Shared Ownership and Homebuy schemes as operated in England and Wales. Whichever of these approaches was adopted, the effect of the more aggressive 'desegregation' policy envisaged for regeneration areas would have the advantage of creating larger, more viable areas for private sector redevelopment, raising land values and reducing the risk incurred by developers in becoming involved in such areas.

Although Atkinson and Kintrea's recommendations seem to be completely at variance with most contemporary thinking, they echo comments by McGregor and MacLennan who argued in the early 1990s that 'there is still a bias towards solving problems in the places where they exist and to put existing residents at the centre stage of action' (1992, p.15). In circumstances where economic and population decline are likely to be protracted, such approaches may be inappropriate.

These views raise fundamental questions about the accepted orthodoxy of targeting public resources according to need, about the role of existing residents in areas requiring regeneration, and about the feasibility of restoring the reputation of an area without radically restructuring its ownership structure.

Further reading

On the policy side, a relatively comprehensive statement of current official thinking on regeneration is provided by the Social Exclusion Unit's *National Strategy for Neighbourhood Renewal* report (SEU 2000). The Urban Task Force's *Towards an Urban Renaissance* report (Urban Task Force 1999) is a wide-ranging critique of recent urban policy packed with proposals on land-use planning, taxation and housing investment.

As far as regeneration research is concerned, Power and Mumford (1999) pick up a number of the Urban Task Force's themes in their study of urban decline. Robson *et al.* (2000) usefully review recent social and economic trends in England's cities. MacLennan (2000) provides an overview of recent studies funded by the Joseph Rowntree Foundation. Much of this work focuses on the effectiveness of ABIs in countering poverty and social exclusion. The study by Nevin *et al.* (2001) is seen as highly influential in having underpinned the government's recent creation of the Housing Market Renewal Pathfinder programme.

The concept of 'sustainable regeneration' is well developed by Carley and Kirk (1998) and Fordham (2002). Similarly, the study by Carley *et al.* (2000) is an insightful exposition of what is meant by that oft-quoted mantra 'partnership working'. The papers by Atkinson and Kintrea (2001) and Cohen (2001) are valuable in bringing a more critical perspective to the regeneration policy debate in their highlighting of the potential conflict between the twin imperatives of strategic planning and community involvement.

10

The Policy System

Introduction

In pulling together the strands of argument and evidence in this book, we adopt a policy analysis framework. Most of what has been discussed in the preceding chapters describes changes impacting on housing in Britain and changes within the housing system responding to wider changes in society, the economy and the environment. How far has policy responded to these changes, which often present a challenge to established approaches? Is the policy system up to the task it now faces? It is interesting that, whilst we have been writing this book, the government has commissioned research from three leading universities (including the present authors) to provide an 'evaluation of English housing policy since 1975'. This indicates a shared view within officialdom that such large questions about the 'fit' between policy and a changing housing system are timely.

What are the essential requirements of an adequate policy response to the changes and challenges described? To address this overall policy question involves answering a number of more specific issues, in relation to the different facets of housing. The key questions are as follows:

1 Does policy recognize the key driving forces?
2 Has policy recognized and adapted to newly-emerging problems?
3 Is resource backing commensurate with the scale of the problems/ challenges?
4 Are institutional and territorial structures adequate, given diversity?
5 Is the policy system geared to learning from evidence?
6 Will policies survive and be sustainable beyond the next change of minister, fashion or government?

These questions provide the structure for this final chapter. Under each heading, we draw on key evidence and conclusions from different chapters, and highlight particular examples which illustrate positive and negative features of policy in these terms.

Does policy recognize the key driving forces?

Underlying forces driving change in the housing system were identified in Chapter 1 and elaborated to varying degrees in the following chapters, particularly 2–5. We pull out half-a-dozen forces for discussion here.

First, and in many ways most fundamental, we see *consumerism* as the defining spirit of contemporary Britain. With increasing affluence, people's concerns shift from basic needs to higher-order aspirations, moving up Maslow's famous hierarchy (Maslow 1943). Aspects of this shift include the greater role of and belief in markets, the decline of 'deference', the emphasis on quality, and the fascination with lifestyle and fashion such that 'shopping' has become the favourite leisure pursuit. Consumers need information to choose from the proliferating array of consumption opportunities, and the mass media feed this hunger. In housing, consumerism is evident in the inexorable rise of owner-occupation, tenants' demand for choice and empowerment, and residents' wishes to be consulted about planning matters. Chapters 7 and 8 discussed aspects of this consumer view of housing.

In some respects the policy system recognizes this fundamental shift, although (as in other sectors like health) it has difficulties reconciling consumers' exploding aspirations with the harder realities of service delivery within constrained resources. Politics itself has become more consumption-oriented. Governments are judged on their delivery of quality public services more than on how they relate to the key producer groups (organized labour, business, the professions, local government). The media closely monitors and sharply highlights shortcomings in service delivery, particularly in sectors such as health, education and transport.

Housing policy has adapted to the consumerist agenda in a number of respects. There is largely bipartisan support for a presumption in favour of owner-occupation as the normal and preferred housing tenure. Reform of public sector housing emphasizes widening choice, tenant empowerment and improved housing management. There is considerable interest in 'choice-based lettings', and longer-term moves through 'rent restructuring' towards a Housing Benefit system incorporating 'shopping incentives' for tenants. Hitherto disadvantaged groups (such as disabled people) seeking greater rights of access to 'normal' lifestyles gain greater recognition, whilst community care policy shifts from supporting specialist housing providers to 'supporting people'.

On the other hand, it could be argued that much housing policy remains focused on the old collectivist, producer-governed social rented sector, rather than on issues which the consumer perspective would highlight such as consumer information, regulation and protection (see Chapter 7).

An essential element of the consumerist perspective is a recognition of diversity: consumers want different things, though this may be strongly influenced by demographic life-stage and household circumstances or by ethnic and cultural heritage. These issues are picked up below but, first and foremost, what people want and what they need assistance with will be very strongly influenced by their material resources. The level and distribution of income and wealth is fundamental to the tasks facing housing policy. Thus, as Chapter 2 made clear, we regard the *new inequalities* which have grown up in the 1980s and 1990s as key challenges for policy (Hills 1996). Post-1997 government has pledged to reverse the strong trend to inequality of the preceding two decades, although to date its achievements here have been limited. For the time being, therefore, housing policy has to factor in profound inequalities between different types of households and occupational groups and also between geographical areas. Housing may itself contribute to widening or narrowing inequalities, chiefly through the effects on personal wealth of housing equity (see Chapter 3), but also through other routes such as labour mobility.

Policy recognizes the significance of income poverty for housing affordability, particularly via the maintenance of a comprehensive Housing Benefit system for tenants. It is more questionable whether policy has yet come to terms with the fact that 'half the poor' (in England) now live in owner-occupation (Burrows and Wilcox 2000). Unlike the situation in some other European countries, there is no general equivalent of HB for owners; income support for mortgage interest has been curtailed, as has spending on grant aid for private sector renovation. Policy is essentially banking on private sector solutions – insurance or borrowing – to the adverse economic contingencies of home-ownership.

Demographic change in the form of changing household structures underlies some of the growth in inequality. Lone parent households, and to some extent single adult households (particularly in the younger and older age groups), are at greater risk of experiencing low income. Policymakers are generally quite well informed about demographic change, as such changes are relatively predictable and widely discussed. Demography, in conjunction with other policy and social trends, may render some traditional policy assumptions less sustainable, however. The combination of student finance reforms with rising participation in higher education means that many new households will start their housing career encumbered with debt. This, combined with an emerging crisis in pension provision, may alter attitudes towards housing debt and investment, which may in turn bring problems of policy co-ordination between government departments.

Closely linked to demography is the issue of migration, and particularly the often-controversial issues of immigration, race and ethnicity. *Diversity* and multiculturalism are matters which obtrude increasingly into national life and politics, and demand a response across all policy sectors. This is most obvious in the context of London and some other English cities, where black and minority ethnic (BME) populations make up large minorities – or in a few boroughs now, majorities – of the population. 'Urban policy' has for some been close to synonymous with BME policy, at least in England, particularly when new phases of policy seem to be ushered in by urban disturbances with racial overtones. A combination of economic progress and rising expectations among BME groups, and the highly publicized attempts to disperse asylum seekers away from London, have combined to raise issues of ethnic diversity across the nations of the UK. Asylum itself may be seen as a by-product of globalization since the ease of communication and travel has facilitated population flows. Whatever the causes, housing is often in the front line of coping with the local impact of such movements, as well as more widely in attempting to promote equality of access.

'Diversity' may also be taken as a much looser shorthand for greater differentiation of demographic patterns, life courses, consumption patterns and lifestyles, which make for more diversity both within and between local communities. As such, it could be seen to encompass all the issues highlighted in this section. In housing, the implications range from planning for a wider range of house types and for 'mixed and balanced communities' (see Chapters 5 and 6) through to management issues of coping with potentially incompatible neighbours or unstable communities (see Chapters 4 and 8). Policy undoubtedly recognizes these as individual issues, but whether the full implications have been taken on board in a holistic way is more questionable. For example, regeneration policies emphasize community involvement and participation, yet this may make untenable assumptions about the cohesiveness or durability of the 'communities' in question. These issues have been highlighted by Atkinson and Kintrea (2000 and 2001), who question the 'inwardness' of some deprived communities.

Another aspect of population movement gives rise to perhaps the central issues in planning for new housing and urban regeneration (Chapters 5 and 9). This is the continuing '*urban–rural shift*' (Champion *et al.* 1998) of population, which poses a major challenge to planning policies for sustainable urban form and urban policies emphasizing urban renaissance (Jencks, Burton and Williams 1996; Urban Task Force 1999). For Britain, as a mature postindustrial society, the transition to 'new urban–rural relationships' may have proceeded further than in other European countries. At the same time, some of the most problematic 'rural' communities are actually dispersed examples of de-industrialization, as in the mining villages of Durham or South Yorkshire. Yet policy for rural areas is often developed separately from urban policy, and indeed in England there has been a recent division of the ministries responsible. Policies promoted for rural areas, to counteract the decline and restructuring of agriculture, and involving diversification and new kinds of rural development, may actually exacerbate the urban–rural shift which threatens urban renaissance.

Overlaying all of this is an economy characterized by ever-greater openness to *international competition* on both a regional and a global scale. Within this, cities and regions are increasingly and self-consciously competing with each other, both within and across the boundaries of nation states, for a share of economic activity. This has several implications for housing. First, traditional regional economic policy (taking work to the workers) is seen as decreasingly viable, because economic activity may be displaced across national boundaries. Such policy is in any case subject to severe limits through European competition rules and structural fund allocations. Housing may have to respond more to the demand for labour where it is manifested, with implications for both planning policies (e.g., land release in attractive areas) and for the orientation and allocation of social/subsidized housing (e.g., key workers), both of which are illustrated by the *Sustainable Communities* plan (ODPM 2003b).

Second, local authorities and regional development agencies may increasingly look at the role of housing in supporting the economic competitiveness agenda. Housing cannot be seen as confined to a box labelled 'social policy', and economically-oriented agencies (such as the Regional Development Agencies, or RDAs, in England) may gain an increasing role in shaping housing development and regeneration. Yet, as Cole (2003) argues, there is a fundamental conflict of outlook between growth-minded RDAs and regeneration-oriented housing agencies.

Third, it is commonly alleged that one of the corollaries of a globalized economy is a more flexible labour market, an end to 'jobs for life' and a much higher level of risk for households in all occupational strata. This is one of the reasons why the financial security of owner-occupation (Chapter 7) is of growing importance.

Again, echoing a repeated theme in this section, policy is responding to these forces in an ad hoc, locally variable fashion. There is little sense of an overall strategic vision for housing policy which recognizes these powerful forces in an overarching way.

Policy recognition of newly-emerging problems

New kinds of problems are emerging in the housing sector, generally reflecting the impact of these driving forces, singly or in combination. Much of this book has been concerned with examining the anatomy of these problems and the nature of policy responses which have been implemented or debated.

The *instability of the British housing market* is not a new problem, with three major booms experienced since the early 1970s. However, as Chapter 3 argued, each boom had distinct characteristics and brought distinctive problems in its wake. The early 1990s' slump, for example, introduced a new phenomenon, negative equity, for which adequate policy responses were not really found other than to wait for market revival to float people out of the problem. Solutions are still being sought for victims unfortunate enough to live in areas of continuing low demand. The severity of the market fluctuations was exacerbated by policy mistakes, and there are some signs that mistakes may be made again in the boom of the new millennium. There is a new problem of macroeconomic control, which is recognized by commentators but which government was perhaps reluctant to acknowledge, possibly because of its rhetoric about macroeconomic competence and having abolished 'boom and bust'. It is really the challenge of European Monetary Union (EMU) which has brought this issue to fore (HM Treasury 2003).

Low demand was perhaps the most dramatic and significant newly-recognized housing problem in the late 1990s. In England, there was a relatively concerted and wide-ranging policy response, reflected in strategic policy documents (DETR 1999c, 2000) and in a range of specific actions, particularly in the field of housing management and allocation (Chapter 8) but extending into areas such as planning (Chapter 5), resource allocation and regeneration (Chapter 9). However, responses to low demand in the private sector have been more halting, reflecting their potential cost and complexity, although 'housing market renewal' was launched as a policy in 2002.

In Chapters 1–2 we identified *residualization* as a longstanding structural trend in the role and profile of social housing in Britain. In the 1990s the implications of residualization became increasingly apparent, not least in the context of low demand where the evidence showed a strong link between unpopularity and concentrations of poverty. This prompted some new policy responses, although these were more in the nature of accommodating an inevitable tendency rather than trying to reverse the fundamental trend. Following the Page (1993) report, social landlords became more careful about allocating tenancies in new developments. National planning guidance in England placed a new emphasis on mixed and balanced communities (DETR 1998, 2000b). Strong interest in choice-based housing allocation (Chapter 8) and mixed tenure/low cost home-ownership (LCHO) in regeneration schemes (Chapter 9) can also be linked to the recognition of residualization problems.

The 1990s were a decade when *environmentally sustainable development* (ESD) became a new mantra informing planning and urban policy across the board (Chapter 5). Within this context, a number of environmental problems emerged to have an impact on housing. An important example is the endemic *traffic congestion* arising from greater affluence and the continuing decentralization of population, jobs and services. There has been underinvestment in transport *infrastructure* and both the resources and delivery mechanisms available are inadequate. There is a strong logic in getting new developments to fund more comprehensive infrastructure provision but, as shown in Chapter 5, the principal mechanism involved, planning agreements, remains very ad hoc, controversial and uncertain in its operation. Whilst government reforms of the planning system are in the offing, a coherent way forward on planning gain remains elusive.

One of the most significant by-products of the housing market boom in southern England at the end of the 1990s was the (re-)emergence of housing affordability problems affecting '*key workers*'. This was, in reality, a cyclical intensification of a problem which has been, to a degree, endemic (particularly in London), and which certainly featured in earlier booms. This time, however, the issue received more policy attention because it coincided with a drive to radically improve public services, and the 'key workers' of particular concern were public service staff such as teachers and police officers. The policy response to date has included a 'starter home initiative', a revival of interest in LCHO, reinforcement of planning and affordable housing policies, and a housing delivery taskforce.

Academics have been writing about *poor owner-occupiers* since the 1970s (Karn 1977), but the perceived extent of overlap between poverty and owner-occupation as a major, widespread problem is much more recent (Burrows and Wilcox 2000). As Chapter 6 shows, the financial safety net mechanisms for owner-occupiers remain inadequate and would be tested by a serious market recession. It is a problem for regeneration when poor households tend to live in the poorer quality housing, when tenure mixing is general and when governments want to see private sector solutions to private sector problems. Chapter 9 shows the weakness of current policies on private sector housing in poor condition, especially when combined with low demand.

Financial products linked to housing are a major area of concern (Chapter 7). At one level this is a concern about lack of any products, as when households have no home insurance; at another level it is a concern that the choices open to consumers are almost too numerous, and indeed confusing, given the technical nature of these products. This is underlined by the succession of scandals about the mis-selling of first personal pensions and more recently by concerns over mortgage endowments and pensions. Government continues to rely heavily on voluntary codes of conduct and regulation, particularly in the critical field of financial information and consumer advice. This area is not recognized as part of mainstream housing policy, but belongs rather in a more esoteric area of 'financial regulation' overseen by the Treasury and the Department of Trade and Industry.

The *Right to Buy* (RTB) has been a flagship housing policy for two decades now. Some of the problems associated with it have only recently been officially recognized. A topical example is the so-called 'abuse' of RTB arising when buyers let their property out or re-sell it to commercial landlords for this purpose. Another problematic area is securing the improvement of common parts of council-constructed blocks containing privatized flats when these leaseholders/flat-owners are reluctant or unable to contribute. Measures to curtail discounts and tighten other RTB rules were introduced in England in 2003 but these measures only apply to a limited number of authorities and, because of being subject to delayed implementation, triggered a predictable stampede of potential purchasers aiming to beat the deadline.

Although not new problems, *crime and anti-social behaviour* have come to be seen as relatively more important challenges for housing management at the local level. Chapter 4 showed that resulting concerns were among the most important in driving unpopularity of areas on a neighbourhood scale; they were more important, for example, than the physical condition of houses. The present government seems to recognize this to a considerable degree, judging by the attention given to these issues in national policy development and within its Neighbourhood Renewal Strategy. It remains to be seen whether all of the measures promulgated here will prove effective; for example, take-up of Anti-Social Behaviour Orders (ASBOs) has been slower than ministers would have wished. However, the renewed interest in 'on the spot' housing and neighbourhood management (Chapter 8) and in better maintenance and supervision of the local public realm (Chapter 6) can be seen as related responses.

One of the issues highlighted by low demand was the apparently *growing competition within the rented sector* between social landlords, and between the social rented sector and a newly resurgent, deregulated private rented sector (Chapter 4). Elements of competition were encouraged in the early 1990s, particularly in England, but the negative side has become more apparent recently. The Housing Corporation has given belated backing to the idea of stock rationalization between housing associations operating in the same areas. Current government policy can be seen as an uneasy mix of condoning choice and diversity, on the one hand, while trying to regulate and limit competition in other respects.

There is a growing awareness of some of the processes which make sustainable area regeneration particularly difficult. One of these is the paradox of *mobility*, or the 'moving up, moving out' phenomenon, identified in Chapter 5 (in relation to migration) as well as in Chapter 9. Success in improving an area, particularly in economic terms, may raise the mobility of its residents and lead to a further net decline in the area, even though for many people the situation has improved. Another tricky issue is that of *displacement*. Attractive new housing in a run-down urban area may well attract willing buyers, but questions need to be asked about where these people are moving from, what happens to the housing they relinquish, and about the fact that other housing they might have bought or rented is not now taken up.

Scale of resources versus scale of problems

It is one thing to recognize a problem, whether emerging or longstanding, but another to develop an effective policy response and allocate resources to match the scale of the challenge. Administrative and analytical resources are needed to develop or change policies, and these may be stretched, particularly for an ambitious government with a wide-ranging reform agenda. Most policies require scarce public expenditure resources. Even where such funding is not needed, the policies may involve imposing fiscal or regulatory burdens on the private sector and these may be politically unpopular.

Governments naturally want to be seen to be responding to problems, and this generates pressure for the announcement of new initiatives. However, if these are not adequately backed by resources for implementation then the policies may be rightly criticized as 'symbolic' (Edelman 1971; Hill and Bramley 1986). A cynical view is that politicians are sometimes more concerned with creating the impression of action than with the substance of policy delivery ('words that succeed and policies that fail'). The present government has been criticized for excessive public relations 'spin' and for creating 'initiative overload'. However, it has also seen the significant development of a style of policymaking involving a stronger emphasis on 'delivery' and the setting of targets for policy 'outputs' and 'outcomes'. This approach places a stronger discipline on the public policy system and increases the risk that policies will be seen as 'failing'. A major current example is the commitment entered into in 2000 to meet the 'decent homes' target for the whole social sector by 2010.

The share of public expenditure devoted to overtly 'housing' policies has generally declined in Britain since the 1970s, at least up to the mid-late 1990s (Chapters 1–2). This has been seen as indicating a decline in the status and salience of housing in the national policy competition for attention and resources (Bramley 1997b; Malpass 1999). However, this decline is arguably not terminal, (a) because – as shown in Chapter 1 – some of the relevant policies are actually in adjacent sectors, and (b) because the emergence of new problems recently, as documented in this chapter, has prompted increased public spending. Nevertheless, the fact remains that resources are limited and the competition from sectors such as health and education is formidable.

As discussed in various chapters, there are important instances where policy responses to identified housing problems have arguably been underresourced.

Chapter 3 discussed the instability of the housing market and its tendency to experience uncontrolled booms leading to a raft of problems, particularly of affordability. In some respects government's ability to control the market has been weakened by such factors as mortgage market deregulation and the adoption of 'hands off' monetary policy. These have brought benefits in low inflation and greater consumer choice, but at some cost in terms of instruments of control which can bear specifically on the housing market. Fiscal tools might be used to supplement control, but there has been a reluctance to introduce significant measures to dampen housing demand, such as more progressive property or wealth taxation or taxation on capital gains. On the other hand, governments have managed to progressively remove mortgage interest tax relief. The political sensitivity of taxation in general, and the association of housing booms with a public 'feel-good factor', clearly lies behind this general reticence.

Chapter 4 showed that the emergence of low demand has prompted a range of policy responses, particularly in England and in relation to social housing. Policies were less coherently or extensively applied to the more intractable problems of low demand in the private sector, where solutions were seen as being significantly more expensive. The recent development of 'housing market renewal' programmes is an attempt to address this problem, but initially through 'pathfinder' projects that entail relatively limited resources for research and planning. Some additional resources have been allocated following the 2002 Comprehensive Spending Review, confirmed in the Sustainable Communities Statement of February 2003, but the £500 million so far allocated remains below the level likely to be required to achieve an overall solution.

Chapter 5 argued that greater land release for housing was required in regions such as the South East to meet demand and keep prices affordable. Response to this need has been delayed and confused to some extent by the strong emphasis on urban renaissance and brownfield land. Currently the main policy initiative is concentrating additional land provision in four designated growth areas, perhaps because this is seen as more achievable in the face of widespread local opposition to new housing on greenfield land. Even this initiative is seen as requiring substantial public investment in infrastructure, and the mechanisms for delivering and paying for this remain very uncertain. Planning is also being called upon to deliver more of the affordable housing required. The policies involved here have experienced many implementation difficulties and their overall performance in terms of additional affordable housing is disappointing.

On the development front (Chapter 6), the central issues facing government have been how to expand the current social housing programme to accommodate unmet need and how to facilitate a substantial improvement in the state of the social housing stock. Public subsidy resources for the former task have remained limited, but these have been stretched to some extent by greater use of private finance, recycling of provider surpluses and levering of some subsidy from land values through planning. Nevertheless, the task is an uphill one because boom conditions have pushed the costs of land and construction ever higher in the regions of greatest pressure. Some additional public spending resources have been committed to the 'decent homes' target, but it is now questioned whether these will be adequate to complete the associated refurbishment programme within a decade. This programme has been predicated on an accelerating programme of stock transfers in larger urban authorities, but these have been beset with difficulties often associated with securing local and tenant agreement.

Consumer issues in owner-occupation (Chapter 7) focus primarily on information about financial products and in the house-buying process, and protection for households getting into difficulties through changing economic circumstances. Here, the mortgage safety nets of ISMI and MPPI have been widely criticized, and the overall policy has been dominated by the drive to curtail public spending liabilities.

Chapter 8 examined key ideas for improving social housing management practice, with a particular emphasis on tenant choice and involvement and a strong regime of regulation. It is fair to question whether these good practice ideas can be delivered with current financial allowances for management and maintenance linked to capped rent levels and involving staff who may be difficult to recruit or retain at current salary scales given the difficulty of the task. Focusing on regeneration issues, Chapter 9 contrasts the decent homes commitment in the public sector with the more limited commitment to private sector renewal. In Scotland, major resources have been committed to the flagship Glasgow stock transfer, but few other authorities appear to be enthusiastic about this route. Repackaging stock transfer as 'community ownership' has done little to bolster support for the idea. A task force has examined private sector housing improvement issues but there is no obvious pot of extra resources to fund the good ideas which have come from this exercise (Scottish Executive 2003c).

Overall, the government faces dilemmas about how it should allocate the modestly enhanced public spending resources it is willing and able to commit to housing. In both England and Scotland there is choice between concentrating on meeting excess demand in the pressured South East, where costs are rising and a given budget can provide fewer units, as against channelling more resources into restructuring the collapsing markets of northern England and west central Scotland. ODPM's recent Sustainable Communities policy statement, and reactions to it, illustrate these dilemmas.

Institutional and territorial structures

The institutional structures of 'governance' in housing have become more complex and diverse. The traditional British model, heavily reliant on local government as the principal vehicle for policy delivery, has been severely criticized and substantially undermined by a combination of resource constraints, diversion of resources into parallel channels, the Right to Buy, stock transfer and regulation. A new social housing industry, based in non-profit RSLs, funded and regulated through quangos such as the Housing Corporation, and backed by private finance institutions, has grown on a major scale. But issues of governance and accountability within this disparate sector are becoming more insistent as its extent has expanded beyond the size for which a reliance on informal structures and mechanisms can suffice.

Although local government has lost legitimacy, power and resources, the treatment of housing problems remains essentially local. Thus it has become clear that local authorities are needed to perform key roles in orchestrating local strategies and enabling action by other agencies. Yet the capacity of local authorities to perform this role remains uneven, for example in terms of their command over research and intelligence about housing needs, problems and market behaviour, or in terms of their ability to use new mechanisms such as the planning system competently and effectively. Whilst some post-stock transfer authorities have embraced the strategic enabling role, others seem to have a mindset that housing has ceased to be a major area of interest for them. And although government urges councils and others to develop more thoroughgoing partnership working, there are problems in managing this process because of the sheer number and complexity of partnerships involved, not just in housing but across the related fields of regeneration, health and social care, community safety and so forth.

We have discussed at various points the increasing diversity of British society and the housing implications resulting. Giving more scope and autonomy to local government to exert leadership and to develop locally appropriate solutions is potentially an important strategic response to this phenomenon. There are some signs that national government is beginning to recognize this, and to draw back from the strong trend towards centralization evident since 1980. However, this remains at the 'green shoots' stage of recovery, with continuing rather mixed messages for local government, typically along the lines of 'you can have some extra freedoms and flexibilities, but only if you earn them by performing well on (a battery of centrally-driven) performance assessments'.

The regional dimension of governance is also receiving renewed attention, even in England, where demands for regional devolution have been voiced very unevenly across the country. Greater London has an elected Mayor and Assembly, but with limited powers and resources and a difficult relationship with central government. Nevertheless, the Mayor has made housing a key priority, has pushed ambitious targets for affordable housing, and has taken a strong interest in spatial development strategy. The English regions have RDAs which are taking a growing role in directing resources for regeneration and becoming more involved in planning and housing investment matters. The relationship between these bodies and existing structures, such as the Housing Corporation and government regional offices (as well as the local authorities), is unclear and still evolving, complicated in some places by the potential arrival of elected regional assemblies. It is clear that there are conflicts and differences in the priorities of these different agencies, and the capacity for strong sub-regional planning seems to be lacking in some cases.

Meanwhile, the most fundamental constitutional and governance change in Britain for generations has been the devolution effected with respect to Scotland and Wales in 1999. This has ushered in an era of increasingly 'variable geometry' in housing and other policies between different parts of the UK. The devolved administrations have often, though not always, sought to distance their policy priorities from those of Westminster and Whitehall. Although broadly the same parties currently hold power in each territory, there have been some significant policy differences (e.g., care of the elderly). In the future, when different parties may be in control of these different centres, such differences will inevitably be accentuated and the mechanisms of policy reconciliation and co-ordination between the territories could prove inadequate to cope with real conflicts. These mechanisms are unavoidable when some of the key policies and resource channels remain 'reserved matters' for Westminster (Housing Benefit, financial regulation and immigration/asylum being three apposite examples).

The devolution arrangements have facilitated the development of new policy and political structures and processes in the devolved territories. In Scotland, for example, elaborate task forces and consultation arrangements have been instituted, giving pressure groups significantly enhanced access to the process. This has contributed to a general raising of expectations which are difficult to satisfy. Although devolution allows diversity to flourish in the realm of policy ideas and debates, it would be a pity if it diverted attention from learning from experience and innovation elsewhere in the UK, which may be relevant to territories where these things have not been done. Planning and affordable housing mechanisms would be a current example of this. There is a general sense of disappointment in some quarters with the devolution project, in the sense that radical new policy ideas have been few in number and that the devolved politicians have been overpreoccupied with detailed, even parochial issues.

Evidence-based policy?

One of the new mantras of the late 1990s was 'evidence-based policy'. As academic researchers we naturally welcome this development, and have perhaps benefited from the expansion of government-sponsored research into housing-related issues. Nevertheless, it is worth asking whether policy is really more 'evidence-based' than in the past, or whether this is just another rhetorical flourish. What is the 'evidence' that policies are more evidence-based? It is probably fair to say, from our experience and observation, that the picture is mixed. A few examples may serve to illustrate this.

In the case of 'low demand' and the associated problems of poor and unpopular neighbourhoods, the authors have had the opportunity to observe some of the policy process at first hand. On the plus side, it is clear that the housing policy system did respond in a significant way to the emergence of evidence about the extent and significance of the problems of low demand. Some policy measures, including geographical redirection of resources, promotion of choice-based allocations and modifications to planning guidance can be attributed to research evidence put forward at this time. On the other hand, some of the policy responses did not appear to take on board some of the lessons from previous experience documented by research. For example, the renewed promotion of small area-based initiatives (e.g., the New Deal for Communities) flew in the face of some of the evidence on their appropriateness which had emerged from previous research and which was rehearsed within the relevant Policy Action Team. There was also a reluctance to recognize criticism of some existing policy mechanisms, such as the convoluted processes involved in compulsory purchase, although there has been some subsequent movement on this issue.

The problems facing owner-occupiers at risk from changing circumstances discussed in Chapters 3 and 7 have been extensively researched. However, whilst evidence generated here has demonstrated the inadequacy of current safety net mechanisms (Ford, Burrows and Nettleton 2001), policy in this area has remained resolutely resistant to developing more effective measures. Any significant recession in the coming period will again reveal these weaknesses as they were exposed in the early 1990s.

Policymakers have blown hot and cold on their attitude to evidence of quantitative housing needs at different times since 1980. In the 1980s, the Conservative government explicitly rejected calls to develop national needs estimates. In the mid-1990s, there was a renewal of interest and some official research was sponsored, as well as work independently commissioned by Rowntree and others. By the late 1990s, however, sentiment seemed to have shifted back against 'numerical' needs projections. However, with the onset of key worker and affordable housing crises in southern England at the beginning of the new millennium, regional need estimates are again in currency, as well as a general drive to improve the rigour of local estimates. Meanwhile, in Scotland there has been a remarkable reticence on the part of government or the national housing agency to quantify housing needs, despite a substantial potential evidence base.

There are policy areas where policymakers have a predisposition towards certain types of solution which, either because it is based on some strongly-held theoretical belief or because it is politically expedient, may persist despite a lack of positive research evidence in support. It could be argued that incentive schemes to tackle underoccupation and social sector rent restructuring represent examples of this kind.

Overall, there is a lot more research commissioned and more efforts at disseminating it through the policy system in relatively accessible ways (pioneered particularly by Rowntree). The research commissioning capability of government is strong, and leading government researchers play a significant part in shaping policy debates. There are extensive consultation procedures about research programmes. All of this is positive in terms of the potential of research to inform policy, as is the strong interest of the media and politicians in certain types of research evidence (e.g., opinion surveys). Evaluation of policy initiatives is routine and in some cases this does influence policy (re-)design; there are good examples of this in relation to regeneration policy, the Pathfinder approach to housing market restructuring, and choice-based lettings.

Nevertheless, for research to influence policy a number of conditions have to be present and this cannot be taken for granted. If policy change faces fundamental obstacles in terms of resource availability, electoral unpopularity, media sensitivity, or conflict with other more strategic values and commitments, then it is less likely to be shifted by particular bits of research evidence.

The sustainability of policies

Policies may be well informed by research and analysis and responsive to current problems and concerns, but how long will they last? Much intellectual attention is devoted to questioning the sustainability of housing design and environmental planning, but should we also consider the sustainability of policies themselves? There are many pressures within the political system for constant change in policy and delivery arrangements. New governments or local administrations wish to be seen to be carrying out reform programmes. New ministers wish to make their mark through frequent policy announcements. There is a rhetoric about public service reform and challenging existing ways of doing things which seems to carry value in the political arena.

Does it actually matter if policies do not in fact have a long shelf life? There seems to be a political logic in suggesting that it does not matter: a week is a long time in politics. If quite a lot of apparent policy change is really just repackaging and representation ('spin'), does this really matter? Also, as argued earlier, there are real changes in the economy and society that policy needs to be responsive to.

We believe that the sustainability of policies, in housing and related urban planning areas, does actually matter. There are a number of fundamental reasons for this. Housing is very durable, and fixed in its location. What is provided now will have to last a long time. We cannot afford to discard lightly what was built before. Investment by individuals or private organizations requires a level of confidence about the fiscal and regulatory environment within which it will function, as well as the physical and socio-economic environment within which it will be placed. The whole edifice of private finance for social housing and other public purposes rests on a model of business planning which looks forward 20–30 years. Political risk threatens the cost-effectiveness of these models, just as it killed off investment in private rented housing over many years up to the 1980s.

Generally, policy cannot be implemented instantly, because of the practical lead times required for administration, financing, design and so forth, but also because of the learning which a myriad of decentralized organizations and policy actors have to go through to make it work properly. Policy mechanisms typically need to attain a certain critical mass before they can be recognized and used effectively by providers and consumers: LCHO through vehicles such as shared ownership provides a clear example of this. Administrative reorganization (a particularly popular form of policy change) has a considerable cost in disruption, organizational politics, motivation and morale. Policy changes which affect property rights (as with planning) have to be introduced gradually, with due consultative process and a working through of new statutory plans and the backlog of existing permissions. It has taken more than a decade to get planning for affordable housing policies working even partially effectively. It took just over a decade to abolish mortgage tax relief, and English rent restructuring looks set to take another decade.

Policies for urban form and spatial planning have even longer timescales, measured in decades. Postwar New Towns took 30 years to grow to maturity and still shape the dynamics of urban growth in the 21st century. Major infrastructure networks, such as the trunk road system, have developed on similar timescales.

Parts of our policy administration system are better geared to this need for a longer-term perspective than others. It is not just politicians who have a short time horizon and attention span. The traditions of the British civil service are to move policy administrators around frequently, and in this situation a considerable responsibility rests upon the professionals, working within government and the wider policy community, to provide the collective memory and the longer-term perspective to see things through. As academics, we should support them in this function.

References

Adams, D. and Watkins, C. (2002) *Greenfields, Brownfields and Housing Development* (Oxford: Basil Blackwell).

Adams, D., May, H. and Pope, T. (1992) 'Changing strategies for the acquisition of residential development land', *Journal of Property Research*, 9, pp.209–26.

Aldbourne Associates (2001) *Implementing Best Value in Housing and Tenant Participation Compacts: The First Year*, www.aldbourneassociates.co.uk.

Aldbourne Associates (2003) *Interim Evaluation of Tenant Participation Compacts* (London: ODPM).

Aldous, T. (1992) *Urban Villages: A Concept for Creating Mixed-Use Urban Developments on a Sustainable Scale* (London: Urban Villages Group).

Anastacio, J., Gidley, B., Hart, L., Keith, M., Mayo, M. and Korwazik, U. (2000) *Reflecting Realities: Participants Perspectives on Integrated Communities and Sustainable Development* (Bristol: Policy Press).

Arnstein, S. (1969) 'A ladder of citizen participation', *Journal of American Institute of Planners*, 35, pp.214–24.

Atkinson, R. and Kintrea, K. (2000) 'Owner-occupation, social mix and neighbourhood impacts', *Policy and Politics*, 28, pp.93–108.

Atkinson, R. and Kintrea, K. (2001) *Neighbourhoods and Social Exclusion: The Research and Policy Implications of Neighbourhood Effects*, Department of Urban Studies, University of Glasgow discussion paper.

Audit Commission (2002) *Housing Benefit; The National Perspective* (London: Audit Commission).

Audit Commission/Housing Corporation (2001) *Group Dynamics: Group Structures and Registered Social Landlords* (London: Audit Commission/Housing Corporation).

Bacon, N. and Davis, R. (1996) *New Directions for Housing Associations* (London: Housing Corporation).

Bailey, N. and Robertson, D. (1996) *Review of the Impact of Housing Action Areas for Improvement*, Scottish Homes Research Report 47 (Edinburgh: Scottish Homes).

Bailey, S. (1999) *Local Government Economics: Principles and Practice* (London: Macmillan).

Balchin, P. (1996a) *Housing Policy: An Introduction* (3rd edn) (London: Routledge).

Balchin, P. (ed.) (1996b) *Housing Policy in Europe* (London: Routledge).

Ball, M. (1983) *Housing Policy and Economic Power* (London: Methuen).

Ball, M. (1996a) *Housing and Construction: A Troubled Relationship?* (Bristol: Policy Press).

Ball, M. (1996b) *Investing in New Housing: Lessons for the Future* (Bristol: Policy Press).

Barelli, J. (1992) *Underoccupation* (London: HMSO).

Barelli, J. and Pawson, H. (2001) *Underoccupation in Social Housing* (London: DETR).

Barlow, J. and Chambers, D. (1992) *Planning Agreements and Affordable Housing Provision* (Brighton: University of Sussex Centre for Urban and Regional Research).

Barlow, J. and King, A. (1992) 'The state, the market and competitive strategy: the house-building industry in the United Kingdom, France and Sweden', *Environment and Planning A*, 24, pp.381–400.

Barlow, J., Cocks, R. and Rich, D. (1994) *Planning for Affordable Housing* (London: HMSO).

Barlow, J., Cohen, M., Ashok, J. and Simpson, Y. (1997) *Towards Positive Partnering: Revealing the Realities of the Construction Industry* (Bristol: Policy Press).

Barton, H. with others (2000) *Sustainable Communities: The Potential for Eco-neighbourhoods* (London: Earthscan).

Bate, R. (1999) *A Guide to Land Use and Housing*, Overview Paper for Joseph Rowntree Foundation Reconciling Environmental and Social Concerns Programme.

Bate, R., Best, R. and Holmans, A. (eds) (2000) *On the Move: The Housing Consequences of Migration* (York: Joseph Rowntree Foundation).

Begg, I. (2002) *Urban Competitiveness: Policies for Dynamic Cities* (Bristol: Policy Press).

Bogdon, A. (2001) 'Monitoring housing affordability', in G. Knaap (ed.), *Land Market Monitoring for Smart Urban Growth* (Cambridge, MA: Lincoln Institute of Land Policy).

Bovaird, T. and Halachmi, A. (2001) 'Learning from international approaches to Best Value', *Policy and Politics*, 29 (4), pp.451–63.

Boyle, R. (1999) 'Urban Education', Paper presented at US/UK Competitive Cities Workshop, Glasgow, November.

Bramley, G. (1993a) 'The enabling role for local housing authorities: a preliminary evaluation', in P. Malpass and R. Means (eds), *Implementing Housing Policy* (Buckingham: Open University Press).

Bramley, G. (1993b) 'The impact of land use planning and tax subsidies on the supply and price of housing in Britain', *Urban Studies*, 30, pp.5–30.

Bramley, G. (1993c) 'Land use planning and the housing market in Britain: the impact on housebuilding and house prices', *Environment and Planning A*, 25, pp.1,021–51.

Bramley, G. (1993d) 'Quasi-Markets and social housing', in J. Le Grand and W. Bartlett (eds), *Quasi-Markets and Social Policy* (London: Macmillan).

Bramley, G. (1994) 'An affordability crisis in British housing: dimensions, causes and policy impacts', *Housing Studies,* 8 (2), pp.128–47.

Bramley, G. (1997a) *Direct State Involvement in Housing Land Development: Australian Experience in Comparative Perspective*, Working Paper (Melbourne: Australian Housing and Urban Research Institute).

Bramley, G. (1997b) 'Housing policy: a case of terminal decline?', *Policy and Politics*, 25 (4), pp.387–407.

Bramley, G. (1998a) 'Housing surpluses and housing need', in S. Lowe, S. Spencer and P. Keenan (eds), *Housing Abandonment in Britain: Studies in the Causes and Effects of Low Demand Housing* (York: University of York: Centre for Housing Policy).

Bramley, G. (1998b) 'Measuring planning: indicators of planning restraint and its impact on the housing market', *Environment and Planning B: Planning and Design*, 25, pp.31–57.

Bramley, G. (1999) 'Housing market adjustment and land-supply constraints', *Environment and Planning A*, 31, pp.1,169–88.

Bramley, G. (2001) 'Monitoring and managing urban growth in the United Kingdom: what have we learned?', in G. Knaap (ed.), *Land Market Monitoring for Smart Urban Growth* (Cambridge, MA: Lincoln Institute of Land Policy).

Bramley, G. (2002) 'Planning regulation and housing supply in a market system', in A. O'Sullivan and K. Gibb (eds), *Housing Economics and Public Policy* (Oxford: Basil Blackwell).

Bramley, G. and Dunmore, K. (1996) 'Shared ownership: short term expedient or long term major tenure?', *Housing Studies*, 11 (1), pp.105–31.

Bramley, G. and Lambert, C. (2002) 'Managing urban development: land use planning and city competitiveness', in I. Begg (ed.), *Urban Competitiveness: Policies for Dynamic Cities* (Bristol: Policy Press).

Bramley, G. and Lancaster, S. (1998) 'Household formation: a suitable case for policy?', *Housing Finance*, May, 38, pp.21–9.

Bramley, G. and Morgan, J. (1998) 'Low Cost Home Ownership Initiatives in the UK', *Housing Finance*.

Bramley, G. and Morgan, J. (2002) *Building Future Living Environments: The Role of New Housing in Competitiveness and Cohesion*, ESRC Cities Central Scotland Research Policy Paper for Communities Scotland and the Scottish Executive.

Bramley, G. and Morgan, J. (2003) 'Building competitiveness and cohesion: the role of new housing in Central Scotland's cities', *Housing Studies*, 18 (4), pp.447–71.

Bramley, G. and Pawson, H. (2002) 'Low demand for housing: extent, incidence and national policy implications', *Urban Studies*, 39 (3), pp.393–422.

Bramley, G. and Russell, J. (2000) (in association with Denise Carlo) *Implications of Private Finance Mechanisms (PFI/PPP) for Project Planning: The Case of NHS Hospitals*, Report to DTI Future Best Practice Task Force on the Planning of Major Infrastructure Projects, under Auspices of Technology Foresight Initiative: Built Environment and Transport Panel. London: DTI.

Bramley, G. and Watkins, C. (1995) *Circular Projections: Housing Need, New Housebuilding and the Household Projections* (London: Council for the Protection of Rural England).

Bramley, G. and Watkins, C. (1996a) 'Modelling the relationship between land availability, the land-use planning system and the supply of new housing', Paper presented at Royal Institute of Chartered Surveyors 'Cutting Edge' Conference, University of the West of England, Bristol, 20–21 September 1996.

Bramley, G. and Watkins, C. (1996b) *Steering the Housing Market: New Building and the Changing Planning System* (Bristol: Policy Press).

Bramley, G., Bartlett, W. and Lambert, C. (1995) *Planning, the Market and Private Housebuilding* (London: UCL Press).

Bramley, G., Morgan, J., Dunmore, K. and Cousins, L. (2002) *Evaluation of the Low Cost Home Ownership Programme in England* (London: ODPM).

Bramley, G., Munro, M. and Lancaster, S. (1997) *The Economic Determinants of Household Formation: A Literature Review* (London: DETR).

Bramley, G., Pawson, H. and Third, H. (2000) *Low Demand Housing and Unpopular Neighbourhoods*, Research Report (London: DETR).

Bramley, G., Kirk, K. and Russell, J. (2001) *Planning Central Scotland. The Role of Infrastructure, Urban Form and New Development in Promoting Competitiveness and Cohesion*, ESRC Cities Central Scotland Integrative Cities Study Policy Discussion Paper (University of Glasgow: Department of Urban Studies).

Bramley, G., Satsangi, M. and Pryce, G. (1999) *The Supply Responsiveness of Private Rented Housing: A International Comparison*, Housing Research Report (London: DETR).

Bramley, G., Satsangi, M., Dunmore, K. and Cousins, L. (2004) *Good Practice in The Planning System for Affordable Housing – Lessons from England*, Report to Communities Scotland.

Breheny, M. (1999) *The People: Where Will They Work?* (London: Town and Country Planning Association).

Breheny, M. and Hall, P. (1996) *The People: Where Will They Go?* National Report of the Town and Country Planning Association Regional Inquiry into Housing Need and Provision (London: Town and Country Planning Association).

Bryant, J. (2001) 'Nine tenths of the law', *Housing Today*, 264, 13 December.

Burrows, R. (1999) 'Residential mobility and residualisation in social housing in England', *Journal of Social Policy*, 28 (1), pp.27–52.

Burrows, R. (2003a) 'How the other half lives? An exploratory analysis of the relationship between poverty and home ownership in Britain', *Urban Studies*, 40 (7), pp.1,223–42.

Burrows, R. (2003b) *Poverty and Home Ownership in Contemporary Britain* (Bristol: Policy Press).

Burrows, R. and Loader, B. (eds) (1994) *Towards a Post-Fordist Welfare State?* (London: Routledge).

Burrows, R. and Wilcox, S. (2000) *Half the Poor: Home Owners with Low Incomes* (London: Council of Mortgage Lenders).

Cairncross, L., Clapham, D. and Goodlad, R. (1997) *Housing Management, Consumers and Citizens* (London: Routledge).

Cambridge Policy Consultants (1999) *An Evaluation of the New Life for Urban Scotland Initiative in Castlemilk, Ferguslie Park, Wester Hailes and Whitfield* (Edinburgh: Scottish Executive Central Research Unit).

Carley, M. and Kirk, K. (1998) *Sustainable by 2020? A Strategic Approach to Urban Regeneration for Britain's Cities* (Bristol: Policy Press).

Carley, M., Chapman, M., Hastings, A., Kirk, K. and Young, R. (2000) *Urban Regeneration through Partnership: A Study in Nine Urban Regions in England, Scotland and Wales* (Bristol: Policy Press).

Carr, H., Sefton-Green, D. and Tissier, D. (2001) 'Two steps forward for tenants?'; in D. Cowan and A. Marsh (eds), *Two Steps Forward: Housing Policy into the New Millennium* (Bristol: Policy Press).

Carter, J. (ed.) (1998) *Postmodernity and the Fragmentation of Welfare* (London: Routledge).

Catterick, P. (1992) *Total Quality Management in Housing* (Coventry: Institute of Housing).

Central Housing Advisory Committee (1969) *Council Housing: Purposes, Policies and Procedures* (Cullingworth Report) (London: HMSO).

Champion, A.J. (2002) *The Containment of Urban Britain; Retrospect and Prospect* (Milan, Italy: Franco Angeli).

Champion, A.J., Atkins, D., Coombes, M. and Fotheringham, S. (1998) *Urban Exodus* (London: Council for the Protection of Rural England).

Chartered Institute of Housing (1998) *Low Demand for Housing: A Discussion Paper* (Coventry: Chartered Institute of Housing).

Chatterton, P. and Bradley, D. (2000) 'Bringing Britain together? The limitatons of area-based regeneration in addressing deprivation', *Local Economy*, 15 (2), pp.98–111.

Cheshire, P. and Sheppard, S. (1989) 'British planning policy and access to housing: some empirical estimates', *Urban Studies*, 26, pp.469–85.

Cheshire, P. and Sheppard, S. (1997) *The Welfare Economics of Land Use Regulation*, Research Papers in Environmental and Spatial Analysis, No. 42 (London: Department of Geography, London School of Economics).

Christie, H. (2000) 'Mortgage arrears and gender inequalities', *Housing Studies*, 15 (6), pp.877–905.

Clark, D. and Dunmore, K. (1990) *Involving the Private Sector in Rural Social Housing* (Cirencester: Action for Communities in Rural England).

Cobbold, C. and Dean, J. (2000) *Views on the Large Scale Voluntary Transfer Process* (London: DETR).

Cohen, J. (2001) 'Abandoned housing: exploring lessons from Baltimore', *Housing Policy Debate*, 12 (3), pp.415–48.

Cole, I. (2003) 'The development of housing policy in the English regions: trends and prospects', *Housing Studies*, 18 (2), pp.219–34.

Cole, I. and Furbey, R. (1994) *The Eclipse of Council Housing* (London: Routledge).

Cole, I. and Goodchild, B. (1995) 'Local housing strategies in England: an assessment of their changing role and content', *Policy and Politics*, 23 (1), pp.49–60.

Cole, I., Hickman, P. and Reeve, K. (2001) *On the Spot Housing Management: A Development Guide for Policy Makers and Practitioners* (London: ODPM); see also www.housing.odpm.gov.uk/information/housingmanage/02.htm.

Cole, I., Kane, S. and Robinson, D. (1999) *Changing Demand, Changing Neighbourhoods: The Response of Social Landlords* (Sheffield: Sheffield Hallam University).

Consumers' Association (2003) *Missold Millions*, press release, 23 January.

Council of Mortgage Lenders (2002) *Housing Finance*, 55.

Council of Mortgage Lenders (2003) 'Statistics', *Housing Finance*, Spring.

Cowan, D. and Marsh, A. (2001) *Two Steps Forward: Housing Policy into the New Millennium* (Bristol: Policy Press).

Cowan, D. (2001) 'From allocation to lettings: sea change or more of the same?' in D. Cowan and A. Marsh (eds), *Two Steps Forward: Housing Policy into the New Millennium* (Bristol: Policy Press).

Crook, A.D.H. and Kemp, P. (1995) *The Supply of Privately Rented Homes Today and Tomorrow* (York: Joseph Rowntree Foundation).

Crook, A.D.H. and Kemp, P. (1996) 'The revival of private rented housing in Britain', *Housing Studies*, 11, pp.51–68.

Crook, A.D.H. and Kemp, P.A. (1999) *Financial Institutions and Private Rented Housing* (York: York Publishing Services).

Crook, T., Currie, J., Jackson, A., Monk, S., Rowley, S., Smith, K. and Whitehead, C. (2002) *Planning Gain and Affordable Housing: Making it Count* (York: York Publishing Services).

Cullingworth, J. B. (1997) *Planning in the USA: Policies, Issues and Processes* (London and New York: Routledge).

Cullingworth, J. B. and Nadin, V. (2002) *Town and Country Planning in the UK* (13th edn) (London: Routledge).

Cutler, J. (2002) 'UK house prices – an accident waiting to happen?', *Housing Finance*, Autumn, pp.11–25.

Daly, G. and Davies, H. (2002) 'Partnerships for local governance: citizens, communities and accountability', in C. Glendinning *et al.* (eds), *Partnerships, New Labour and the Governance of Welfare* (Bristol: Policy Press).

Danielsen, K., Lang, R. and Fulton, W. (1999) 'Retracting suburbia: smart growth and the future of housing', *Housing Policy Debate*, 10 (3), pp.513–40.

Dean, J. and Hastings, A. (2000) *Challenging Images: Housing Estates, Stigma and Regeneration* (Bristol: Policy Press).

Dear, M. and others (2001) *Sprawl Hits the Wall: Confronting the Realities of Metropolitan Los Angeles* (Washington: The Brookings institution, www.brookings.edu/dybdocroot/es/urban/la/color.pdf).

Delargy, M. (2003) 'Who's counting? no-one, yet', *Roof*, March/April, pp.18–19.

Dennis, I. and Guio, A.C. (2003) 'Poverty and social exclusion in the EU after Laeken – part 1', *Statistics in Focus: Population and Social Conditions* (Luxembourg: Eurostat).

Department of the Environment (1981) *Difficult to Let Investigation* (Vols 1 and 2), Housing Development Department Occasional Papers 4/80 and 5/80 (London: Department of the Environment).

Department of the Environment (1994a) *Housing Attitudes Survey* (London: HMSO).

Department of the Environment (1994b) *Planning Policy Guidance Note 13: Transport* (London: HMSO).

Department of the Environment (1995a) *Our Future Homes* (London: HMSO).

Department of the Environment (1995b) *Projections of Households in England to 2016* (London: HMSO).

Department of the Environment (1996) *Household Growth: Where Shall we Live?*, Cm 3471 (London: The Stationery Office).

Depres, C. (1991) 'The meaning of the home: literature review, directions for further research and theoretical development', *Journal of Architectural and Planning Research*, 8, pp.96–115.

DETR (1997) *An Economic Model of the Demand and Need for Social Housing* (London: DETR).

DETR (1998a) *A New Deal for Transport: Better for Everyone*, White Paper on the Future of Transport, Cm 3950 (London: The Stationery Office).

DETR (1998b) *Planning and Affordable Housing*, Circular 6/98 (London: DETR).

DETR (1998c) *Planning for the Communities of the Future* (London: DETR).

DETR (1998d) *Rethinking Construction* (The Egan Report), www.Rethinkingconstruction. org/documents/rethinking%20construction%20Report.pdf.

DETR (1998e) *Sustainable Development: Opportunities for Change* (London: DETR).

DETR (1999a) *Developing Good Practice in Tenant Participation* (London: DETR).

DETR (1999b) *Housing Management: National Strategy for Neighbourhood Renewal, Report of Policy Action Team 5* (London: DETR).

DETR (1999c) *Unpopular Housing: National Strategy for Neighbourhood Renewal, Report of Policy Action Team 7* (London: DETR).

DETR (1999d) *Projections of Households in England to 2021* (London: The Stationery Office).

DETR (1999e) *Tenant Participation Compacts: A Guide for Tenants* (London: DETR).

DETR (2000a) *Joining it up Locally, Report of Policy Action Team 17* (London: DETR).

DETR (2000b) *Planning Policy Guidance Note 3: Housing* (London: HMSO).

DETR (2000c) *Quality and Choice: A Decent Home for All – The Housing Green Paper* (London: DETR).

DETR (2001) 'Guidance Notes to Local Authority Housing Strategy Statistical Appendix Statistical Return' (unpublished).

Dorling, D. and Cornford, J. (1995) 'Who has negative equity: how house price falls in Britain have hit different groups of house buyers', *Housing Studies*, 10 (2), pp.151–78.

Dorling, D. and Rees, P. (2003) 'A nation still dividing: the British census and social polarisation 1971–2001', *Environment and Planning A*, 35 (7), pp.1,287–313.

Downs, A. (1997) 'Challenge of our declining cities', *Housing Policy Debate*, 8 (2), pp.359–408.

DTLR (2001) *Planning: Delivering a Fundamental Change*, Planning Green Paper (London: DTLR).

DTZ Pieda (2000) *Demolition and New Building on Local Authority Estates* (London: DETR).

Duncan, P. and Thomas, S. (2000) *Neighbourhood Regeneration: Resourcing Community Involvement* (Bristol: Policy Press).

Dunmore, K., Strode, M., Cousins, L., Stewart, J. and Bramley, G. (1997) *A Critical Evaluation of the Low Cost Home Ownership Programme* (London: HMSO).

Edelman, M. (1971) *Politics as Symbolic Action* (Chicago, IL: Markham).

Ellaway, A. and MacIntyre, S. (1998) 'Does housing tenure predict health in the UK because it exposes people to different levels of housing-related hazards in the home or its surroundings?', *Health and Place*, 4, pp.141–50.

Evans, A. and Smith, R. (2002) *Closing the Gap: Working Together to Reduce Rent Arrears* (Cardiff: Audit Commission in Wales).

Evans, A.W. (1973) *The Economics of Residential Location* (London: Heinemann).

Evans, A.W. (1991) 'Rabbit hutches on postage stamps: planning, development and political economy', *Urban Studies*, 28 (6), pp.853–70.

Evans, R. (1998) 'Tackling deprivation on social housing estates in England: an assessment of the housing plus approach', *Housing Studies*, 13 (5), pp.713–26.

Farthing, S. (1995) 'Landowner involvement in local plans: how patterns of involvement both reflect and conceal influence', *Journal of Property Research*, 12, pp.41–61.

Featherstone, A. (1991) *Postmodernity and Consumer Culture* (London: Sage).

Fischel, W. (1990) *Do Growth Controls Matter? A Review of Empirical Evidence on the Effectiveness and Efficiency of Local Government Land-use Regulation*, Lincoln Institute of Land Policy Working Paper (Boston, MA: Lincoln Institute of Land Policy).

Ford, J. (2000a) 'Housing and the flexible labour market: responding to risk' in P. Taylor-Gooby (ed.), *Risk Trust and Welfare* (London: Macmillan).

Ford, J. (2000b) *MPPI Take up and Retention: Evidence from Existing Research* (London: Council of Mortgage Lenders).

Ford, J., Burrows, R. and Nettleton, S. (2001) *Home Ownership in a Risk Society: A Social Analysis of Mortgage Arrears and Possessions* (Bristol: Policy Press).

Fordham, G. (2002) *Regeneration that Lasts* (London: ODPM).

Forrest, R. (1983) 'The meaning of home ownership', *Environment and Planning D: Society and Space*, 1, pp.205–16.

Forrest, R. and Murie, A. (1987) 'The affluent home owner: labour market position and the shaping of housing histories', *Sociological Review*, 35, pp.370–403.

Forrest, R. and Murie, A. (1988) *Selling the Welfare State: The Privatisation of Public Housing* (London: Routledge).

Forrest, R. and Murie, A. (1993) *New Homes for Homeowners: A Study of New Building and Vacancy Chains in Southern England* (London: HMSO).

Forrest, R., Murie, A. and Williams, P. (1990) *Home Ownership: Differentiation and Fragmentation* (London: Unwin Hyman).

Freeman, A., Holmans, A. and Whitehead, C. (1996) *Is the UK Different? International Comparisons of Tenure Patterns* (London: Council of Mortgage Lenders).

Freeman, A., Holmans, A. and Whitehead, C. (1999) *Evaluating Housing Affordability – Policy Options and New Directions* (London: Local Government Association).

Furbey, R., Reid, B. and Cole, I. (2001) 'Housing professionalism in the United Kingdom: the final curtain or a new age?', *Housing, Theory and Society*, 18 (1–2), pp.36–49.

Garnett, D. (2000) *Housing Finance* (Coventry: Chartered Institute of Housing).

Geddes, M. (2001) 'What about the workers? Best Value, employment and work in local public services', *Policy and Politics*, 29 (4), pp.497–508.

Gibb, K., Munro, M. and McGregor, A. (1995) *The Scottish Housebuilding Industry: Opportunity or Constraint?*, Research Report 44 (Edinburgh: Scottish Homes).

Gibb, K., Munro, M. and Satsangi, M. (1999) *Housing Finance in the UK* (2nd edn). (London: Macmillan).

Giddens, A. (1998) *The Third Way: The Renewal of Social Democracy* (Cambridge: Polity Press).

Giles, C., Johnson, P., McCrae, J. and Taylor, J. (1996) *Living with The State: The Incomes and Work Incentives of Tenants in the Social Rented Sector* (London: Institute for Fiscal Studies).

Glennerster, H., Lupton, R., Noden, D. and Power, A. (1999) *Social Exclusion and Neighbourhood: Studying the Area Bases of Social Exclusion,* CASE Paper (London: Centre For Analysis of Social Exclusion, London School of Economics).

Goodlad, R. (1998) *Creating a New Future: The Strategic Role of Scottish Local Authorities* (Edinburgh: Chartered Institute of Housing).

Goodlad, R. (2001) 'Developments in tenant participation: accounting for growth', in D. Cowan and A. Marsh (eds), *Two Steps Forward: Housing Policy into the New Millennium* (Bristol: Policy Press), pp.179–98.

Grant, M. (1992) 'Planning law and the British land use planning system', *Town Planning Review*, 63 (1), pp.3–12.

Griffiths, M., Parker, J., Smith, R., Stirling, T. and Trott, T. (1996) *Community Lettings: Local Allocation Policies in Practice* (York: Joseph Rowntree Foundation).

Gurney, C. (1999) 'Pride and prejudice: discourses of normalisation in public and private accounts of home ownership', *Housing Studies*, 14, pp.164–85.

HACAS Chapman Hendy (2002) *Beyond Bricks and Mortar: Bringing Regeneration into Stock Transfer* (Coventry: Chartered Institute of Housing).

Hague, C. (1996) 'The development and politics of tenant participation in British council housing', *Housing Studies*, 5, pp.242–56.

Hall, P., Thomas, H., Gracey, R. and Drewett, R. (1973) *The Containment of Urban England* (London: George Allen & Unwin).

Hamnett, C. and Seavers, J. (1996) 'Home ownership, housing wealth and wealth distribution in Britain', in J. Hills (ed.), *New Inequalities: The Changing Distribution of Income and Wealth in the United Kingdom* (Cambridge: Cambridge University Press), pp.348–13.

Hamnett, C. (1999) *Winners and Losers: Home Ownership in Modern Britain* (London: UCL).

Hamnett, C., Harmer C. and Williams P. (1991) *As Safe as Houses: Housing Inheritance in Britain* (London: Paul Chapman).

Harries, A. and Vincent-Jones, P. (2001) 'Housing management in three metropolitan local authorities; the impact of CCT and implications for Best Value', *Local Government Studies*, 27 (2), pp.69–92.

Harrison, M. with Phillips, D. (2003) *Housing and Black and Minority Ethnic Communities: Review of the Evidence Base* (London: ODPM).

Harvey, R. and Ashworth, A. (1997) *The Construction Industry of Great Britain* (Oxford: Butterworth-Heinemann).

Hawksworth, J. and Wilcox, S. (1995) 'The PSBR handicap', in S. Wilcox (ed.), *Housing Finance Review 1995/96* (York: Joseph Rowntree Foundation).

Healey, P., Doak, P., MacNamara, P. and Elson, M. (1985) *The Implementation of Planning Policies and the Role of Development Plans* (2 vols) (Oxford: Department of Town Planning, Oxford Polytechnic).

Healey, P., Doak, P., MacNamara, P. and Elson, M. (1988) *Land Use Planning and the Mediation of Urban Change: The British Planning System in Practice* (Cambridge: Cambridge University Press).

Healey, P., Purdue, M. and Ennis, F. (1993) *Gains from Planning? Dealing with the Impacts of Development* (York: Joseph Rowntree Foundation).

Heneberry, J., Guy, S. and Bramley, G. (2003) 'Urban properties: spaces, places and the property business', in I. Turok, N. Buck, I. Gordon and A. Harding (eds), *City Matters* (Basingstoke: Palgrave Macmillan).

Henney, A. (1984) *Inside Local Government: A Case for Radical Reform* (London: Sinclair Brown).

Hill, M. and Bramley, G. (1986) *Analysing Social Policy* (Oxford: Basil Blackwell).

Hills, J. (1991) *Unravelling Housing Finance: Subsidies, Benefits and Taxation* (Oxford: Clarendon).

Hills, J. (ed.) (1996) *New Inequalities: The Changing Distribution of Income and Wealth in the United Kingdom* (Cambridge: Cambridge University Press).

Hills, J. (1997) *The Future of Welfare: A Guide to the Debate* (2nd edn) (York: Joseph Rowntree Foundation).

Hills, J. (1998) *Income and Wealth: The Latest Evidence* (York: Joseph Rowntree Foundation).

HM Government (1990) *This Common Inheritance*, Environment White Paper (London: HMSO).

HM Government (1994) *Sustainable Development: The UK Strategy*, Cm 2426 (London: HMSO).

HM Treasury (2003) *Housing Consumption and EMU*, EMU Studies (London: The Stationery Office). www.hm-treasury.gov.uk/documents/the_euro/assessment/studies/euro_assess03_studindex.cfm.

Holmans, A. (1991) *Estimates of Housing Equity Withdrawal by Owner-occupiers in the United Kingdom 1970 to 1990*, Government Economic Service Working Paper No. 116 (London: Department of the Environment).

Holmans, A. (1995) 'The changing relationship between tenure and employment', in H. Green and J. Hansbro (eds), *Housing in England 1993/94* (London: HMSO).

Holmans, A. (2000) 'Estimates of future housing needs and demand', in S. Monk and C. Whitehead (eds), *Restructuring Housing Systems: From Social to Affordable Housing* (York: York Publishing Services).

Holmans, A. and Simpson, M. (1999) *Low Demand: Separating Fact from Fiction* (Coventry: Chartered Institute of Housing).

Hood, C., James, O. and Scott, C. (2000) 'Regulation of government: has it increased, is it increasing, should it be diminished?', *Public Administration*, 78 (4), pp.283–304.

Hooper, A., Dunmore, K. and Hughes, M. (1998) *Home Alone* (Amersham: Housing Research Foundation).

Houston, D., Barr, K. and Dean, J. (2002) *Research on the Private Rented Sector in Scotland* (Edinburgh: Scottish Executive Central Research Unit).

Hutton, W. and Giddens, A. (eds) (2001) *On the Edge: Living with Global Capitalism* (London: Vintage).

Industrial Systems Research (1999) *Political Barriers to Housebuilding in Britain: A Critical Case Study of Protectionism and its Industrial-commercial Effects* ISR Business and Political-Legal Environment Reports (Manchester: ISR).

Inkson, S. (1999) 'From acute to critical: the low demand condition in Wales', *Welsh Housing Quarterly*, 35, pp.14–16.

Institute for Public Policy Research (2001) *Building Better Partnerships: Final Report of the Commission on Public–Private Partnerships* (London: Institute for Public Policy Research).

Jacobs, J. (1969) *The Economy of Cities* (New York, NY: Vintage).

Jencks, M., Burton, E. and Williams, K. (eds) (1996) *The Compact City: A Sustainable Urban Form?* (London: E. & F. Spon).

Jones, C. and Murie, A. (1999) *Reviewing the Right to Buy* (Birmingham: University of Birmingham).

Jones, C. and Watkins, C. (1999) 'Planning and the housing system', in P. Allmendinger and M. Chapman (eds), *Planning Beyond 2000* (Chichester: Wiley).

Joseph Rowntree Foundation (1994) *Inquiry into Planning for Housing* (York: Joseph Rowntree Foundation).

Joseph Rowntree Foundation (2000) *Key Steps to Sustainable Area Regeneration*, Foundations D10 (York: Joseph Rowntree Foundation).

Joseph Rowntree Foundation (2003) 'Private landlords and buy-to-let', *Housing Research Findings* 013. http://www.jrf.org.uk/knowledge/findings/housing/013.asp.

Jowell, R. and others (2000) *British Social Attitudes: Focussing on Diversity* (17th edn) Report by National Centre for Social Research (London: Sage).

Jupp, B. (1999) *Living Together: Community Life on Mixed Tenure Estates* (London: Demos).

Karn, V. (1977) 'Low income owner-occupation in the inner city', in C. Jones (ed.), *Urban Deprivation and the Inner City* (London: Croom Helm).

Karn, V., Kemeny, J. and Williams, P. (1985) *Home Ownership in the Inner City – Salvation or Despair?* (London: Croom Helm).

Kearns, A., Hiscock, R., Ellaway, A. and MacIntyre, S. (2000) ' "Beyond four walls": the psycho-social benefits of home: evidence from West Central Scotland', *Housing Studies*, 15, pp.387–410.

Keenan, P., Lowe, S. and Spencer, S. (1999) 'Housing abandonment in inner cities – the politics of low demand for housing', *Housing Studies*, 14 (5), pp.703–16.

Kemeny, J. (1981) *The Myth of Home Ownership: Private vs. Public Choices in Housing Tenure* (London: Routledge).

Kemp, P. (1998) *Housing Benefit: Time for Reform* (York: Joseph Rowntree Foundation).

Kemp, P. (2000) *'Shopping Incentives' and Housing Benefit Reform* (York: Joseph Rowntree Foundation/Charted Institute of Housing).

Kemp, P., Wilcox, S. and Rhodes, D. (2002) *Housing Benefit Reform: Next Steps* (York: York Publishing Service).

Kintrea, K. and Clapham, D. (2000) 'Community based housing organisations and the local governance debate', *Housing Studies*, 15 (4), pp.533–59.

Kintrea, K., McGregor, A., McConnachie, M. and Urquhart, A. (1995) *Interim Evaluation of the Whitfield Partnership* (Edinburgh: Scottish Office Central Research Unit).

Kleinman, M., Matznetter, W. and Stephens, M. (1998) *European Integration and Housing Policy* (London: Routledge).

Knaap, G. (2001) *Land Market Monitoring for Smart Urban Growth* (Cambridge, MA: Lincoln Institute of Land Policy).

Kullberg, J. (1997) 'From waiting lists to adverts: the allocation of social rental dwellings in the Netherlands', *Housing Studies*, 12 (3), pp.393–403.

Kullberg, J. (2002) 'Consumers' response to choice based letting mechanisms', *Housing Studies*, 17 (4), pp.549–79.

Lambert, C. (1990) *New Housebuilding and the Development Industry in the Bristol Area*, Working Paper 86 (Bristol: Bristol University, School for Advanced Urban Studies).

Lambert, C. and Malpass, P. (1998) 'The Rules of the Game: Competition for Housing Investment', in N. Oatley (ed.), *Cities, Economic Competition and Urban Policy* (London: Paul Chapman).

Latham, M. (1994) *Constructing the Team* (London: HMSO).

Le Grand, J. and Bartlett, W. (1993) *Quasi-markets and Social Policy* (London: Macmillan).

Le Grand, J., Propper, C. and Robinson, R. (1992) *The Economics of Social Problems* (3rd edn) (London: Macmillan).

Leach, R. and Percy-Smith, J. (2002) *Local Governance in Britain* (Basingstoke: Palgrave/ Macmillan).

Leather, P. (2000) 'Grants to home owners: a policy in search of objectives', *Housing Studies*, 15, pp.149–68.

Leather, P. and Anderson, K. (1999) *The Condition of Former Right to Buy Properties and Innovative Approaches to the Management and Financing of Repair Work* (Edinburgh: Scottish Homes).

Leather, P. and Mackintosh, S. (1997) 'Towards sustainable policies for housing renewal in the private sector' in P. Williams (ed.), *Directions in Housing Policy: Towards Sustainable Housing Policies for the UK* (London: Paul Chapman).

Leather, P. and Morrison, T. (1997) *The State of UK Housing* (Bristol: Policy Press).

Leather, P., Munro, M. and Littlewood, A. (1999) *Make Do and Mend: Homeowners' Attitudes to Repair and Maintenance* (York: Joseph Rowntree Foundation).

Lee, P. and Murie, A. (1997) *Poverty, Housing and Social Exclusion* (York: Joseph Rowntree Foundation).

Leishman, C., Jones, C. and Fraser, W. (2000) 'The influence of uncertainty on house builder behaviour and residential land values', *Journal of Property Research*, 17 pp.147–68.

Levačić, R. (1987) *Economic Policy-making in Theory and Practice* (Brighton: Wheatsheaf).

Lewis, M. and Hartley, J. (2001) 'Evolving forms of quality management in local government; Lessons from the Best Value Pilot Programme', *Policy and Politics*, 29 (4), pp.477–96.

Loughlin, M. (1984) *Local Needs Policies and Development Control Strategies: An Examination of the Role of Occupancy Restrictions in Development Control*, Working Paper 42 (Bristol: School for Advanced Urban Studies).

Lowe, S., Spencer, S. and Keenan, P. (1998) *Housing Abandonment in Britain: Case Studies in the Causes and Effects of Low Demand Housing* (York: University of York).

Lowry, I. (1966) *Migration and Metropolitan Growth: Three Models* (San Francisco, CA: Chandler).

Maclennan, D. (1997) 'The UK housing market: up, down and where next?' in P. Williams (ed.), *Directions in Housing Policy: Towards Sustainable Housing Policies for the UK* (London: Paul Chapman).

Maclennan, D. (2000) *Changing Places, Engaging People* (York: Joseph Rowntree Foundation).

Maclennan, D., Muellbauer, J. and Stephens, M. (1998) 'Asymmetries in housing and financial market institutions and EMU', *Oxford Review of Economic Policy*, 14, pp.54–80.

Magnusson, L. and Turner, B. (2002) *Countryside Abandoned? Suburbanisation and Mobility in Sweden*, Institute for Housing and Urban Research, Uppsala University, Sweden (unpublished).

Maile, S. and Hoggett, P. (2001) 'Best value and the politics of pragmatism', *Policy and Politics*, 29 (4), pp.508–19.

Malpass, P. (1999) 'Housing policy: does it have a future?', *Policy and Politics*, 27 (2), pp.217–28.

Malpass, P. (2000) *Housing Associations and Housing Policy: A Historical Perspective* (London: Macmillan).

Malpass, P. and Mullins, D. (2002) 'Local authority housing stock transfer in the UK: from local initiative to national policy', *Housing Studies*, 17 (4), pp.673–86.

Malpass, P. and Murie, A. (1999) *Housing Policy and Practice* (5th edn) (London: Macmillan).

Malpezzi, S. (1996) 'Housing prices, externalities and regulation in US Metropolitan Areas', *Journal of Housing Research*, 7 (2), pp.209–41.

Maslow, A. (1943) 'A theory of human motivation', *Psychological Review*, 50, pp.370–96.

McCrone, G. and Stephens, M. (1995) *Housing Policy in Britain and Europe* (London: UCL Press).

McGregor, A. and MacLennan, D. (1992) *A Review and Critical Evaluation of Strategic Approaches to Urban Regeneration*, Scottish Homes Research Report No. 22 (Edinburgh: Scottish Homes).

McGregor, A., Kintrea, K., Fitzpatrick, I. and Urquhart, A. (1995) *Interim Evaluation of the Wester Hailes Partnership* (Edinburgh: Scottish Office Central Research Unit).

McIntosh, A. (2002) 'Too Much Bumf', *Inside Housing*, 27 September, p.27.

Meen, G. (1995) 'Is housing good for the economy?', *Housing Studies*, 10, pp.405–24.

Meen, G. (1996) 'Ten propositions in UK housing macroeconomics: an overview of the Eighties and early Nineties', *Urban Studies*, 33, pp.425–44.

Meen, G. (1998) 'Modelling sustainable home ownership: demographics or economics?', *Urban Studies*, 35, pp.1919–34.

Merrett, S. (1979) *State Housing in Britain* (London: Routledge & Kegan Paul).

Miles, D. (1994) *Housing Financial Markets and the Wider Economy* (Chichester: Wiley).

Monk, S. and Whitehead, C. (1996) 'Land supply and housing: a case study', *Housing Studies*, 11 (3), pp.407–23.

Monk, S. and Whitehead, C. (1999) 'Evaluating the economic impact of planning controls in the United Kingdom: some implications for housing', *Land Economics*, 75 (1), pp.74–93.

Monk, S. and Whitehead, C. (2000) *Restructuring Housing Systems: From Social to Affordable Housing?* (York: York Publishing Services).

Monk, S., Pearce, B. and Whitehead, C. (1991) *Planning, Land Supply and House Prices: A Literature Review*. Monograph 21, Department of Land Economy, University of Cambridge (London and Cambridge: Granta).

Morgan, J. and Talbot, R. (2000) 'Sustainable social housing for no extra cost?' in K. Williams, E. Burton and M. Jencks (eds), *Achieving Sustainable Urban Form* (London: E. & F. Spon).

Muellbauer, J. (1990) 'The great British housing disaster', *Roof*, May/June.

Mullen, T. (2001) 'Stock transfer', in D. Cowan and A. Marsh (eds), *Two Steps Forward: Housing Policy into the New Millennium* (Bristol: Policy Press).

Mullins, D. (1999) *Survey of Registered Social Landlord Best Value Activity 1999: A Baseline for the Future* (London: National Housing Federation).

Mullins, D. and Riseborough, M. (2000) *Changing with the Times* (Birmingham: University of Birmingham).

Munro, M and Madigan, R. (1993) 'Privacy in the private sphere', *Housing Studies*, 9, pp.25–45.

Munro, M. and Tu (1996) 'The dynamics of UK national and regional house prices', *Review of Urban and Regional Development Studies*, 8, pp.186–201.

Murie, A. (1997) 'Beyond state housing', in P. Williams (ed.), *Directions in Housing Policy: Towards Sustainable Housing Policies for the UK* (London: Paul Chapman).

Murie, A. and Nevin, B. (2001); 'New Labour Transfers', in D. Cowan and A. Marsh (eds), *Two Steps Forward: Housing Policy into the New Millennium* (Bristol: Policy Press).

Murie, A., Nevin, B. and Leather, P. (1998) *Changing Demand and Unpopular Housing*, Working Paper 4 (London: Housing Corporation).

Muth, R. (1969) *Cities and Housing* (Chicago, IL: University of Chicago Press).

Muthesius, S. and Glendinning, M. (1994) *Tower Block: Modern Public Housing in England, Wales, Scotland and Northern Ireland* (New Haven, CT, and London: Yale University Press).

National Audit Office (2003) *Improving Social Housing through Transfer* (London: The Stationery Office).

Needham, B. and Lie, R. (1994) 'The public regulation of property supply and its effects on private prices, risks and returns', *Journal of Property Research*, 11, pp.199–213.

Nettleton, S. and Burrows, R. (2000) 'When a capital investment becomes and emotional loss: the health consequences of the experience of mortgage possession', *Housing Studies*, 15, pp.463–79.

Neuberger, J. (2003) *House Keeping: Preventing Homelessness through Tackling Rent Arrears in Social Housing* (London: Shelter).

Nevin, B. and Battle, J. (2002) 'Filling the void', *Inside Housing*, 22 February, pp.24–5.

Nevin, B., Lee, P., Goodson, L., Murie, A. and Phillimore, J. (2001) *Changing Housing Markets and Urban Regeneration in the M62 Corridor* (Birmingham: University of Birmingham).

Newton, P. (2000) 'Urban form and environmental performance', in K. Williams, E. Burton and M. Jencks, (eds), *Achieving Sustainable Urban Form* (London: E. & F. Spon).

Nicol, C. and Hooper, A. (1999) 'Contemporary change and the housebuilding industry: concentration and standardisation in production', *Housing Studies*, 14, pp.57–76.

O'Leary, K and Farquhar, J. (2003) 'Offset mortgages: the consumer viewpoint', *Housing Finance*, 57, pp.28–38.

O'Sullivan, A. and Gibb, K. (eds) (2002) *Housing Economics and Public Policy* (Oxford: Basil Blackwell).

Oatley, N. (2000) 'New Labour's approach to age-old problems: Renewing and revitalising poor neighbourhoods – the national strategy for neighbourhood renewal', *Local Economy*, 15 (2), pp.86–97.

ODPM (2002a) *Allocation of Accommodation Code of Guidance for Local Housing Authorities* (London: ODPM).

ODPM (2002b) *A Decent Home: The Revised Definition and Guidance for Implementation* (London: ODPM) and www.housing.odpm.gov.uk/information/dhg/pdf/guidance.pdf.

ODPM (2002c) Housing Statistics 2002 Great Britain; www.odpm.gov.uk.

ODPM (2003a) *English House Condition Survey 2001: Building the Picture* (London: ODPM) and http://www.odpm.gov.uk/stellent/groups/odpm_housing/documents/page/odpm_house_022942.pdf.

ODPM (2003b) *Sustainable Communities: Building for the Future* (London: HMSO).

Ove Arup and others (1998) *Planning for Sustainable Development: Towards Better Practice*, Report to DETR (London: The Stationery Office).

Page, D. (1993) *Building for Communities: A Study of New Housing Association Estates* (York: Joseph Rowntree Foundation).

Page, D. (2000) *The Reality of Social Exclusion on Housing Estates*, Findings 120 (York: Joseph Rowntree Foundation).

Palmer, G., Rahman, M. and Kenway, P. (2002) *Monitoring Poverty and Social Exclusion 2002* (York: Joseph Rowntree Foundation).

Pannell, B. (2002) 'Affordability – how much higher can UK house prices go?', *Housing Finance*, Autumn, pp.26–35.

Pawson, H. (1998) 'Gravity defied: local authority lettings and stock turnover in the 1990s', in S. Wilcox (ed.), *Housing Finance Review 1998/99* (York: Joseph Rowntree Foundation).

Pawson, H. (2001) 'Pilots set for take-off', *DTLR Choice-based Lettings Newsletter*, No. 1 http://www.odpm.gov.uk/stellent/groups/odpm_housing/documents/page/odpm_house_6 02510.hcsp.

Pawson, H. (2002a) *Allocations and Choice in Scotland: A Discussion Paper* (Edinburgh: Chartered Institute of Housing in Scotland).

Pawson, H. (2002b) *Assessing Stock Transfer in Scotland* (Housing Quality Network); see www.hqnetwork.org.uk.

Pawson, H. and Bramley, G. (2000) 'Understanding recent trends in residential mobility in council housing in England', *Urban Studies*, 37 (8), pp.1,231–59.

Pawson, H. and Fancy, C. (2003) *Maturing Assets: The Evolution of Stock Transfer Housing Associations* (Bristol: Policy Press).

Pawson, H. and Ford, T. (2002) *Stock Turnover and Evictions in the RSL Sector*, Sector Study 14 (London: Housing Corporation).

Pawson, H. and Mullins, D. (2003) *Changing Places: Housing Association Policy and Practice on Nominations and Lettings* (Bristol: Policy Press).

Pawson, H. and Sinclair, S.P. (2003) 'Shopping therapy? Incentive schemes and tenant behaviour: lessons from underoccupation schemes in the UK', *European Journal of Housing Policy*, 3 (3), pp.289–311.

Pawson, H., Munro, M., Carley, M., Lancaster, S., Kintrea, K. and Littlewood, A. (1998) *Smaller Urban Renewal Initiatives: An Interim Evaluation*, Scottish Homes Research Report No. 63 (Edinburgh: Scottish Homes).

Pawson, H., Kirk, K. and McIntosh, S. (2000) *Assessing the Impact of Tenure Diversification: The Case of Niddrie, Edinburgh*, Scottish Homes Research Report No. 79 (Edinburgh: Scottish Homes).

Pawson, H., Levison, D., Lawton, G., Parker, J. and Third, H. (2001) *Local Authority Policy and Practice on Allocations, Transfers and Homelessness* (London: DETR).

Pawson, H., Currie, A., Currie, H., Hayhurst, W. and Holmes, J. (2004) *Performance Management in Local Authority Housing Services* (Edinburgh: Communities Scotland).

Pdogzinski, H.U. and Sass, T.R. (1991) 'Measuring the effects of municipal zoning regulations: a survey', *Urban Studies*, 28 (4), pp.597–621.

Pearl, M. (1997) *Social Housing Management: A Critical Appraisal of Housing Practice* (London: Macmillan).

Perri 6 (1997) Escaping Poverty: From Safety Nets to Networks of Opportunity (London: DEMOS).

Perry, J. (2000) 'The end of Council housing?', in S. Wilcox (ed.), *Housing Finance Review 2000/01* (Coventry, London and York: Chartered Institute of Housing, Council of Mortgage Lenders and Joseph Rowntree Foundation).

Perry, J. (2002) 'Taking stock: partial transfers can play a key role in urban regeneration', *Housing*, September, pp.34–5.

Petersen, A., Barns, I., Dudley, J. and Harris, P. (1999) *Poststructuralism, Citizenship and Social Policy* (London: Routledge).

Phelps, L. and Carter, M. (2003) *Possession Action – the Last Resort? CAB Evidence on Court Action by Social Landlords to Recover Rent Arrears* (London: Citizens Advice Bureau).

Piachaud, D. and Sutherland, H. (2002) *Changing Poverty Post-1997*, Centre for Analysis of Social Exclusion (CASE) paper 63 (London: London School of Economics).

Pollhammer, M. and Grainger, P. (2003) *Housing on the Horizon; The Brave New World of Empowerment in Housing Allocations* (Newcastle-upon-Tyne: Northumbria University).

Power, A. (1987) *Property before People* (London: Allen & Unwin).

Power, A. and Mumford, K. (1999) *The Slow Death of Great Cities Urban Abandonment or Urban Renaissance* (York: York Publishing Services).

Pryce, G. (1999) 'Construction elasticities and land availability: a two-stage least squares model of housing supply using the variable elasticity approach', *Urban Studies*, 36 (13), pp.2,283–304.

Rae, D. and Calsyn, D. (1996) cited in. J. Cohen (2001), 'Abandoned housing: exploring lessons from Baltimore', *Housing Policy Debate*, 12 (3), pp.415–48.

Randolph, B. (1993) 'The Re-privatisation of Housing Associations', in P. Malpass and R. Means (eds), *Implementing Housing Policy* (Buckingham: Open University Press).

Ravetz, A. with Turkington, R. (1995) *The Place of Home: English Domestic Environments 1914–2000* (London: E. & F. Spon).

Richardson, J.J. and Jordan, A.F. (1979) *Governing under Pressure* (Oxford: Martin Robertson).

Riseborough, M. (1998) 'More control and choice for users? Involving tenants in social housing management', in A. Marsh and D. Mullins (eds) *Housing and Public Policy: Citizenship, Choice and Control* (Buckingham: Open University Press).

Robson, B., Parkinson, M., Boddy, M. and Maclennan, D. (2000) *The State of English Cities* (London: DETR).

Royal Commission on Environmental Pollution (1995) *Transport and the Environment*, Eighteenth Report, presented to Parliament, October 1994 (Oxford: Oxford University Press).

Royal Town Planning Institute (2000) *Green Belt Policy: A Discussion Paper* (London: Royal Town Planning Institute).

Rybczynski, W. (1987) *Home: A Short History of an Idea* (New York: Penguin Putnam).

Saunders, P. (1978) 'Domestic property and social class', *International Journal of Urban and Regional Research*, 2, pp.233–51.

Saunders, P. (1984) 'Beyond housing classes', *International Journal of Urban and Regional Research*, 8, pp.207–7.

Saunders, P. (1986) 'Comment on Dunleavy and Preteceille', *Environment and Planning A*, 4, pp.155–63.

Saunders, P. (1989) 'The meaning of "home" in contemporary English culture', *Housing Studies*, 4, pp.177–92.

Saunders, P. (1990) *A Nation of Home Owners* (London: Unwin Hyman).

School of Planning and Housing (2001) *The Role of the Planning System in the Provision of Housing* (Edinburgh: Scottish Executive Central Research Unit).

Schoon, N. (2001) *The Chosen City* (London: Spon Press).

Scott, S., Currie, H., Dean, J. and Kintrea, K. (2001a) *Good Practice in Housing Management: Case Studies, Conclusions and Recommendations* (Edinburgh: Scottish Executive).

Scott, S., Currie, H., Fitzpatrick, S., Keoghan, M., Kintrea, K., Pawson, H. and Tate, J. (2001b) *Good Practice in Housing Management in Scotland: Review of Progress* (Edinburgh: Scottish Executive).

Scottish Executive (1999) *Development of a Policy on Architecture for Scotland* (Edinburgh: Scottish Executive) http://www.scotland.gov.uk/library3/construction/apoa-10.asp.

Scottish Executive (2001a) *Better Homes for Scotland's Communities – The Executive's Proposals for the Housing Bill* (Edinburgh: Scottish Executive).

Scottish Executive (2001b) *Review of Strategic Planning*, Consultation Paper (Edinburgh: Scottish Executive Development Department, Planning Services).

Scottish Executive (2003) *Scottish Planning Policy (Edinburgh: Scottish Executive)*.

Scottish Executive (2003a) *Modernising Scotland's Social Housing: A Consultation Paper* (Edinburgh: Scottish Executive) and www.scotland.gov.uk/consultations/housing/mssh.pdf.

Scottish Executive (2003b) *Scottish Planning Policy 3: Housing* (Edinburgh: Scottish Executive).

Scottish Executive (2003c) *Stewardship and Responsibility: A Policy Framework for Private Housing in Scotland*, The Final Report and Recommendations of the Housing Improvement Task Force (Edinburgh: Scottish Executive), www.scotland.gov.uk/library5/housing/pfph-00.asp.

Scottish Homes (1997) *Scottish House Condition Survey* (Edinburgh: Scottish Homes).

Scottish Homes (1998) *Group Structures, Subsidiaries and Other Related Organisations*, Scottish Homes Guidance Note SHGN 98/10 (Edinburgh: Scottish Homes).

Scottish Homes (2000) *Group Structures Including Non-RSLs and Related Organisations*, Scottish Homes Guidance Note SHGN 2000/08.

Scottish Homes (2001) *Investment Programme 2001/02* (Edinburgh: Scottish Homes).

SEU (1998) *Bringing Britain Together: A National Strategy for Neighbourhood Renewal* (London: The Stationery Office).

SEU (2000) *Bringing Britain Together: A National Strategy for Neighbourhood Renewal* (London: Cabinet Office).

Sim, D. (1993) *British Housing Design* (London and Coventry: Longman/Institute of Housing).

Slade, M. and Roberts, M. (2003) 'The rise and rise of mortgage churn in the UK', *Housing Finance*, 57 (Spring), pp.11–27.

Smith, G.R. (1999) *Area-based Initiatives: The Rationale and Options for Area Targeting*, Paper 25 (London: Centre for Analysis of Social Exclusion, London School of Economics).

Smith, J. (2003) 'Mortgage equity withdrawal: evidence from CML market research', *Housing Finance*, 57 (Spring), pp.50–63.

Smith, S.J. and Mallinson, S. (1997) 'Housing for health in a post-welfare state', *Housing Studies*, 12, pp.173–200.

Smith, S.J., Easterlow, D., Munro, M. and Turner, K. (2003) 'Housing as health capital: how health trajectories and housing paths are linked', *Journal of Social Issues*, 59 (3), pp.501–26.

Smith, S.J., Ford, J. and Munro, M. (2002) *A Review of Flexible Mortgages* (London: Council of Mortgage Lenders).

Somerville, P. (2001) 'Allocating housing or "letting" people choose?', in D. Cowan and A. Marsh (eds), *Two Steps Forward: Housing Policy into the New Millennium* (Bristol: Policy Press).

Steinlieb, G. and Burchell, R. (1974) 'Housing abandonment in the urban core', *Journal of the American Institute of Planners*, 4, pp.321–32.

Stephens, M. (1993) 'Housing finance deregulation: Britain's experience', *Netherlands Journal of Housing and the Built Environment*, 8, pp.159–75.

Stevenson, F. and Williams, N. (2000) *Sustainable Housing Design Guide* (Edinburgh: Scottish Homes/The Stationery Office).

Stewart, M. and Taylor, M. (1995) *Empowerment and Estate Regeneration* (Bristol: Policy Press).

Stirling, T. and Smith, R. (2003) 'A matter of choice? Policy divergence in access to social housing post-devolution', *Housing Studies*, 18(2), pp.145–58.

Stoker, G. (1993) *The Politics of Local Government* (London: Macmillan).

Taper, T., Walker, S. and Skinner, G. (2003) *LSVTs: Staff Impacts and Implications* (London: ODPM).

Taylor, M. (1995) *Unleashing the Potential: Bringing Residents to the Centre of Estate Regeneration* (York: Joseph Rowntree Foundation).

Tewdwr-Jones, M. (1996) *British Planning Policy in Transition: Planning in the 1990s* (London: UCL Press).

Third, H., Wainwright, S. and Pawson, H. (1997) *Constraint and Choice for Minority Ethnic Home Owners in Scotland* (Edinburgh: Scottish Homes).

Thorns, D. (1992) *Fragmenting Societies? A Comparative Analysis of Regional and Urban Development* (London: Routledge).

Turner, B. and Whitehead, C. (2001) 'Reducing housing subsidy: Swedish housing policy in an international context', *Urban Studies*, 39 (2), pp.201–17.

University of Newcastle-upon-Tyne, University of Leeds and Greater London Authority (2002) *Development of a Migration Model: Research Report to ODPM* (London: ODPM).

Urban Task Force (1999) *Towards an Urban Renaissance* (London: DETR).

US Department of Housing and Urban Development (1999) *The State of the Cities 1999: Third Annual Report*, Report to the President by Department of Housing and Urban Development.

Van Kempen, R., Schutjens, V. and Van Weesep, J. (2000) 'Housing and social fragmentation in the Netherlands', *Housing Studies*, 15 (4), pp.505–31.

Vincent-Jones, P. (2001) 'From housing management to the management of housing: the challenge of Best Value', in D. Cowan and A. Marsh (eds), *Two Steps Forward: Housing Policy into the New Millennium* (Bristol: Policy Press).

Walker, B. and Marsh, A. (1998) 'Pricing public housing services: mirroring the market?', *Housing Studies*, 13 (4), pp.549–66.

Walker, R. (1998) 'New Public Management and housing associations: from comfort to competition', *Policy and Politics*, 22 (1), pp.71–87.

Walker, R. (2001) 'How to abolish public housing: implications and lessons from public management reform', *Housing Studies*, 16 (5), pp.675–96.

Walker, R.M. (2000) 'The changing management of social working: the impact of externalisation and managenalisation', *Housing Studies*, 15(2), pp.281–99.

Walsh, K. (1995) *Public Services and Market Mechanisms: Competition, Contracting and the New Public Management* (London: Macmillan).

Webster, D. (1998) 'Employment change, housing abandonment and sustainable development: structural processes and structural issues', in S. Lowe, S. Spencer and P. Keenan (eds), *Housing Abandonment in Britain: Studies in the Causes and Effects of Low Demand Housing* (York: University of York).

Wellings, F. (2001) *Private Housebuilding Annual 2001* (London: Credit Lyonnaise Securities).

Welsh Assembly Government (2003) *The Welsh Qualtiy Housing Standard: Guidance for RSLs on the Assessment Process and Achievement of the Standard*: www.housing.wales.gov.uk/pdf.asp?a=e39.

Wenban-Smith, A. (1999) *'Plan, Monitor and Manage': Making it Work* (London: Council for the Protection of Rural England).

Westra, H. (2001) 'Housing Allocation: The Delft Model', Paper presented to Chartered Institute of Housing Conference, Dundee, March.

Wilcox, S. (1996) 'Help with housing costs', in S. Wilcox (ed.), *Housing Review 1996/97* (York: Joseph Rowntree Foundation).

Wilcox, S. (2000) *Housing Finance Review 2000/01* (Coventry, London and York: Chartered Institute of Housing, Council of Mortgage Lenders and Joseph Rowntree Foundation).

Wilcox, S. (2002) *UK Housing Review 2002/03* (Coventry, London and York: Chartered Institute of Housing, Council of Mortgage Lenders and Joseph Rowntree Foundation).

Wilcox, S. (2003) *UK Housing Review 2003/04* (Coventry, London and York: Chartered Institute of Housing, Council of Mortgage Lenders, Joseph Rowntree Foundation).

Wilcox, S. and Sutherland, H. (1997) *Housing Benefit, Affordability and Work Incentives* (London: National Housing Federation).

Wilcox, S., Bramley, G., Ferguson, A., Perry, J. and Woods, C. (1993) *Local Housing Companies: New Opportunities for Council Housing* (York: Joseph Rowntree Foundation).

Williams, K., Burton, E. and Jencks, M. (2000) *Achieving Sustainable Urban Form* (London: E. & F. Spon).

Williams, P. (ed.) (1997) *Directions in Housing Policy: Towards Sustainable Housing Policies for the UK* (London: Paul Chapman).

Wilson, D., Margulis, H. and Ketchum, J. (1994) 'Spatial aspects of housing abandonment in the 1990s: the Cleveland experience', *Housing Studies*, 9 (4), pp.493–510.

World Commission on Environmental Development (1987) *Our Common Future* (The Brundtland Report) (Oxford: Oxford University Press).

Name Index

Subject Index